# IN ETHIOPIA WITH A MULE

Dervla Murphy was ⟨...⟩ County
Waterford, where her ⟨...⟩ r father
and most of his fan ⟨...⟩ e Irish
Republican Movemer ⟨...⟩ ... ... the Ursuline

Convent, Waterford until 1945 when she came home to keep
house and nurse her mother who was an invalid. Her education
was continued by reading whatever took her fancy, with occasional breaks to cycle on the continent. In 1963 she was free to
make her bicycle journey to India, after which she worked with
the Tibetan refugee children in Dharamsala. She still lives in
Lismore, County Waterford where she was brought up.

Foreigners were not encouraged to travel alone through
Ethiopia's remote regions, and it was against official advice that
Dervla Murphy planned her highland trek in 1966. She bought
an amiable pack-mule, Jock, and at the end of December she
and Jock set out to walk north to Aksum. From Aksum they
went south, negotiated the formidable sweltering Takaze
Gorge, climbed into the icy High Semiens and descended to
Gondar. By then both travellers were so emaciated that they
rested for a week before continuing around the little-known
northern and western shores of Lake Tana. At Bahar Dar they
again turned north to climb further high ranges and cross an
uninhabited, pathless drought-area on their way to Lalibela.
Jock was now suffering from malnutrition and his sad owner
exchanged him for an unco-operative donkey. The last stage of
the journey to Addis Ababa was across the gruelling plateau of
Manz.

Three times Dervla Murphy was robbed, but in general the
highlanders were hospitable. As the weeks passed she realised
that her total dependence on them and her increasing familiarity with their strange ways were breaking down the original
barriers. In Addis Ababa she reviewed her trek and concluded
'A traveller who does not speak their language cannot presume
to claim any deep understanding of the Ethiopian highlanders.
But it is the gradual growth of affection for another race, rather
than the walking of a thousand miles or the climbing of a
hundred escarpments, that is the real achievement and the
richest award of such a journey.'

Dervla Murphy

# IN ETHIOPIA WITH
# A MULE

CENTURY PUBLISHING
LONDON

LESTER & ORPEN DENNYS DENEAU
MARKETING SERVICES LTD
TORONTO

First published in 1968 by John Murray (Publishers) Ltd
This edition published in 1984 by Century Publishing Co. Ltd,
Portland House, 12–13 Greek Street, London WIV 5LE

Published in Canada by
Lester & Orpen Dennys Deneau Marketing Services Ltd,
78 Sullivan Street, Ontario, Canada

Reprinted 1985

ISBN 0 7126 0344 1

Cover shows a detail of a lithograph by Henry Salt
courtesy of Eyre & Hobhouse Ltd

*To Patsy, John & William with love*

Reprinted in Great Britain by
Richard Clay (The Chaucer Press) Ltd, Bungay, Suffolk

# Contents

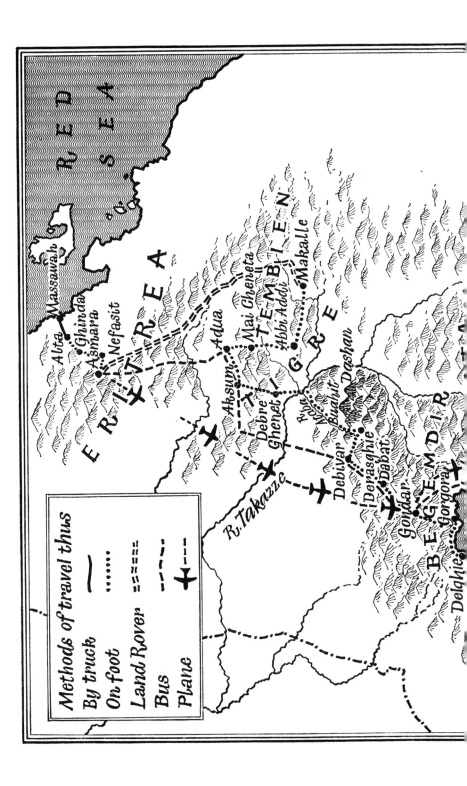

R E D   S E A

Alta
Massawa
Ghinda
Asmara
Nefasit

E R I T R E A

Adua
Aksum
Mai Cheneta
TEMBIEN
Abbi Addi
Makalle
G R E
Debre Ghenet
Aba Gerima
Buahit
Mt. Dashan
Debivar
Dabat
Devasghie
Gondar
Gorgora
Delghie
B E G I E M D I R

R. Takazze

Methods of travel thus
By truck ———
On foot ·······
Land Rover =====
Bus – – –
Plane ✈ – ✈

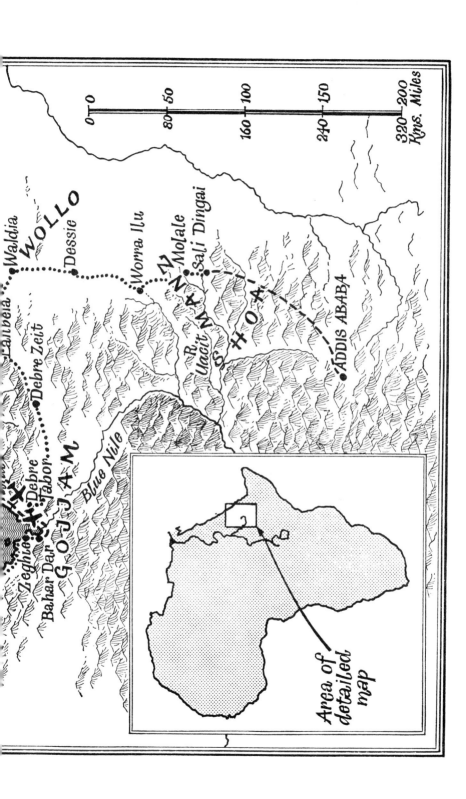

A diversification among human communities is essential for the provision of the incentive and material for the Odyssey of the human spirit. Other nations of different habits are not enemies: they are godsends. Men require of their neighbours something sufficiently akin to be understood, something sufficiently different to provoke attention, and something great enough to command admiration.

A. N. Whitehead: *Science & the Modern World*

'They tell us this is a table land. If it is, they have turned the table upside down and we are scrambling up and down the legs.'—*A British soldier's comment on Ethiopian scenery, during the Napier Expedition,* 1867–8.

# Prologue

When I am asked, 'Why did you go to Ethiopia?' I find it impossible to give a short, clear answer. From earliest childhood the romantic names of Prester John, Rasselas, the Queen of Sheba and the Lion of Judah are linked with Abyssinia and, in one's reading, occasional references to the country build up a picture of some improbable land of violence and piety, courtesy and treachery, barrenness and fertility.

Ethiopia has always been difficult to explore and much of it remains so; yet for centuries it was less inaccessible than most parts of Africa and, since the early sixteenth century, a sufficient number of travellers have visited the highlands to maintain Europe's interest. Latterly these travellers had commercial or political motives, but the earliest European explorers were Portuguese missionaries, whose excessive zeal inspired an era of xenophobia that is only now coming to a close.

Most of the Europeans who were lucky enough to return from Ethiopia wrote wondrous accounts of the mountain empire, and gradually the name of Ethiopia or Abyssinia became synonymous with beauty, danger, solitude and mystery. Often the lure of such places operates subconsciously. Then one fine morning the traveller wakes and surprises himself by saying—'I'm going to Ethiopia'.

Modern Ethiopia is about five times the size of Britain. Its southern tip is 250 miles from the Equator and its coastline on the Red Sea is 500 miles long. The region generally known as 'the highlands' is a vast, fissured plateau between the Upper Nile valley and the Somaliland desert; this plateau lies six to ten thousand feet above sea level, rising in certain areas to twelve to fifteen thousand, and its height gives it—despite the nearness of the Equator—a climate said to be the healthiest and one of the most agreeable in the world.

I

The country is divided into fourteen provinces, inhabited by people of many different races, religions and cultures—among them the Danakils, the Falashas, the Gurages, the Somalis, the Konsos, the Waytos and the Wollamos. But the true Abyssinians are the Amharas and the Tigreans, who form almost the entire population of the six highland provinces through which I travelled—Eritrea, Tigre, Begemdir, Gojjam, Wollo and Shoa. Until the latter half of the nineteenth century the eight other provinces were either completely independent of or only vaguely associated with the Amharic Empire.

It is thought that the original highlanders were of the same Hamitic stock as the Danakils, Somalis and Nubians. Then, probably between 1,000 and 500 B.C., tribes of Yemeni Arabs began to cross the Red Sea to settle in the fertile northern highlands, where the ruins of large cities indicate that their civilisation thrived during the centuries immediately before and after the birth of Christ. One of these tribes was called the Habashat and from this derives 'Habesh'—by which name Ethiopia is still known in Muslim countries—and from 'Habesh' European tongues produced Abyssinia. However, the highlanders now resent being called Abyssinians and their wish to be known as Ethiopians creates a complication. All the Emperor's multiracial subjects are legally Ethiopians, so it would be inexact to write 'Ethiopians' when one is referring specifically to Amharas or Tigreans, who have nothing in common with their non-Abyssinian fellow-subjects. Therefore I avoid 'Ethiopians' for the sake of accuracy and 'Abyssinians' for the sake of politeness and refer to 'Amharas', 'Tigreans' or 'highlanders'.

Following the Arab migrations the Semitic language and culture replaced the old Hamitic civilisation, of which nothing is definitely known, though some scholars believe it to have been highly developed. The newcomers also intermarried with the indigenous population and, though the Hamitic strain remained dominant, the Semitic influence is still obvious and this cross has produced a race of outstandingly handsome men and beautiful women.

An Egyptian trader named Cosmos travelled from the Red Sea port of Adulis to Aksum in about A.D. 524, shortly before the decline of the Aksumite Empire. This Empire had been founded by the Semitised Hamitic peoples of the present-day provinces of Eritrea and Tigre, but neither Cosmas nor anyone else is very informative about it and little is known of its six hundred years of glory. It was the centre from which the Semitic language and culture and the Christian religion seeped south until, by the thirteenth century, the provinces of Begemdir, Gojjam and Shoa had ceased to be pagan.

The rise of Islam quickly isolated these Christian highlands and, after Cosmos' departure, a thousand years passed before the arrival at Massawah of the next foreign visitor to give an account of Ethiopia. His name was Francisco Alvarez, and he spent six years in the country as chaplain to a diplomatic mission sent by King Manoel I of Portugal to the court of the Emperor Lebna Dengel—whose grandmother, while ruling as regent during the Emperor's minority, had appealed for Portuguese aid when Ethiopia was being threatened by the Ottoman Empire.

This millennium of isolation inspired Gibbon's frequently quoted—'Encompassed on all sides by the enemies of their religion, the Ethiopians slept near a thousand years, forgetful of the world by whom they were forgotten'. But, in fact, the Ethiopians were much more wide awake then than they are now. During these centuries they produced their finest paintings and illuminated manuscripts, many extraordinarily beautiful rock-churches, of which Lalibela's eleven examples are the most famous, and the best of what little original literature they possess.

Alvarez is the only European to have described Ethiopia as it was before the terrible Muslim invasions, which began in 1527—a year after the departure of the Portuguese mission. The invaders were led by Mohammed Gragn, a remarkably able general who took full advantage of the firearms which had recently been made available by the Turks, from whom he also obtained a small corps of about two hundred matchlockmen. 'The effect produced by this tiny body of disciplined regulars, skilled in the use of firearms, was catastrophic. The Abyssinian armies broke and fled like chaff before the wind. The whole of Abyssinia was overrun. . . . The treasure fortresses were captured and the accumulated wealth of the Kingdom was carried off. The churches and monasteries were looted and burnt . . . and the princes of the Solomonian line put to the sword. In the words of the Abyssinian chronicles, nine men out of ten renounced the Christian faith and turned Muslim. Only the King with a scanty band of faithful followers maintained the struggle . . . in the mountain fastnesses of the interior'.*

In about 1535 Lebna Dengel succeeded in sending an appeal for help to the Portuguese and six years later four hundred Portuguese troops landed at Massawah, commanded by Christopher da Gama, a son of the navigator. In the fighting that followed the Portuguese and Muslim leaders were both killed, and without Mohammed Gragn the invaders faltered and were expelled from the highlands during the reign of Lebna Dengel's son, Claudius.

By then the Empire had been miserably weakened, and immediately there was a new threat from the Galla. These pagan nomadic tribesmen, being harried by the Somali, began to invade the southern region of the Ethiopian plateau; and when they had acquired horses from the highlanders they soon became formidable cavalrymen, penetrating as far north as Begemdir. 'The Galla came to the highlands not as raiders alone, but also as settlers. Wherever they settled, they made travel dangerous and uncertain for the Abyssinians, isolated entire provinces from one another, and broke up the empire. The Abyssinians fought many battles against the Galla, but though individual groups were defeated, the force of the Galla migration could not be stopped. . . . Many of them, because of their warlike propensities, were recruited into the armies of the Abyssinian rulers . . . [and] . . . it is said that during this period only the sacred character of the Abyssinian monarchy preserved the dynasty from extinction, so that the Galla, even though they wielded great power, never took over the throne itself.'†

During the ninety years or so between the expulsion of the Muslims and the beginning of the Gondarine era there was yet another disruptive element in highland life, which briefly

---

\* *A History of Ethiopia:* Jones & Monroe.
† *Northwest Ethiopia:* Frederick J. Simoons.

threatened 'the sacred character' of the monarchy. This was
the excessive missionary zeal already mentioned. In 1632 the
conversion, by Jesuits, of the Emperor Susenyos, and the
Catholics' intolerant attempts to convert the whole Empire,
led to the banishment from Ethiopia of all foreigners and was
followed by a relapse into isolation. However, Ethiopian history
since 1632 is reasonably well documented, and in my diary I
have referred to some of the main characters and events.


There is a certain similarity between the developments of
Ethiopian Christianity and Tibetan Buddhism. In both cases,
when alien religions were brought to isolated countries the
new teachings soon became diluted with ancient animist super-
stitions; and so these cuttings from two great world religions
grew on their high plateaux into exotic plants, hardly recognisable as offshoots of their parent faiths. But there the similarity
ends. Of the two religions Tibetan Buddhism is much more
advanced philosophically and has a far greater civilising influence on the peasants. Lamas rarely encourage bigotry and
racial arrogance—as Ethiopian Coptic priests frequently do,
by teaching that Ethiopian Christians are the only true Christians in the whole world. This defect is not exclusive to Coptic
priests, but it is extra-pernicious in such a remote land, where
a pathetic national superiority complex tends to run wild for
lack of sobering comparisons with other nations.

Though so little is known about early Ethiopian history, the
romantic story of the Empire's conversion is believed by
scholars to be substantially true. In the first half of the fourth
century Meropius, a philosopher of Tyre, was voyaging in
search of knowledge with two young relatives, Aedesius and
Frumentius, who were being educated by him. Their ship put
in for water at a port (Adulis?) where it was boarded by
'barbarians'. These tribesmen massacred Meropius and his
companions, but spared the boys—who were found on shore,
studying under a tree—and brought them to the court of Ella
Amida at Aksum. The King became very fond of both boys,
and made Aedesius his cupbearer and Frumentius, who was
already learned and wise, his secretary and treasurer; but

before long Ella Amida died, leaving an infant son, Aeizaras, as heir. The Queen begged the young men to help her bear the burden of the regency and, during the years when he was virtual ruler of the country, Frumentius encouraged Christian Roman merchant settlers to spread their faith.

When Aeizaras had been crowned Aedesius and Frumentius handed over their trust and returned to the Roman Empire, though both the King and his mother implored them to stay. Aedesius hurried back to visit his family in Tyre, where he later became a priest, but Frumentius went direct to Alexandria and urged Athanasius to send a bishop to foster Christianity in Ethiopia. Athanasius decided to consecrate Frumentius himself and sent him back to his mission-field—where he converted countless pagans, ordained priests and after many years converted Aeizaras himself, thereby firmly establishing the Coptic Church in Ethiopia.

From the appointment of Frumentius by Athanasius until 1951 the Abuna (head of the Ethiopian Church) has always been an Egyptian monk, chosen by the Patriarch of Alexandria from the monastery of St Antonius. Inevitably there were long intervals—sometimes one or two decades—between an Abuna's death and the arrival of his successor; and the suffragan bishops who were occasionally appointed could not ordain. Moreover, as a solitary exile for life, with a language, training and background which completely isolated him from his strange diocese, the Abuna never formed a real link with orthodox Christian traditions—so there was no check on the uninstructed Ethiopians' peculiar scriptural interpretations.

Many animist strands still run through Ethiopian Christianity, which also reveals a considerable Jewish influence. The Amharic words for 'alms', 'idol', 'purification', 'Hell' and 'Easter' are of Hebrew origin, though the only version of the scriptures ever known to the Ethiopian Church was a translation into Ge'ez of the Septuagint. A. H. M. Jones thinks that before the rise of Islam Yemeni Jews may have been proselytising in Ethiopia, 'which had at this time very close commercial and political relations with South-Western Arabia and was closely akin to it in language and culture. . . . The conversion of the royal house to Christianity . . . prevented Judaism from becoming the official religion of the Abyssinian Kingdom, but was not in time to prevent the conversion of various independent Agau tribes to Judaism, nor the adoption by the Abyssinians of certain Jewish practices.'

These aboriginal Agau converts are called Falashas (exiles) by the Coptic highlanders, and some of them still speak an Hamitic language as well as Amharic. Their traditional stronghold was in the Semien mountains and, though they now number only about 30,000, they were sufficiently powerful in the seventh century for Professor Simoons to suspect that they aided the collapse of the Aksumite Empire by blocking the southward spread of Christianity.

Among the Falashas, as among their Christian neighbours, isolation has led to various eccentric beliefs and practices, and a number of Coptic traditions—including a monastic system—eventually merged with their own archaic form of Judaism. Never having had a written language of their own they are dependent on the Ge'ez version of the Old Testament and they do not possess the Mishra or the Talmud. According to Wolf Leslau most of their laws and precepts are based on the apocryphal *Book of Jubilees*. These 'Black Jews' are now scattered throughout the provinces of Tigre and Begemdir, where they are not allowed to own land, but must rent it from the Christians, who despise them for being non-Christians—though this doesn't worry the Falashas, who like to keep well away from unclean non-Falashas.

This, then, was the background to my journey—a country not quite of Africa nor of Asia, with a civilisation that became completely introverted as time passed. During many centuries the currents of new thought merely lapped the Red Sea coast, reaching the interior as disturbing rumours to be at once rejected for seeming far less credible than the legends of the saints in the monastery manuscripts.

The preparations for a walking-tour are simple. I only had to buy a large rucksack, a strong pair of boots, a one-gallon plastic water-bottle, a Husky outfit of jacket, pants and socks that was light to carry but warm to wear, a few basic medical supplies, half-a-dozen notebooks and a dozen ball-point pens. To maintain contact with my own civilisation I also packed a Shakespeare anthology, *Tom Jones*, W. E. Carr's *Poetry of the Middle Ages*, Cooper's *Talleyrand* and Boros' *Pain and Providence*. Unfortunately other books inexplicably accumulated in my rucksack between London and Massawah and when climbing to the 8,000 foot Eritrean plateau I found myself carrying a weight of fifty pounds.

I had been warned—by people who knew people who knew people who had been to Ethiopia—that the Ethiopian authorities distrust foreigners and would only give me a thirty-day tourist visa. Happily this proved to be nonsense. When I had presented my passport at the Ethiopian Embassy in London, filled in an application form for a six-months' Business Visa and paid the fee, I was asked to call again at 10 a.m. the next day. I came at 10.05 a.m., expecting to encounter a large snag; but my passport had been duly signed and sealed and was at once delivered.

The real difficulty concerned maps. There is no such thing as a good map of Ethiopia, but Barbara Toy generously presented me with the Italian maps that she had used on her Ethiopian journey and these suited me perfectly. They were inaccurate enough to give me, at times, the gratifying illusion of being an explorer in trackless wastes—yet accurate enough to tell me that Addis Ababa is due south of Massawah. So it didn't matter if I went mildly astray every day en route, provided I didn't go east or west for too long at a stretch.

My homework was a little more arduous. I read most of the recently published books on Ethiopia and carefully studied *Wax and Gold**—which greatly increased the pleasure of my journey, for without Dr Levine's sympathetic analysis of the Amharic culture I would have gone wandering through the highlands in a permanent daze of incomprehension.

Then, having had my 'shots', I flew to Cairo on 3 December, 1966, and eight days later boarded a Norwegian boat, at Port Said, for the five-day voyage to Massawah.

* University of Chicago Press, 1965.

# 1

# *Finding my Four Feet*

All day the coast was in sight—a long line of low mountains, often indistinguishable from the pale clouds that hung above it. No one could tell me where the Sudan ended and Ethiopia began, but at 5.40 p.m. we were approaching Massawah and a crimson sun slid quickly out of sight behind the high plateau of Abyssinia.

We anchored a mile off-shore, to await our pilot, and as I stood impatiently on deck a tawny afterglow still lay above the mountains and a quarter-moon spread its golden, mobile sheen across the water. Near here stood Adulis, the principal port of the Aksumite Empire, and in the first century A.D. the anonymous author of the *Periplus of the Erythraean Sea* wrote, 'There are imported into these places double-fringed mantles; many articles of flint glass; brass, which is used for ornament and in cut pieces instead of coin; iron, which is made into spears used against wild beasts, and in their wars; wine of Laodicea and Italy, not much; olive oil, not much; for the King gold and silver plate made after the fashion of the country—— There are exported from these places ivory and tortoise-shell and rhinoceros-horn'. Then the traders feared the attacks of 'barbarous natives'. Now my luxury-loaded Italian fellow-passengers fear the attacks of *shifta* (bandits) on their way to Asmara tomorrow.

Following the arrival of our pilot-boat we spent two hours with easy-going Immigration and Sanitary officials. The Passport officer was a small-boned, dark-skinned little man, with an expression like a grieved monkey, and he warned me against the natives of Massawah—a pack of 'murderous, thieving Muslims'. From this I rightly deduced that he was a highlander.

9

His home is in Tigre and he hates the climate here, but says that because the locals are so ignorant and unreliable highlanders have to fill all responsible posts.

At last the Customs officers deigned to come on duty and we were permitted to go ashore. The Customs shed was comically vast—it could easily have held two hundred passengers instead of seven. My rucksack and general appearance gave the usual convenient impression of grinding poverty, and I was chalked and sympathetically waved on my way with a three months' supply of tax-free cigarettes undetected.

I cannot remember feeling so alien during my first hours in any other country. One doesn't think of Massawah as being Ethiopian, in any sense but the political, and I should find the atmosphere of an essentially Arab town quite familiar. Yet enough of the singularity of the tableland has spilled over to the coast for newcomers to be at once aware of Ethiopia's isolation—even where contact with the outside world is closest.

Certainly there is no outward evidence of isolation here. I walked first along the sophisticated Italianate street that faces the quays and passed many groups of foreign sailors or local officials sitting at little tables drinking iced beer, or coffee, or smuggled spirits. Several beggars tried to 'help' by getting hold of my rucksack and leading me to the doss-house of their choice; but they were easily deterred and no one followed when I turned into a rough, narrow, ill-lit lane between tall houses. Most of these houses were brothels, and young Tigrean girls were sitting in the doorways playing with their toddlers (prostitution and family life are not incompatible here), or dressing each other's hair in the multitudinous tiny plaits traditional among Tigrean women. In the gloom I was often mistaken for a customer and, on realizing their error, most of the girls either jeered at me rather nastily or sent their children to beg from me.

However, this 'hotel' is congenial. The friendly owner—an elderly, handsome Tigrean woman—thinks I'm the funniest thing that has happened in years. She is now sitting nearby, with two neighbours, watching me write. Apparently the neighbours were called in because such a good joke has to be shared.

From the alleyway outside a high door—marked *Pensione*—

opens into a large, square room where a few ugly metal tables and plastic chairs stand about on a wilderness of concrete floor-ing. Ethiopian Christians are very devoted to the Blessed Virgin, and two pictures of Our Lady of Good Counsel hang on the walls between several less edifying calendar ladies advertising Italian imports. Behind this 'foyer'—separated from it by wooden lattice-work—is a small, unroofed space, with a tiny charcoal cooking-stove in one corner and some unsteady wooden stairs leading up to a flat roof, off which are five clean three-bed bedrooms. Other hideous tables and chairs furnish this 'lounge', where I'm now sitting beneath a corrugated iron roof. The shutters of the unglazed windows and the upper half of the bedroom walls are also of lattice-work—attractive to the eye, but not conducive either to privacy or quiet. The loo hangs opposite me, adhering most oddly to the next-door wall, and the plumbing is weird and nauseating in the extreme. Theoreti-cally all should be well, since it is a Western loo with a plug that pulls successfully—one can see the water running towards it through transparent plastic pipes fixed to the roof. The snag is that nothing seems to get any further than a cess-pool, covered with an iron grill, which stands in the centre of the kitchen floor.

Tonight the heat is appalling and, while writing this, I've absorbed five pints of *talla*—the cloudy, home-brewed highland beer. As far as I can feel it is totally unintoxicating, though very refreshing and palatable.

## *17 December*

At lunch-time today I had my first meal of *injara* and *wat*. *Injara* has a bitter taste and a gritty texture; it looks and feels exactly like damp, grey foam-rubber, but is a fermented bread made from *teff*—the cereal grain peculiar to the Ethiopian high-lands—and cooked in sheets about half-an-inch thick and two feet in circumference. These are double-folded and served beside one's plate of *wat*—a highly spiced stew of meat or chicken. One eats with the right hand (only), by mopping up the *wat* with the *injara*; and, as in Muslim countries, a servant pours water over one's hands before and after each meal.

During the afternoon a blessed silence enfolds sun-stricken Massawah and I slept soundly from two to five. By then it was a little less hellish outside, so I set forth to see the sights—not that there are many to see here. Visitors are forbidden to enter the grounds of the Imperial Palace and women are forbidden to enter the mosques—of which there are several, though only the new Grand Mosque looks interesting. It was built by the Emperor, presumably to placate his rebellious Eritrean Muslim subjects.*

In the old city, south of the port, the architecture is pure Arabic, though many of the present population have migrated from the highlands. The narrow streets of solid stone or brick houses seem full of ancient mystery and maimed beggars drag themselves through the dust while diseased dogs slink away at one's approach, looking as though they wanted to snarl but hadn't enough energy left.


*18 December. Nefasit*

The process of converting a cyclist into a hiker is being rather painful. Today I only walked eighteen miles, yet now I feel more tired than if I had cycled a hundred and eighteen; but this is perhaps understandable, as I'm out of training and was carrying fifty pounds from 3,000 to 6,000 feet. At the moment my shoulder muscles are fiery with pain and—despite the most

* Throughout Ethiopian history Massawah has been important in a negative sense, for it was the highlanders' inablity to hold their natural port that isolated them so momentously. At the beginning of the fifteenth century King Yeshaq took Massawah from the Muslims, who had been in possession for seven centuries, but within eighty years it had been lost again to the coastal tribes then warring against the highlanders. From 1520 to 1526 it was occupied by the Portuguese, from 1527 to 1865 by the Turks, and from 1865 to 1882 by the Egyptians. The British next took over, promising the Emperor John IV that on leaving Massawah they would return it to the highlanders. They left three years later, but their anxiety to counter French influence along the Red Sea coast led them to hand Massawah over to the Italians —for whom it was the capital of their new colony until 1897, when Asmara was built. After World War II the British again took possession and not until 1952 did Massawah, with the rest of Eritrea, become part of the Ethiopian Empire. To-day this province is a troublesome part, for many Eritreans resent being ruled from Addis Ababa, and foreign Muslim powers are busy transforming this resentment into a modern nationalistic ambition to have Eritrea declared an independent state.

comfortable of boots—three massive blisters are throbbing on each foot.

Yesterday Commander Iskander Desta of the Imperial Navy kindly suggested that I should be driven across the coastal desert strip in a naval jeep, which collected me from my *pensione* at eight o'clock this morning. The Eritrean driver spoke fluent Italian, but no English, and the dozen English-speaking cadets, who were going to spend Sunday at the 4,000-feet Embatcallo naval rest-camp, were not disposed to fraternise with the *faranj* (foreigner).

Beyond a straggle of new 'council houses' our road climbed through hillocks of red sand, scattered with small green shrubs. Then these hillocks became hills of bare rock—and all the time the high mountains were looming ahead in a blue haze, sharpening my eagerness to get among them. We passed one primitive settlement of half-a-dozen oblong huts, which is marked as a village on my map—perhaps because Coca-Cola is sold outside one of the shacks—and a few miles further on the road tackled the steep escarpment in a series of brilliantly-engineered hairpin bends.

By 10 a.m. I had been released from the truck at 3,000 feet, where mountains surrounded me on every side. Here the climate was tolerable, though for an hour or so sweat showered off me at every step; then clouds quickly piled up and a cool breeze rose. On the four-mile stretch to Ghinda I passed many other walkers—ragged, lean Muslim tribesmen, highlanders draped in *shammas* (white cotton cloaks) and skinny children herding even skinnier goats. Everyone stared at me suspiciously and only once was my greeting returned—by a tall, ebony-skinned tribesman. One doesn't resent such aloofness, since surprise is probably the main cause, but I soon stopped being so unrewardingly amiable. Already I notice a difference between cycling and walking in an unknown country; on foot one is even more sensitive to the local attitude and one feels a little less secure.

Ghinda is described in my official guide-book as 'a small resort city' to which people come to escape the cold of Asmara or the heat of Massawah. In fact it is a small town of tin-roofed hovels from which I personally would be glad to escape in any direction.

Just beyond Ghinda a squad of children advised me to avoid the main road and guided me up a steep short cut for about two miles. Later I took two other short cuts and discovered that on this loose, dry soil what looks like a reasonable climb is often an exhausting struggle. The busy Massawah–Asmara railway runs near the road and when I was attempting one short cut, up the embankment, I went sliding down on to the track just as an antiquated engine, belching clouds of black smoke, came round the corner twenty yards away. Happily this line does not cater for express trains; extermination by a steam-engine would be a prosaic ending to travels in Ethiopia. During the abrupt descent my knees had been deeply grazed and my hands torn by the thorny shrubs at which I clutched; but this was merely the initiation ceremony. When one has been injured by a country, then one really has arrived.

From Ghinda to the outskirts of Nefasit the rounded mountains and wooded gorges appear to be almost entirely uninhabited and uncultivated. Even this colonised fringe of Ethiopia feels desolate and the silence is profound. Many of the lower slopes are covered in green bushes, giant cacti and groves of tall trees; one lovely shrub blazes with flowers like the flames of a turf-fire and vividly coloured birds dart silently through the undergrowth. Around the few villages some terracing is attempted, but it looks crude and ineffective. My impression so far is of a country much more primitive, in both domestic architecture and agriculture, than any Asian region I know.

At intervals the week-end traffic passed me—Italian or American cars returning to Asmara in convoys of six or eight as a precaution against *shifta*. (There are 5,000 Americans stationed at the Kagnew Military Base near Asmara.) As another precaution two policemen sat watchfully by the roadside every five miles, leaning on antediluvian rifles. The *shifta* are said to be far better armed than the police, their foreign backers having equipped them well. Many cars stopped to offer me a lift, and soon this kindness became tiresome; it is difficult to persuade motorists that two legs can also get one there—at a later date. The last five miles were a hell of muscular exhaustion. At every other kilometre stone I had to stop, remove my rucksack and rest briefly.

Here I'm staying in a clean Italian doss-house and being overcharged for everything by the Eritrean-born proprietress. While writing this I've got slightly drunk on a seven-and-six-penny bottle of odious vinegar called 'vino bianco'—produced by the Italians in Asmara.

*19 December. Asmara*

I awoke at 6.30 to see a cool, pearly dawn light on mountains that were framed in bougainvillea. The Eritrean servant indicated that *mangiare* was impossible, so by 6.50 I was on the road. After ten hours unbroken sleep my back felt surprisingly unstiff, though my feet were even more painful than I had expected.

From Nefasit the road zig-zagged towards a high pass and before I had covered four miles all my foot-blisters burst wetly. During the next two hours of weakening pain only my flask of 'emergency' brandy kept me going. It seemed reckless to use it so soon, yet this did feel like a genuine emergency. Several cars stopped to offer me tempting lifts, but I then supported a theory (since abandoned) that the quickest way to cure footsores is by walking on them.

Here the road ran level, winding from mountain to mountain, and the whole wide sweep of hills and valleys was deserted and silent. These mountains are gently curved, though steep, and despite the immense heights and depths one sees none of the expected precipices or crags.

The sky remained cloudless all day, though a cool breeze countered any sensation of excessive heat. However, the sun's ultra-violet rays are severe at this altitude and the back of my neck has been badly burned.

It takes a few days for one's system to adjust to being above 6,000 feet and as I struggled towards the 8,000 foot plateau my head was throbbing from too little oxygen and my back from too much weight, though I hardly noticed these details because of the pain of my feet. Then at last I was there—exultantly overlooking a gleaming mass of pure white cloud that concealed the lower hills. But on this exposed ridge a strong, cold wind blew dust around me in stinging whirls and pierced through my sweat-soaked shirt; so I soon began to hobble down the slight incline towards Asmara.

On the last lap I passed a big British War Cemetery and gazed into it enviously, feeling that a cemetery rather than an hotel was the obvious resting place for anyone in my condition. Fifteen minutes later I was approaching the uninspiring suburbs of Asmara and looking out for a bar. At 1.30 I found one, pushed aside a curtain of bottle-tops on strings and in a single breath ordered three beers. Since morning I had only walked fifteen miles, yet my exhaustion was so extreme that I had to be helped to remove my rucksack.

By three o'clock I had found this Italian-run *pensione* in the centre of the city, conveniently opposite the British Consulate. Sitting on the edge of my bed, I took off my boots and socks and saw the worst. It is no longer a question of blisters: with my socks I had peeled off all the skin from both soles, leaving what looks like two pounds of raw steak. Undoubtedly this is where I forget 'mind-over-matter' and sit around for some days industriously growing new skin.

*20 December*

This morning I hobbled over to the Consulate to ask for the name of a reliable doctor; but the Consul, Major John Bromley, is on duty in Massawah today and his Ethiopian staff were vague—though friendly and anxious to help. The next few hours were spent limping around in a daze of pain searching for sound medical advice—not that there is any shortage of doctors here, but in my insular way I distrust foreign medicine-men whose names are followed by a rearrangement of the whole alphabet. Eventually I chanced to meet a kind nurse from the Lutheran Red Sea Mission, who recommended Professor Mario Manfredonia as being Ethiopia's best doctor; but he, too, is in Massawah today, so I could only make an appointment for tomorrow morning.

*21 December*

By this morning my right foot had begun to heal but my left had turned into a suppurating mess. Professor Manfredonia did a lot of skilful pressing and prying, before plastering it with antibiotic ointment, putting on an imposing bandage and telling me to rest for four or five days. He is the sort of doctor who makes you imagine that you are better long before you possibly could be, so I left his surgery feeling quite un-infected.

Today the Bromleys returned from Massawah. Major Brom-ley has lived in Ethiopia for thirty years and he gave me much practical advice on conditions in the highlands, telling me that it will be necessary to carry a full water-bottle and supple-mentary food rations. When I explained that I couldn't pos-sibly carry one ounce more than my present load we decided on the purchase of a pack-mule. Apart from pack-carrying, it is wise to have an animal that can be ridden in an emergency, should one fall ill or break a bone at the back of beyond.

During the afternoon, as I was dutifully resting in my room, Mrs Bromley telephoned and nobly invited me to stay. So I'm now happily installed in this agreeably happy-go-lucky house-hold.

## 22 December

Fortunately I'm a rapid healer; tonight my right foot has a nice new tough skin and my left is no longer throbbing.

This morning's mule-search was unsuccessful. The Bromleys' servant reported that it had been a poor market; but on the twenty-fourth he will try again, as the most important market of the week is held on Saturdays.

## 23 December

To-day I took a sedate stroll through Asmara, which was founded by the Italians seventy years ago and looks like a lost suburb of Milan, with many Arab shanty-settlements, nomad camps and highlanders' hovels scattered around the periphery. The Catholic Cathedral, the Grand Mosque and the Coptic Church were all designed by Italians. Mussolini was among the chief contributors to the cathedral building fund and the design is said to have been inspired by the Lombardic school of architecture; but this inspiration seems to have flagged quite soon and I much preferred what I was allowed to see of the mosque. Apart from one Latin flourish—a fluted Roman column at the base of the minaret—this is a fine no-nonsense example of Arab architecture. Near the mosque is St Mary's Coptic church (rectangular, with mock-Aksumite stone-work) and I spent a couple of hours sitting in its enclosure—not because I was riveted by the building, but because the worshippers interested me. Ethiopian churches are locked after morning Mass, yet as I sat in the sun on the steps, surrounded by spectacularly-maimed beggars, people were all the time praying vigorously at each door. Having crossed themselves, and made three little curtseys, they went to the door, pressed their bodies close to it and, between whispered prayers, kissed and stroked the smooth, golden wood. Many were women, with fly-covered infants tied to their backs. Five wild-looking men seemed to be new-comers to Asmara; they had ebony skins, pure Hamitic features, a fuzzy disorder of long hair and tall, thin bodies, draped in the ragged remains of one-piece, knee-length, cotton garments. Probably they belonged to some lowland tribe recently converted to Christianity. When they had finished their prayers they stood back to view the enormous, gaudy mosaic which decorates the facade, and for twenty minutes these apparently ferocious tribesmen remained on the steps animatedly discussing angels and saints.

Meanwhile a distinguished-looking elderly man had joined the worshippers around the main door. He had iron-grey hair, almost black skin, handsome features and tremendous dignity; in his well-tailored suit and snow-white shirt he was conspicuous indeed among this filthy, bare-footed throng. Having completed his ritual devotions he withdrew from the mob, carrying highly-polished shoes, and stood erect and motionless for over an hour in the shade of a nearby bell-tower, staring intently at the church and praying *sotto voce*. He was still there when I left.

This afternoon I bought ten pounds of imported emergency rations—dried fruit, and tins of cheese and fish. The prices were astronomical, for in addition to freight charges there are import duties of 65 per cent to 100 per cent on all foreign goods. These taxes may seem unreasonable, but they are the Government's chief source of revenue and the *faranjs* who buy most of the imported goods can better afford to pay taxes than can the Ethiopians. At present Ethiopia desperately needs more money, because in many ways this is the least advanced African country—a result of never having been colonised and a sore point among the few Ethiopians who can bring themselves to face the Empire's backwardness.

In general, relations between the Eritreans and the Italian colony seem to be excellent. The majority of the resident Italians have been born here and the fact that they chose to remain, after the union with Ethiopia, proves that to them Eritrea is 'home'. All the locals to whom I have spoken declare that the Italians are their favourite *faranjs*; but a regrettable bond between the settlers and the Eritreans is their shared contempt for the rest of the Emperor's 'uncivilised' subjects.

During the past few days the weather has been quite cool. This plateau has an extraordinary even temperature. In May, the hottest month, the Asmara average is 65°F and in December, the coldest month, it is 58°F. Yet the Danakil desert, immediately west of the tableland, is one of the hottest places in the world. The mountains which make things so pleasant up here also bring to the highlands the Indian Ocean monsoon, from June to September.

## 24 December

Today's mule-buying effort also failed. The servant reported that though he had seen a few good animals the prices were exorbitant—two hundred dollars, which is thirty pounds. He therefore advised buying at a smaller market, where it should be possible to get an equally good animal for half the price. This development coincided with an announcement by Major Bromley that on the twenty-sixth he must take two vehicles to Makalle; so we decided to make a minor expedition of it, Mrs Bromley (known as Peter) and myself going by car, the Major and the children by Land-Rover.

In Makalle lives Her Highness Leilt (Princess) Aida Desta, eldest grandchild of the Emperor. She is an old friend of the Bromleys, who say that she will be happy to help me buy a good mule at a reasonable price. I can then spend a few days getting acquainted with the animal, and start trekking from Makalle when my foot is completely re-soled.

My original route did not include Makalle, which lies south-east of the Asmara–Adua–Aksum trail that I had planned to take on my way to the Semien Mountains. I'll now have to walk north-east to Adowa, before turning due south towards the Takazze Gorge, which divides the provinces of Tigre and Begemdir.

*25 December*

Having two children in the house—Christopher and Nicola Bromley—gives some point to the tedious ballyhoo of our modern Western Christmas. Ethiopian Christians celebrate this feast on 7 January, by which time I hope to be celebrating with them in the middle of nowhere.

*26 December. Makalle*

On our drive from Asmara my first glimpse of the highlands overwhelmed me. Their magnificent, ferocious beauty is beyond all expectation, imagination or exaggeration—even to think of it makes my heart pound again.

We left Asmara at 10.30 and immediately outside the city were on an arid, red-brown plain, with low hills ahead and high mountains to the east. Then, beyond Decamere, the road swooped down and up for many miles through mountains whose configuration was so extraordinary that I felt I must be dreaming. Often we were driving on the verge of immense chasms, which lay between escarpments of pink or yellow rock that had been eroded to the most grotesque contrasts—and this tormented splendour is sustained for hundreds of miles.

We covered 200 miles today, and one gets such a confused impression from a car that already I've forgotten where we saw what. I think we were near Adigrat when the Semiens first appeared, some eighty miles away to the south-west—a fantastic array of powder-blue ruggedness, their 12 to 15,000-foot summits seeming deceptively near and clear. Never have I seen such strange mountains; they look like peaks in a cartoon film. We were then on a 9,000-foot plateau and between us and the Semiens lay this fissured wilderness of gorges, cliffs and lesser mountains. In the middle distance was a curiously perfect cone, and there were several solitary, flat-topped, steep-sided *ambas*, rising abruptly from a surrounding area of level ground. These *ambas* form almost impregnable natural fortresses and their rôle in Ethiopian history has been so important that one looks at them with awe, rather as though they were the venerable veterans of some remote and famous battle.

My map marks six 'important' towns between Asmara and Makalle, yet none of them seems more than a large, shoddy village. Those in Eritrea were important once, but since the Italians left the bigger houses have become roofless ruins, on which faint lettering indicates that thirty or forty years ago Italian grocers, barbers and hotel-keepers were in residence. The locals never moved into these comparatively solid and spacious houses, preferring to live on in their own rickety, cramped, tin-roofed shacks. Here corrugated-tin roofs are not merely a status-symbol, as in Nepal, but a means of collecting precious rain; and in such a barren region the use of every raindrop justifies even this ugliness.

Though we were driving on one of Northern Ethiopia's only two motor-roads we passed no other private cars and saw not more than six or seven trucks. Between Decamere and Senafé a convoy of nine buses approached us, escorted by two smart army vehicles, bristling with machine-guns. This is the hub of the *shifta* country, where private cars rarely travel unescorted unless flying a flag that denotes diplomatic privileges. I noticed that here even Peter, who has nerves of steel, was slightly tensed up, despite the large Union Jack fluttering conspiciously on our bonnet. But she assured me that the danger was minimal as *shifta* specialise in buses; if the owners of Transport Companies don't regularly pay a protection fee their vehicles are pushed over precipices.

Makalle lies west of the road and previously it was necessary to overshoot it and then turn back north from Quiha; but a few years ago Leilt Aida's husband, H. H. Leul Ras Mangasha Seyoum, the Governor-General of Tigre, designed a direct ten-mile jeep track to the town, and did most of the construction work himself with a bulldozer and tractors.

As we hairpinned steeply down the mountainside I had my first glimpse of Tigre's provincial capital—a little town sheltered by eucalyptus trees on the edge of a wide and windswept plain. My guidebook claims that Makalle 'gives the impression of a boom town'—and perhaps it does, to those who knew it ten years ago. To me it gives the impression of a neat feudal settlement, gathered happily around the somewhat misleadingly named 'palace' of the Emperor Yohannes IV. It has such an atmosphere of remote tranquillity that neither the turmoils of its past nor the progress of its present are easily credited. We drove straight to the new tourist hotel, a converted eighty-year-old castle, managed by Indians, which stands small and square on a low hill. Here prices are reasonable (about twenty-five shillings for bed and breakfast) and, though tourist hotels are not my natural habitat, I find the wall-to-wall carpeting and the pink-tiled bathroom sufficiently compensated for by eccentric electricity and a moody water supply. When countless servants had pitted themselves against the plumbing for over an hour we achieved baths, before setting off to dine at the palace—me in my Husky outfit, which seemed one degree less removed from palatial evening-wear than a pair of ill-fitting Cairo-tailored shorts.

At present Ras Mangasha is away in the mountains, building another road, so Leilt Aida appeared alone in the courtyard to receive us. It can be disconcerting to meet a princess who seems like a princess; one feels as though a fairy-tale had come true—especially with a background of high turrets standing out blackly against a moon-blue sky. Haile Selassie's eldest grandchild is very elegant and very beautiful—olive skinned, with a triangular face, large and lovely eyes and the finest of bones. The likeness to her grandfather is at first quite intimidating, but is soon countered by a subtle sense of humour and a kindly graciousness. Clearly she is going to be a wonderful ally

—concerned for my safety, but only to a sensible extent. She has not opposed my setting out through the Tembien *sans* guide, *sans* guard, though she insists on giving me letters to the various district governors, who are being instructed to help me if I'm in difficulty.

Yohannes IV's stone palace-fortress was constructed by an Italian workman, named Giuseppe Naretti, and its practical solidity fittingly commemorates one of Ethiopia's greatest warrior Emperors. But the many cavernous reception rooms are not very suitable for a family of eleven and innumerable servants, so an inconspicuous bungalow has recently been built on to the south wing.

As I write a fiendish gale is tearing around the hotel, incessantly howling, whining, rattling and roaring. Makalle is renowned for these strong, cold winds, which rise during the late afternoon and continue until dawn.


## 27 December

This morning I mentioned mule-buying to Leilt Aida—and such is the Imperial Magic that within twenty minutes no less than six pack-mules were being paraded before me, by hopeful owners, in the stable-yard behind the palace.

My choice was quickly made, for one animal looked much superior to the rest. He is about thee years old, with perfect feet, a good coat and an apparently docile nature. It seemed auspicious that he meekly allowed me to open his mouth and pick up his feet, and when I took the halter he followed me around the yard like a lamb. He is dark grey, with a black off-foreleg, a white saucer-sized spot on the withers, a large chestnut patch on the near flank and a few white stripes on his belly. But the most important—and surprising—thing is his endearing expression. It had never occurred to me that one could be on more than civil terms with a mule, yet I can foresee myself becoming fond of this creature, for whom I willingly paid 105 dollars (fifteen guineas). The owner was an affable character, who considerately admitted that his animal had never seen a motor vehicle until today, and would therefore be inclined to ballet-dance on main roads.

I immediately named my new comrade 'Jock', in honour of a friend of mine who is noted for his kind dependability and capacity for overworking every day of the year—qualities which one hopes will be encouraged in Jock II by this talisman of a mutual name. I trust the friend in question will appreciate the compliment of having a mule named after him. As compliments go it is perhaps a trifle opaque at first sight.

Watering Jock in the stable-yard proved to be a little difficult; he had never before drunk from anything save a stream and was shy of both tank and bucket. When he had at last followed the example of a palace mule, I led him into a stable and left him settling down to a feed of barley. The buying of accessories was postponed till to-morrow, as Leilt Aida had arranged to take us to the Leul's road-building camp for a picnic lunch.

The age when arrogant, energetic highland princes were the *de facto* rulers of their provinces has passed, but one can see traces of it in Ras Mangasha's career as Governor-General of Tigre. His position is a curious one. Officially he is a senior civil servant in a centralised bureaucracy; actually he remains the hereditary prince of the Tigreans—a people to whom bureaucrats mean nothing and feudal lords everything. This vigorous great-grandson of Yohannes IV has shown a traditional independence in organising his latest project. Instead of submitting his scheme to the relevant procrastinating ministry in Addis he designed the road himself (though without academic training as an engineer), appealed to the peasants to help him, took off his shirt—literally—and got on with it. The peasants are now willingly contributing unpaid labour, though if an unknown official from Addis requested this sort of co-operation he would get a stony stare from these same people. The work has been in progress for only fifteen days, yet ten miles of road have been completed; and it must give Ras Mangasha considerable satisfaction personally to lead the peasants in this communal effort as his forefathers led their forefathers in battle.

At 11 a.m. we left Makalle in a battered chauffeur-driven Mercedes and followed the main road towards Addis for an hour and a quarter, seeing no traffic except large mule and camel caravans on their way to the Danakil Desert to fetch salt. When we turned off the main road to begin our nine-mile climb the new track rounded many well engineered hair-pin bends and near the summit of the range's highest mountain we stopped at a tiny caravan—Ras Mangasha's temporary home. Today's work-party was visible at the end of the road, and soon the Leul came slithering expertly down a cliff to greet us—stocky, self-confident and dark-skinned, with bright, enthusiastic eyes and work-roughened hands. He has none of his wife's calm depth and his conversation at once reveals a certain naïvety of approach to this complex transition period in Ethiopian history; but one feels that he genuinely loves his people and that they love him.

We sat on a boulder, and were served with *injara*, *wat*, *talla* and *tej* while watching a giant bulldozer edging its way along a precipice, pushing over the verge tons of rock already loosened by the herculean endeavours of ill-equipped peasants. It was thrilling to see and hear these colossal chunks of mountain go rolling and rumbling through the undergrowth into the invisible depths of the valley below. Apart from the workers, scores of men, women and children walk for miles every day just to watch, and they feel that this machine which moves mountains must be operated by some high-powered magic, lately discovered through the cleverness and virtue of their Prince. Frequently, during our picnic, Ras Mangasha leaped to his feet and yelled frantic warnings at open-mouthed onlookers who had chosen to stand and stare in the path of lethal boulders. As Leilt Aida remarked, these recurrent dramas were very bad for everyone's digestion. Not to mention the fact that from our angle the bulldozer itself looked in imminent danger of following the rocks.

Despite the bulldozer, the tractors and the Mercedes this scene was essentially of another age. As we ate, several peasants approached Ras Mangasha to present gifts of bread. They came towards us bent double, holding out the leaf-wrapped loaves with both hands and not daring to raise their eyes; but when a servant had accepted the gift some of the bolder spirits came closer and, after a moment's hesitation, reverently touched the muddy princely boot with their fingertips.

Archbishop Mathew has remarked that until the accession of Yohannes IV 'the sustained element of the picturesque, which was so marked a feature of court life in Ethiopia, was lacking in the viceroyalty of the Tigre. . . . These viceroys were without a sense of dynasty, armed chief had followed armed chief. . . . There could be nothing withdrawn or sacred in such a feudal history.' However, since the reign of Ethiopia's only Tigrean Emperor this province has adopted the rigid, stylized etiquette that for so many centuries regulated the behaviour of the Gondarine and Shoan courts—though the differing traditions are remarkably reflected in the personalities of Leilt Aida Desta and Leul Ras Mangasha Seyoum. Yet neither is pure-blooded, for theirs is not the first marriage alliance between the rival royal houses of Tigre and Shoa. When Yohannes IV was dying on the battlefield of Gallabat he named as his heir Ras Mangasha, an illegitimate son by his brother's wife (his legitimate heir had already been poisoned), and this man became the future Emperor Menelik's only serious competitor. Soon Menelik had vanquished the Tigrean prince on the battlefield and he then compelled Ras Mangasha to divorce his wife and marry a niece of the Empress Taitu. It was after this Mangasha's son—Seyoum—had been killed in the 1960 revolution that the present Leul became head of the family.

As I watched the peasants paying homage to their Prince I thought of all this tangled background—which partly explains why Ras Mangasha maintains no royal aloofness. His noted accessibility is a reversion to type, though it bewilders the Tigrean peasants, who know little of their own history and have long since accepted the formal Amharic code.

When we got back to the palace I hurried out to see Jock, who was looking a little forlorn in his new quarters. We took a short stroll, and I then decided that since both my feet feel comfortably re-skinned we can start our trek on the twenty-ninth.

For dinner Leilt Aida provided us with a sheep roasted whole on a spit. It looked romantic and tasted delicious.

*28 December*

This morning I woke at 6.30 to see Christopher and Nicola standing by my bed, pleading to come with me as far as Aksum. They are a tough pair—born and bred in Southern Ethiopia—so I said that of course they could come, if parental permission were granted. But in the end this day-dream was reduced to Christopher's accompanying me on tomorrow's stage and being retrieved in the evening by a palace car.

When the other Bromleys had left for home Christopher and I went to the open-air market, where I hoped to find a suitable walking-stick. The market-place covers about two acres and scores of villagers from surrounding districts—the majority women suckling babies—sat on the dusty ground behind small piles of eggs, grain or unfamiliar herbs. All these highlanders wear rags and look filthy beyond description—which is hardly surprising, with water so scarce.

We found that *dulas* (heavy sticks) are not marketed here, since people prefer to cut and prepare their own weapons, so I looked for a substitute at several of the poky Arab huckster-stalls that line the narrower streets. My enquiries had to be made in sign language and, remembering the highlanders' predilection for hitting each other over the head, I used this gesture—with the result that I soon became a popular turn. A delighted crowd followed me up the street, all perfectly understanding what I meant but none willing to part with his beloved *dula*. Then an Arab trader offered his own light stick for fifty cents (one and fivepence) and I gladly accepted it—against the advice of my Tigrean followers, who despise light sticks.

After lunch Jock and I went for a stroll around the 'estate', which is delightfully unpretentious. Broken-down farm machinery and the displaced statues of stone lions litter the forecourt, a chihuahua bitch complacently suckles three almost invisible pups in a cardboard box on the bungalow verandah and donkeys and mules graze on nothing in particular inside the imposing arched gateway—while the Prince's standard flutters importantly above them.

For centuries Ethiopia's emperors and nobles lived nomad

lives, their courts elaborate camps set up at various points throughout troubled domains, and here one realises that two generations of 'settledness' have not counteracted the effects of this wandering tradition, which bred indifference to comfort and beauty. The Ras Mangasha who succeeded Yohannes IV stabled his riding horses within his palace to mark the esteem in which they were held—a natural gesture, for someone reared in a robust society immemorially centred on good horses and good horsemanship. Many Ethiopian emperors and chieftains were intelligent men, but they devoted their skills and energies to intriguing, hunting, repelling invasions or warring with neighbouring chieftains; and when the Imperial Court did settle in Gondar it soon became degenerate.

At tea-time I went indoors, and soon several servants appeared at the french windows, holding up sundry bits of terrifyingly complicated pack-mule equipment. Leilt Aida asked my opinion of these items, but I hastily confessed that I'd never seen the like in my life before and couldn't possibly pronounce on their quality or suitability. The palace staff are taking this matter of Jock's equipment very seriously and soon we heard them arguing vehemently about the relative reliability and convenience of various bridles, bits, pack-saddles and ropes. Finally it was decided that a servant, Gabne, should accompany me to a saddler in the bazaar to advise me on the purchase of a bit and bridle.

Because today is one of Ethiopia's many important religious feasts the saddler's shop was shut, so Gabre led me on to the man's home, through alleyways where mounting-blocks stood outside most of the sturdy little stone houses. (Compared with other highlanders the Tigreans are noted for their solid buildings.) In the saddler's compound some forty men and women were being entertained to *talla* and *dabo* (substantial wheaten bread) and I was taken to a small room, where much saddlery hung on the mud walls and women were baking on a fire in the centre of the earthen floor. The general reaction to this unprecedented intrusion of a *faranj* was interesting. I sensed a mixture of curiosity, amusement, shyness and suspicion; and, despite the status of my escort, I was given no special treatment —as one inevitably would be by Asians in similar circumstances.

A minor Ethiopian official would have been received with much more ceremony, and one could see that the Princess' servant was regarded as a person of far greater consequence than the Princess' foreign friend. I was glad to observe so much today, before setting out on my trek. It is always a help to know one's place from the start.

# 2

# *Tamely through the Tembien*

*29 December. A Hovel on a Hilltop*

This morning's assembly in the palace farmyard was comical —one long-suffering mule, one clueless *faranj*, one anxious-to-help but (in this context) equally clueless princess and five bewildered farm-hands. (All these men are expert mule-loaders, but none had ever before encountered such an intractable miscellany of baggage.) The pack-saddle is a simple square of well-padded, soft sacking and we began by roping on my rucksack, flea-bag, box of emergency rations and water-bottle, topping them with Jock's natty plastic bucket (bought in Asmara) and Leilt Aida's bulky contribution of imported foods.

After a forty-minute struggle everything seemed secure, so all good-byes were said and everyone industriously waved to everyelse as Christopher and I left the farmyard behind Jock and Gabre Maskal—the servant who had been deputed to guide us on to the Adua track. Then, on the verge of the road, a hooting Red Cross jeep caused Jock to buck frantically, and everything slowly slid under his belly and thence to the ground.

As we retreated to the yard I decided that two evenly weighted sacks would have to replace my awkwardly-shaped rucksack. In due course these were produced and I impatiently tumbled into them a conglomeration of books, clothes, matches, medicines, candles, pens, soup-cubes, cigarettes, toothpaste, torch batteries, notebooks, maps and insecticides. Then, after much testing and balancing of sacks, and tying and retying of ropes and leather thongs, reasonable security was assured. Undoubtedly Jock is a patient animal: there he stood, the picture of bored resignation, while the men crowded around him yelling argumentatively and heaving on the ropes like sailors in a storm. Their loading method is impossibly complex and I am

30

singularly inept at acquiring such skills—so we will be dependent on hypothetical passers-by if we have to camp out at night.

Much of the route from Makalle to Adua follows a makeshift motor-track constructed during the Italian occupation but neglected for the past quarter of a century. Our guide evidently disapproved of Leilt Aida allowing *faranjs* to travel unescorted and he asked several peasants who were walking in our direction if they would take charge of us; but all were soon turning off this main track towards their settlements and eventually Gabre Maskal was persuaded to turn back.

For the next four miles our track ran direct over a light-brown, stony plain, bounded to east and west by low mountains. I walked ahead, leading Jock, and Christopher followed a little way behind, displaying remarkable stamina for a ten-year-old. Already I could see that he would never admit to being tired, so an early lunch seemed advisable and we stopped near the edge of the plateau, where a solitary, gnarled tree provided meagre shade. Here too was the first settlement we had seen—a few round, thatched huts (*tukuls*) clumsily constructed of stakes and mud. Several locals at once gathered around us and one young man asked if we were Italian or American; on being told that we were British and Irish he and his companions looked blank. These people must be quite used to seeing *faranjs* at Makalle, but beneath their formal courtesy I sensed—or imagined—a mixture of hostility, suspicion and contempt.

From the edge of the plateau we took a short cut down a steep, narrow path which wound around a mountain covered in low green scrub. This path was so rough that I urged Jock to go ahead and choose his own way, since my stumbling progress was making things more difficult for him, and on rejoining the main track he stood meekly waiting for me to catch up. All day his behaviour was angelic, apart from one slight aberration when he suddenly lay down beside a shallow river and attempted to roll in the fine sand; but the moment I tugged at the halter—exclaiming 'Jock!' in a horrified tone—he scrambled to his feet and consoled himself with a long drink. This docility was especially encouraging because I had by then removed the bit, which was obviously causing him great discomfort. At our next rest-halt I experimented further by letting him graze loose, and as a reward for my increasing trust he didn't withdraw even a step when I went to catch him.

During the afternoon we were sometimes accompanied by groups of men and boys, driving mule or donkey caravans towards their invisible settlements in the folds of the hills. Everyone stared at us with astonishment and amusement— the amusement being caused by Jock's eccentric load. Amidst surroundings innocent of the garishness that now disfigures many European landscapes my simple possessions look horribly ostentatious—a canary-yellow nylon flea-bag, a vivid green plastic bucket and a white and red plastic water-bottle. No wonder the locals are amused, as they stride along in their off-white *shammas* behind sober-hued, professionally-balanced loads of hides and salt-blocks.

There is a disconcerting lack of spontaneity in the highlanders, reactions to a *faranj*. No doubt it is illogical to deduce hostility from restraint, yet one misses the friendly, unrepressed interest aroused in Asia by wandering foreigners.

All afternoon our track switchbacked through easy hills— some scrub-covered, some barren—and despite this region's appearance of infertility the many herds of wide-horned cattle and small, fat-tailed sheep seemed in excellent condition.

As the sun declined pale colours softened the hills, and then came the quiet glory of the highland sunset. Without clouds there are no spectacular effects, but this evening broad bands of pastel light merged dreamily into one another above the royal blue solidness of a long, level escarpment some hundred yards west of our track.

When we heard the distant roar of the palace jeep I led Jock on to some ploughland and murmured soothingly in his ear; but as the noise came closer he began to tremble, and much to his disapproval I hastily replaced the bit, lest he should try to bolt. However, he managed to retain his self-control and quietly followed me back to the track after the vehicle had pulled up nearby.

To our surprise it was not the jeep, but the Mercedes—and Leilt Aida was sitting in front with a picnic-basket. As Christopher and I gulped cups of steaming tea she and the driver discussed what seemed to them a Problem—where I would sleep to-night. We had walked only fourteen miles, so both Jock and I were fresh enough to cope with the remaining four miles to the next village. But Leilt Aida forbade me to continue —ostensibly because hyenas might attack Jock after dark, though I suspect that her real fear was of *shifta* attacking me. She then sent the driver to reconnoitre a steep, uncultivated mountainside that rose directly from the track on our right; there was no trace of an upward path and it would never have occurred to me to look for shelter in such an apparently unpopulated area.

By now it was dark and as we sat waiting, on a low stone wall, Leilt Aida repeated that I must telephone her whenever possible and not hesitate to ask for help if in need. I thought then of the words spoken by one of her ancestors to the 1841 British trade mission. His Majesty Sahela Salassie, seventh King of Shoa, had said, 'My children, all my gun-people shall accompany you; may you enter into safety. Whatsoever your hearts think or wish, that send word unto me. Saving myself, ye have no relative in this distant land.' The difference here was that no gun-people were accompanying me, and it was obvious that Leilt Aida had already begun to reproach herself for not insisting on an escort.

Fifteen minutes later a favourable report was shouted from the hilltop and, waving goodbye to Leilt Aida and Christopher, I began to lead Jock up the steep slope, scrambling blindly over or around rough rocks and through excruciatingly prickly scrub. We were guided by the driver above and Leilt Aida below. He would yell down in Amharic, 'More to the right,' or 'A little left there!' and she would yell the translation up to me. Reaching the top, I saw by starlight that we were on a level, scrub-covered plateau. Here the driver produced as my guide an awe-stricken, speechless youth—whose name I later discovered to be Marcos—and then he bounded down to the track, while Leilt Aida and I yelled final good-byes.

Ten minutes later, as we were being led along a narrow path, I saw the car jolting slowly away towards Makalle, which was visible as a cluster of dim lights on a plateau level with this. Across all the intervening countryside no other lights glimmered, though there must be many settlements among these hills, and the dwindling headlights of the Mercedes seemed pleasingly symbolic.

When we reached this compound it, too, was in darkness—apart from the flicker of a dying wood-fire in the smallest of the three stone huts—and it took me fifteen minutes to unload Jock. (It was the measure of today's disorganisation that my torch lay at the bottom of a sack and could only be got at after the untying of countless complicated knots.) Marcos must be used to unloading mules, but he seemed to have been mentally numbed by astonishment—or else he believes that there is some special mystique connected with *faranj*-owned pack-animals. He made no attempt to help until I had somehow induced everything to come to pieces; then, while I fumbled through the sacks for food, torch, insecticide-powder and notebook, he led Jock to a shelter, before carrying my load into the smallest hut. This was round and solidly built, with a pointed grass roof and two-foot thick walls. A quarter of the floor space was taken up by a mud 'stove', some eighteen inches high, another quarter by two six-foot mud-and-wicker grain storage bins, and the rest by an uneven mud couch, covered with a stiff cow-hide and raised two feet above the floor. Marcos dumped my load on this bed, bent down to blow the embers and, when a handful of twigs had begun to blaze, gave me an uneasy, sideways glance. I grinned cheerfully in reply—without saying anything, since my earlier attempts at communication had seemed only to scare him. He was a handsome youth, with a broad brow, a straight nose, slightly prominent cheek-bones and fine eyes. Beneath his unease I sensed a nice nature and now he responded to my grin with a quick, shy smile, before adding more twigs to the fire and putting a rusty basin of water to heat. I wondered if some beverage would in due course be produced from the basin; but instead, when the water was hot, Marcos began to remove my boots and socks, keeping his head respectfully bent. For the next ten minutes he violently massaged my legs from knees to toes, pouring water over them before each attack. Even without today's severe sun-burn—just where he was concentrating on my calf-muscles—such treatment would have been trying enough; but now my legs feel comfortably relaxed.

While replacing my boots I heard voices, and then saw, through the low doorway, a few vague shapes wrapped in *shammas*. The arrival of his family had an interesting effect on Marcos. He leaped up, his face shining with delighted relief, and only then did I realise that he had been seriously frightened of me. I hope this Italian-bred fear of *faranjs* is not common throughout Tigre, since fear can express itself in many ways.

As Marcos told his news three men and two women crowded up to see me, the women half-hiding behind their menfolk, covering the lower part of their faces with their *shammas*.

Released from the strain of my undiluted company, Marcos beamed at me in a proprietary way, as though my presence here were all his own work, and began self-importantly to make free with my possessions, which earlier he had dropped as if they might bite him. He held up my sleeping-bag and bucket to be admired—but was at once sharply reprimanded by his father for unnecessarily touching a guest's belongings. By now the men had edged into the *tukal* and we were all sitting close together on the bed, while outside the women excitedly discussed me. Soon they had decided that I must be transferred to the main dwelling-house—a rectangular, high-ceilinged, single-story building, which consists of one large room, where several tree-trunks support the wooden beams of the mud roof and many grain bins take up most of the floor-space. Here the mud bed—which has been sacrificed to me—is about three feet high and built four feet out from the wall. The younger members of the family sleep on the floor around the fire and the poultry roost on crude shelves directly above the bed.

When Marcos began to move my luggage I tried to stop him; but everyone insisted that it must remain beside me, so it has been stacked at the end of the bed. This attitude seems to indicate an endemic lack of trust. In similar circumstances elsewhere a host would store my kit in the most convenient spot—not necessarily anywhere near my sleeping quarters—after assuring me that it would be safe.

Having recovered from the initial shock, everyone wanted to talk to me. Marcos' parents speak a little Italian and I do too; but a little Italian, spoken with strong Tigrean and Irish accents, doesn't really facilitate conversation and we soon gave up.

However, mutual attempts to communicate always warm the atmosphere and now I don't feel at all excluded from the family circle, though I've been writing non-stop while everyone else chatters away ninety to the dozen. Just occasionally someone looks at me and laughs kindly at my dumbness, or Marcos leans over to count the pages I've written, or his mother urges me to move closer to the fire.

It is almost thirteen months since I last stayed in a peasant's hut. That was in Nepal, and now it is somehow reassuring to be in similar surroundings on another continent, following the old routine of writing by firelight with wood-smoke in my eyes and sleepy hens clucking beside me and a variety of footloose vermin swarming over my body.

### 30 December. Migua Selassie

Bug-wise, last night was hell. My insecticide powder proved unequal to the occasion and repeatedly I woke from a restless doze to scratch. These African devils seem even more vicious than their Asian cousins and my body is now covered with inflamed lumps.

I was on the trail by 6.30, without sleep or breakfast, but full of the joys of life—as who wouldn't be, in cool, clear air, amidst a silent wilderness of mountains, with a companionable mule following to heel and twelve sunny hours ahead. All day our track went up and down and round and down and up and round again. On every side the mountains lay in long, smooth lines, and the midday heat haze gave a familiar look to their lower slopes, whose mixture of red clay and green scrub produced a heathery tinge. We passed one very beautiful teff-harvesting scene. This cereal has grain and straw of the palest gold and for miles the whole countryside was glowing against the strong blue of the sky or the faint powder-blue of distant mountains. After the straw has been threshed by bullocks the women winnow the grain by tossing it on huge wicker trays.

For two hours this morning we accompanied a donkey-caravan on its way to a market-village on a mountain-top. The five men and boys registered the usual unsmiling astonishment when they first saw us, but I soon realised that despite

their silence and inscrutability they had 'taken charge' of me
—obviously as a duty rather than as a pleasure. If I stopped to
examine a shrub or try to identify a bird they also stopped
and waited politely for me to continue—which was very nice of
them, though I would have preferred being left to dawdle un-
inhibitedly at my own pace. However, I soon had reason to feel
genuinely grateful. Jock had been clumsily loaded by Marcos
and on one steep slope everything suddenly fell off. Without
even glancing at me, two of my escort went into action and
professionally reloaded in a matter of moments; but had I been
alone I might have spent hours sitting by the wayside waiting
for help.

Today also taught me that it is less tiring to drive a pack-
animal with a caravan. Even the nicest mules have definite
personal opinions and Jock feels that there is something un-
dignified about a single animal walking over one and a half
miles an hour when loose, or two and a half miles when being
led; and this go-slow policy causes a certain amount of frustration as my average speed is three and a half miles an hour.
However, when we are with trotting donkeys he imagines the
honour of muledom to be at stake, so he canters into the lead
and effortlessly averages four miles per hour. This morning he
sometimes went so far ahead that I could only distinguish him
by the bouncing green bucket.

At half-past eleven, after a steep climb, we reached the village
of Enda Mikael Tukul—a long straggle of round huts and
rectangular stone shacks. Most highland towns and villages are
marked by tall groves of the quick-growing Australian eucalyptus (or blue-gum), which was imported into Ethiopia by
Menelik II, on French advice; now this is by far the commonest
tree in the north and at midday its shade is welcome, despite
the altitude.

When I stopped to rest, on the outskirts of the village, my
companions characteristically continued towards the market-
place without any word or gesture of farewell. They had done
their duty by me and were doubtless relieved to be rid of the
responsibility of escorting an inexplicable female *faranj*.

Beneath the aromatic blue-gums I ate the remains of a Palace
fruit-cake while Jock grazed on next-to-nothing with every

appearance of satisfaction. Already we're such good buddies that when I turn him loose he never moves far away, though in Makalle I was warned never to leave him untethered.

Beyond the village—where everyone stared curiously at us, showing neither hostility nor friendliness—our path plunged down a precipice—and here I acquired the knack of allowing Jock to help me on steep, rough, slithery slopes. Instead of sending him ahead I continued to lead him, hanging on to the halter with one hand and leaning on my *dula* with the other. If he were at all unreliable this could be a dangerous technique, but he seemed to understand exactly what was required of him.

Soon afterwards I heard an extraordinary zooming sound overhead and looked up to see an enormous eagle dive-bombing towards a little brown civet-cat—which heard the zoom too and swerved to safety under a rock. The disappointed eagle then resumed its slow gliding over the valley; once the first surprise attack has failed a bird of prey has no hope of capturing any nimble animal and within moments the civet-cat emerged from his air-raid shelter and strolled on casually through the boulders.

At two o'clock we approached a settlement set among junipers on a slope above a murky stream. Coarse green grass grew thickly on the near bank and when Jock had drunk his fill he settled down to some serious grazing while I topped up my water-bottle and added two more purifying pills. In theory one should only water a pack-animal at the end of the day's trek: but it would indeed be rash to try to stop a thirsty mule from drinking when and where he gets the chance.

Thirty yards upstream cattle were standing in ankle-deep water beneath an ancient wild-fig tree. Near them half-a-dozen men sat watching their women-folk washing clothes in the trickle of discoloured water and soon, to my surprise, these men came towards me, shouting friendly questions. Then the women abandoned their laundrying and came too, and everyone sat around on the grass laughing uproariously. The fact that I don't understand Tigrinya seems always to be a source of incredulous amusement, but I discovered that in this case my relationship with Jock was the joke. On arriving at the stream I had given him a little well-earned stroking on the neck and murmured a few sweet nothings in his ear—and to the locals this looked as comic as the stroking of a motor-truck would look to us.

While discussing my eccentricities the men were eating *atar* —a type of green pea which thrives in dry soil and is planted after the rains. These peas are often dried and stored for use in *wat*—especially during the long fasts—and they are also ground to make savoury puddings and breads. Two men had gone to pick some for me in an adjacent field, where I had previously noticed the little green bushes—about eighteen inches high—on which the pods are almost invisible among dense, fern-like foliage. Each pod contains two to four seeds and I was stupidly surprised to see these familiar green peas. They taste like our variety, though their shape is less regular.

This encounter made me feel more at ease in the Tigrean countryside and I set off happily on the next lap, my friends expressing great astonishment at the docility with which Jock allowed himself to be caught.

Two hours later we came to a bigger settlement, scattered over a hillside. Here the jeep-track went due west, and a well-defined animal-track went north-west towards Abbi Addi and Adua. A consultation with my map merely revealed the map's limitations, so I approached three harvesters, pointed to the animal-track and said 'Abbi Addi?' All three men stared at me blankly, and when I pointed to the jeep-track and repeated 'Abbi Addi?' their blankness remained total. I then decided that since Adua lay to the north, and the animal-track went north, and I wanted to get to Adua, we would now leave the jeep-track—though I was aware that in this sort of terrain logical decisions can have dire consequences.

The men impassively watched us turning off the main track: but we were also being observed from the settlement, and soon five breathless young men overtook us. Their leader, who was dressed in European fashion, at once grabbed Jock's halter, said '*Yellum! yellum!*' ('No! no!') and released an argumentative spate of Tigrinya, flecked with unenlightening Italian and English phrases. Again I pointed ahead and inquired 'Abbi Addi? Adua?' and he replied 'Yes' in English, rapidly followed by 'No' and an elaborate series of gestures which, despite my fluency in sign language, conveyed nothing to me—except extreme disapproval of our continuing along this track. I reckoned that his objection might conceivably have a sensible basis, and to ignore such emphatic local advice, when one couldn't find out what lay behind it, seemed distinctly unwise. So I turned back.

Ayela proved to be the headman's son and as he led Jock up the slope he asked 'American? Italian?' On hearing that I was 'Irish—from Ireland' he nodded cheerfully and carefully pronounced 'American—you are American. Ethiopian—I am Ethiopian.' As it happens I find it peculiarly irritating to be mistaken for an American; but it is hardly reasonable to expect Ethiopians to have heard of Ireland, so I let the matter go.

The headman's round, stone, tin-roofed *tukul* is unusual, being both white-washed and two-storeyed, with an outside stairway of uneven rocks leading up to the granary, where I'm now writing by the light of a smoky oil-lamp, leaning on a shaky wooden table and sitting on a disintegrating iron chair. Downstairs is the all-purpose living room and there are three smaller huts in the compound—one a kitchen, the others the homes of married sons. The headman and his wife and sister-in-law are splendid old people—gracious and warm-hearted— and on meeting them I was glad that we had been forced to stop here. *Faranjs* are obviously a rarity in their lives but these elders have an air of dignified assurance, though the younger people (except for the Adua-educated Ayela) are timid enough. Highland society has always been organised on strictly hierarchical lines and each headman wields considerable power within his own little realm.

When I arrived my host ordered this table and chair (status symbols of the first magnitude) to be brought up to the granary, which is also the guest-room, and soon we were being served with cups of freshly-ground coffee and roasted whole barley— a palatable combination. Crowds of children came to stare and were periodically shooed away by Ayela—only to return to squat around the doorway a moment later, having been emboldened by my distribution of Palace toffees.

Then my host raised the question of where I was to sleep. In sign-language he said, 'Downstairs, with the family,' and in the same language I firmly replied, '*No!* Up here on the floor.' (Undoubtedly bed-bugs are my Achilles' heel.) But, as everyone was appalled at the idea of my sleeping alone, the headman announced that his sister-in-law would sleep here too, to 'protect' me. At once I foresaw her importing bug-laden hides into this possibly bug-free granary, so at the risk of seeming rude I again said 'No!'—and eventually my obstinacy was accepted as a strange *faranj* fetish. However, half-an-hour later I saw, to my horror, an iron bedstead and a hair mattress being carried across the mountainside from the priest's compound. At the very sight of the mattress I felt itchy and frantically explained that I had my own bed to put on the floor: whereupon Ayela shouted through the doorway and the generous little procession went into reverse and disappeared.

I haven't yet discovered why we were prevented from continuing and I'm not even speculating about whether or not it will be in order for us to go north-west tomorrow. The first essential for the enjoyment of this sort of trek is to take each day as it comes.

### 31 December. Workhsegeh

Mercifully my liquid insecticide proved effective last night and I slept soundly until an odd message was shouted through the door, in warped English, at 5 a.m. At first I thought I must be dreaming, it all sounded so improbable—something about two policemen having arrived to escort me to Abbi Addi on Leilt Aida's instructions, because yesterday *shifta* had been observed in the intervening mountains. Crawling out of my flea-bag I opened the door and saw by moonlight two armed policemen smartly coming to attention—and they were accompanied by the Chief Clerk of the Governor of Abbi Addi.

The senior policeman was the linguist; he said urgently—'Hurry! Quick! Big hurry! Much quick!' I had no idea why the hurry was big, but since these unfortunates had apparently been walking all night on my behalf I felt obliged to be much quick. So I hurled everything into those confounded sacks and when Jock had been loaded, in the odd, 'stagey' glow of mingled moonlight and dawnlight, we turned towards the north-west trail.

Our party was led by a tall, handsome police lieutenant, carrying his rifle at the ready and followed by me. Next came the Chief Clerk's armed servant, leading Jock, then a group of five armed local men, on their way to an animal-market at Abbi Addi, then the portly Chief Clerk on his riding mule (which he had gallantly offered to me) and finally the junior policeman. The locals take *shifta** very seriously and were delighted to have police protection this morning. It seems odd that most Asians, and apparently most highland Ethiopians, are so much more jittery than we are about dangers of this

* Dr Levine clearly defines the position of *shifta* in highland society. He writes, 'The one area in which communal sentiments have seemed fairly strong among the Amharas has been in connection with the pursuit of outlaws. It is customary—in some Amhara districts, at least—for the local inhabitants to band together in informal posses when threatened by the presence of one or more *shifta*, or "outlaw". Yet even here, in his attitude towards the *shifta*, the Amhara reveals an ambivalence regarding the maintenance of civil order and security.

'The term *shifta* had, in former times, primarily a political connotation. It referred to someone who rebelled against his feudal superior and was applied only to persons of relatively high status. More recently the term has been vulgarised and broadened to include any sort of outlaw in the rural areas. In any case the *shifta* is a man apart, who makes his home in uninhabited mountainous country or lowlands and lives by stealing cattle and robbing travellers. Some Amhara become *shifta* because of a passion for this way of life; this is particularly true of soldiers who, after a long campaign, prefer the continuation of a predatory and free existence to a return to the hard work of the fields. Others do so involuntarily, in order to escape punishment after committing some violence in the course of a personal dispute.

'The attitudes of civilian Amhara towards the *shifta* combine fear and dislike with a strong tendency towards idealisation. The *shifta* is feared because he is a killer; if a person happens to witness him performing some act of theft or murder, he will usually keep quiet about it for fear of reprisal. He is disliked because he lives parasitically off the productive activities of others. But the *shifta* is widely admired, on the other hand, because he possesses a number of qualities that are dear to the Amhara. He is reputed to be an expert singer. . . He is credited with unusually handsome features because . . . he has plenty to eat and no arduous work. . . . Above all he is *guabaz*—the great Amhara virtue that embodies bravery, fierceness, hardihood and general male competence. . . .

'The Amhara's admiration for the *shifta* is reminiscent of American attitude towards the outlaw in "western" films. . . [but] is not balanced by a corresponding idealisation of the sheriff-figure as the representative of civil order. . . There is no feeling. . . that the *shifta* must be captured simply because he is an outlaw. Instead. . . [he] is acknowledged as a legitimate social type and is tolerated at a distance so long as his killing does not become wanton or excessive. This approach . . . bespeaks a relatively weak commitment to the value of civil order.' *Wax and Gold* by Donald N. Levine, The University of Chicago Press (Copyright 1965 The University of Chicago).

sort; if they lived in Europe they would probably refuse to drive trucks after dark lest they should be hi-jacked.

Our walk was extremely frustrating; had I been alone I could have spent a day on this stretch, but we kept going non-stop until 10.30 a.m.

For a few miles we were crossing recently harvested, level fields. Then came a gradual descent, followed by a steep climb up a forested ridge, with a gloriously deep valley on our right and beyond it an array of jagged, tumbled mountains. (A 'forest' in the highlands usually means an area covered not with tall, green, shady trees, but with thick, thorny bush and scrub and low acacia trees.)

At the top of this ridge we were on the edge of a thousand foot drop, overlooking miles of volcanic chaos—harsh, magnificent, unreal—and all around were violent colours and unbelievable contours. From the base of the escarpment savagely broken land fell away for another thousand feet and in the distance Abbi Addi's tin roofs glinted on the plain. Even the highlanders, born and bred amidst geological dramas, paused here for a moment and smiled wryly at me, making gestures to indicate that they considered this a bloody awful stretch of country.

I would have thought it impossible for any non-mountaineer to tackle such a precipice; yet down we plunged, Jock and the riding-mule leading the party, lest they should concuss us with dislodged rocks, and myself thinking how much more dangerous this was than any *shifta* attack. Deep grey or red dust concealed round stones and pebbles that moved beneath our feet at every step and never before has my sense of balance—or power of regaining balance—been so severely tested. The locals, who are accustomed to this route, leaped down like baboons; but the police were perceptibly apprehensive and the Chief Clerk was soon a nervous wreck. Thorny scrub reaches out over the path —which, understandably, is not much used—and I was too

It is interesting that in Eritrea the word *shifta* has now regained a political connotation. Of course the men concerned repudiate the term and call themselves the Eritrean Liberation Army; but the government speaks of *shifta*, hoping that the 'fear and dislike' provoked by the traditional outlaws will also be aroused by the new political bandits—though the peasants are more likely to 'idealise' them as *shifta* than as foreign supported political agitators.

busy avoiding a lethal slip to avoid the thorns, so this evening
my painfully sunburnt legs are badly torn. Yet these barbs give
only surface scratches to the highlanders' tough skins.

At the base we waited for the Chief Clerk and the junior
policeman, who were holding hands like a pair of frightened
children as they came slowly slithering down in a cloud of dust.
A moment before the sun had reached the top of the escarpment, and I gazed up with joy at those grotesquely eroded
pinnacles, now looking as though freshly drenched in burgundy.

During the next half-hour we were crossing an already-too-
hot area of black lava-beds, interspersed with deep, powdery,
white ash and bluish chunks of rock which made a tinkling
cinder-sound beneath our feet. Then came a steep descent,
through an unexpected tangle of lush greenery, into the
shadowed, narrow ravine of a dry river bed. Here walking was
made difficult by unsteady stones lying hidden beneath fine,
pale dust; but occasionally I paused to look up at the serrated
tops of gold and crimson cliffs that were rising gloriously against
a deep blue sky.

We passed many pools of scummy water—the breeding sites
of malarial mosquitos—and now it was the mules' turn to feel
frustrated. They paused often to sniff at these pools, but had
too much sense ever to drink from them.

Within the past few hours we had descended from 8,000 to
6,000 feet and, as the ravine widened, I began to suffer from
the strong rays of this equatorial sun; but soon we turned up
a cul-de-sac side-valley and came to a grotto where sparkling
spring water dripped from the rock into a deep pool. The object
of this detour was to water the animals and give everyone an
opportunity to wash all over.

Abbi Addi is the administrative centre of the Tembien district, yet it is misleading to refer to the place as a 'town'. Walking through its laneways one has to negotiate small boulders
and minor gorges, and all the houses are single-storey, roughly-
constructed shacks. The headquarters of the district administration is an extraordinary building, made of iron-sheeting, even
to the floors; and because many sheets are missing one has to
jump over six-foot-deep holes, half filled with chunks of rock.

When we reached the Governor's office a pleasant man of

about forty, dressed in a dark lounge suit, respectfully received me. He was sitting behind a paperless desk on which stood an antique winding telephone, and he looked so pitifully perplexed by my presence that I wanted to pat him on the head and tell him not to worry—though this wouldn't have done much good, as he spoke not a word of English. There is no post office here, but an Italian-initiated telephone link of uncertain temper is maintained with Adua and Makalle, so I pointed to the machine and said loudly and clearly, 'Leilt Aida'.

It took an hour to get my call through and while I was waiting the policemen, who had been standing to attention in the background, were signed off duty and eagerly came towards me to request a written testimonial for presentation to their superior officer. The possibility of any Ethiopian ever being able to decipher my hand-writing—even if he could read English—is incalculably remote, but here the collection of such chits has become an obsession, which again indicates a deep-rooted lack of trust. Subordinates feel it necessary always to *prove* that they have done their duty well, where in our society this would be taken for granted.

After a brief argument with Leilt Aida, on the subject of bodyguards, she relented and spoke reassuringly to the perplexed Governor—though it was obvious that even her permission did not quite reconcile him to the idea of a lone *faranj* wandering around his district.

I then went to a *talla-beit* to drink several pints in preparation for the next eight-mile stage to this settlement. Jock had already been unloaded and provided with straw; he looked disillusioned on being reloaded so soon—by a group of local experts—but resignedly followed me when I set off in the cruel midday heat.

At first the track was ankle-deep in stifling volcanic ash and, as it wound between heat-reflecting boulders, I streamed sweat; but here the air is so dry that clothes never get damp—though my hair, under a wide straw hat, quickly becomes saturated. After a few miles I saw a woman and her filthy toddler sitting under a wild fig-tree beside a fat earthenware jar of *talla*. Assuming this to be the highland version of a roadside pub I collapsed nearby—to the terror of the toddler—and downed a quart at one draught. It was a thickish, grey-green brew, full of husks and unidentifiable bits and scraps, but I only cared that it was wet and had been kept cool by green leaves stuffed into the narrow mouth of the jar. The gourds used as drinking vessels never encounter washing-water; they are merely rinsed with a little *talla* before one's drink is poured. While I was imbibing my second quart two old men came along and stopped to look wistfully at the *talla*-jar—and then hopefully at me. I stood them a drink each, and that was the end of my solitude for today. They too were coming here, so they insisted on accompanying me, one leading Jock. (It is considered frightfully non-U for a *faranj* to walk instead of riding and the absolute bottom for a *faranj* personally to lead a pack-animal.) The only traffic we saw was a man on a cantering mule, escorted by two servants running alongside—one armed with a rifle. Highlanders rich enough to own riding-mules never travel unprotected and their servants are natural long-distance runners. No wonder Ethiopia's representative has won two Olympic Marathons—he probably regarded the twenty-six mile race as a sort of pre-breakfast stroll.

The track was easy, running smoothly over a burnt-up golden-brown plain, with dusty-blue mountains in the middle distance and contorted red cliffs nearby. The highest of these cliffs was used for exterminating Italians during the war and one can still see a few bleached human bones lying at its base.

This settlement is on a hilltop from which superb mountains are visible in every direction and when we arrived, at half-past-four, it seemed that my appearance was the most shattering local event since the Italian invasion. A ten-year-old boy who goes to school at Abbi Addi was summoned as interpreter; his English is minimal, but he conveyed that soon the headman would come to welcome me. This encounter took place fifty yards from the edge of the settlement and pending the headman's investigation I was not encouraged to approach any nearer. None of the many staring men who had surrounded me seemed at all well-disposed—which is understandable, when one remembers what this region suffered during the occupation and how impossible it is for these peasants to distinguish between Italians and other *faranjs*.

Indicating that Jock could safely be left, Yohannes, my young guide, led me to a nearby Italian military cemetery where scores of graves lie in neat rows—their headstones smashed or defaced —at the end of an avenue of mathematically-planted giant candelabra. In a country where neither building nor cultivation is planned or arranged, but everything appears merely to have 'happened', this little corner of forlorn orderliness was alien indeed—the epitome of the whole Italian–Ethiopian tragedy.

On our return we found Jock surrounded by Workhsegeh's entire male population and the headman stepped forward to greet me ceremonially. He looked rather ill-at-ease in rumpled khaki slacks and a patched tweed jacket, so I deduced that he had been delayed by a compulsion to don these garments of state in my honour. It is sad that Western clothes have become status symbols—the highlanders look so dignified and right in even the most tattered *shammas*, which hang around them in swinging folds and gracefully emphasise their proud, erect bearing.

Yohannes explained that I was to stay in a hut in the chief's sister's compound; but another long delay followed because the hut was being cleaned out for my reception. There are some forty compounds here, each containing two or three *tukuls* and all securely fenced in by thorn bushes as a protection against hyenas and leopards. This hut is used only as a bed-room-cum-storeroom. A narrow mud platform runs around half the circumference and opposite is a mud 'double-bed', with a built-in 'pillow bump' at one end. The cow-hides and goat-skins must secrete bugs by the million so I have already sprayed fanatically, uncharitably wishing the livestock on the three children who will be my hut-mates. As I write, by the light of a tiny wick floating in oil, a clay vat of *talla* is fermenting audibly beside me.

The chief's elderly sister is friendly though shy. When I entered the compound *talla* was immediately produced and each time I half-emptied my quart-measure gourd it was filled to the brim by Yohannes.

My supper consisted of two minute raw eggs, sucked from their shells, and a rusty tinful of fresh milk. Then I sat by the door watching the sunset colours and the first stars darting out in a still-blue sky. The men were all sitting on their haunches in the compound, talking and drinking *talla*, their *shammas* wrapped tightly around them against the evening air—which to me feels only pleasantly cool. The women were pounding peppers for *wat* in a hollow piece of tree-trunk, or cooking *injara* over a wood-fire in the main hut; probably none was offered to me because of a mistaken idea that it is unacceptable to *faranjs*.

My attempts to buy barley for Jock have failed and he is tethered to a gnarled, dry-leaved tree, mournfully chewing pale *teff* straw—which contains no nourishment whatever, though presumably it will take the edge off his hunger. This whole compound is rather miserable; a few thistles grow in corners and a little enclosed patch of cotton-bushes is the 'garden'. But the people are very handsome, like most highlanders. Both men and women have the basic bone-structure that good looks become even more pronounced with old age and everyone shows the finest of teeth that seem never to decay. Few highlanders are conspicuously tall, though the young sub-chief here is well over six feet and devastatingly handsome. I suspect that he and several of his contemporaries have some Italian blood. This is not because of any difference in colouring (many of the highlanders are quite fair-skinned, owing to their part-Semitic ancestry), but because of a difference in physique. The spindly limbs of the highland men and the exaggerated buttocks of the women clearly distinguish them from any European race.

Ten minutes ago ferocious fighting broke out nearby. The roars and screams of pain and rage were rather alarming, but Yohannes calmly explained that it was only a quarrel about cattle-stealing between neighbours armed with mule-whips. Now all is silent again, and as the boys have just come in to sleep I'll do likewise—I hope!


*1 January 1967. Mai Cheneta*

This has been an irritating New Year's Day. When I was ready to start at 6.30 a.m. disaster befell me, for Yohannes was unequal to explaining (or the chief was unwilling to believe) that Leilt Aida had said I might travel alone. Therefore an escort of two was inflicted upon me and as these youths were anxious to get home this evening we arrived here at 2 p.m., having covered sixteen miles of rough terrain in six hours.

Our departure was delayed by the chief's insistence on giving my escort a chit, to be delivered to the police on our arrival here; then the boys would be given a receipt from the police for the chief, confirming my safe delivery, and another chit from me informing all whom it might concern that they had done their duty in proper fashion. Such a preoccupation with the written word seems odd in a country where at least 99 per cent of the rural population is illiterate; but possibly it is because of this illiteracy that chits are considered so immensely significant. The sub-chief was the only person in Workhsegeh who could write and, when I had provided paper and pen, all the elders held a long and inexplicably acrimonious discussion about what was to be inscribed. Then the young man began his anguished struggle to form the Tigrinya characters. Merely to watch this effort made me feel mentally exhausted—and when we arrived here the whole performance was repeated, with variations.

Before we left I shocked everyone profoundly by trying to pay for my lodgings; looking at me with scorn Yohannes said— 'Here we don't like money.'

At 10.30 we stopped briefly for the boys to eat hunks of dark brown, bone dry *dabo*, which they wished to share with me. I can't imagine how they swallow it without water: and they never seemed to get thirsty, despite the heat.

All day we climbed steeply up and down countless arid grey-brown hills, dotted with thorny scrub. An amount of white marble was mixed with the rock and clay—great chunks of it glistened in the sun and sometimes marble chips lay in such profusion that the slopes looked like urban cemeteries. No settlements were visible, though we passed several herds of cattle and flocks of goats—tended, as usual, by small, naked, circumcised boys. In the heat of the day these children wear their folded *shammas* as thick pads on top of their shaven heads.

Our toughest climb was during the hottest noon hour—up a precipitous mountain of bare rock on a rough, dusty path. Yet in these highlands a strong, cool breeze often relieves even the midday heat. This climb ended on a high pass, where I paused to drink deeply from my water-bottle while gazing across the hills that we had traversed since morning. Already the weirdly shaped ridges around Workhsegeh were blurred by haze and distance.

My impatient bodyguard had hurried on with Jock and, as I trotted downhill after them, I reflected that the machine-age has dangerously deprived Western man of whole areas of experience that until recently were common to the entire human race. Too many of us are now cut off from the basic sensual gratifications of resting after violent exercise, finding relief from extremes of heat or cold, eating when ravenously hungry and drinking when the ache of thirst makes water seem the most precious of God's creations.

My map proclaims that Mai Cheneta is another town and I'm beginning to get the idea: any village with a police post and a primary school is a 'town'.

My arrival here almost caused a riot. Hundreds of people raced to stare at me, the children trampling on each other in an effort to see the *faranj* clearly. Then a Muslim tailor invited me into his tiny workshop, ordered tea and sent his son to summon an English-speaking teacher. As I gulped the black syrupy tea three men had to stand by the door, beating back the populace with their *dulas*: in my experience this was an unique scene.

Soon the teacher arrived—a quiet, kind young man named Haile Mariam, who at once offered me his room for the night. I'm now installed in it, being attacked by apparently spray-proof bugs, while small rats scuttle round my feet. The Italians are responsible for most of Mai Cheneta's solid buildings, of which this is one—high-ceilinged, about fifteen foot square, with a tin roof, an earth floor inches deep in dust, once white-washed stone walls and a small, unglazed window. When I arrived the only piece of furniture was an iron bedstead with a hair mattress. (All the teacher's possessions hang on the walls.) Then a battered table and chair were imported from the police station, so that I might write in comfort, and a few moments ago Haile Mariam came in with a big, bright oil-lamp.

When Jock had been looked after the three teachers urged me to visit their school-house on the summit of a hill overlooking the town. This house was built as the Italian C.O's residence and is now a semi-ruin. All the windows and doors have been removed, part of the tin roof has collapsed and hundreds of pigeons roost in the rafters and cover the floor with their droppings. There are four fine rooms, completely unfurnished save for small hanging blackboards and rows of stones brought in from the hillside as seats for the pupils. Two years ago, when the school opened, there were thirty on the roll; now there are ninety, despite much opposition from local parents and clergy. As is usual in such communities many parents are anti-school, preferring their children to herd flocks rather than to study; and the highland clergy resent the recent intrusion of the state on a domain that hitherto has been exclusively theirs.

Looking at a diagram of the planetary system on one of the blackboards I wondered how the parents of these children would react if their youngsters had the temerity to discuss astronomy when they went home from school. The highlanders still think that the earth is flat: some imagine it to be square, some see it as a disc and others believe it to be limitless. For them day and night are caused by the rotation of the sun above the earth, and the moon is responsible for the crops' progress after the sun has brought the seedlings above ground. Theoretically it is desirable that such ignorance should be dispelled; but will these children be any better off, as they till their fields throughout the years ahead, for having had their conception of the cosmos thoroughly disorganised?

On returning here I found the Chief of Police, the headman and a character described as 'the Sheriff' sitting in a row on the bed debating how best to deal with the problem of me. A group of privileged children—presumably the offspring of the officials—had been permitted into the room and were squatting motionless along the walls, gazing at me as though hypnotised, while various other locally important personages stood around joining in the argument.

Had I been willing to 'do in Rome . . .' I would have accepted an escort for tomorrow's trek; but escorts are so ruinous to my enjoyment that I remained obstinate—and eventually won the battle. I was then asked to write out and sign a statement (in triplicate: one copy for each official) declaring that I had been warned of the dangers and offered an escort, but had insisted on continuing alone. Obviously if I believed in these dangers I wouldn't be such a fool; but the risk of being shot at by *shifta* while walking through Ethiopia is probably no greater than the risk of being strangled by a maniac while hitch-hiking through Britain.

In the course of our argument Haile Mariam had said reproachfully, 'It is not part of our culture to travel alone'; and I suspect that the unconventionality of my trek upsets these people as much as the possibility of a *faranj* being murdered and local officials getting the blame. They cannot understand why anyone should want to travel alone—and not understanding they disapprove.

While our dispute was in progress a touching number of gifts were being brought to me by the locals—dozens of eggs, gourds of curds, flat slabs of different kinds of *dabo* and four chickens, all squawking frantically in premonition of the pot. (The teachers will benefit greatly from my visit.) Meanwhile the headman's wife was pouring us tea from a kettle and handing round an earthen bowl of damp, roasted flour, rather like the Tibetans' *tsampa*: we all dipped in for our handfuls and then kneaded them into little balls. The curds, too, were delicious; they tasted strongly of wood-smoke, as do some types of *talla*. One of the chickens became *durro-wat* for my supper, which I shared with the teachers.

Like many semi-educated young highlanders, these teachers despise their own Church. Haile Mariam ridiculed the Ethiopian fasting laws and said that the people endure them only because of a superstitious fear of the priests. Perhaps there is an element of truth in this, yet fasting is so emphasised by Ethiopian Christianity that to the average highlander 'keeping the fast' and 'being a Christian' are synonymous. These fasts have long been known to weaken the highlanders. Both Muslims and Gallas repeatedly attacked the highlands during Lent, but throughout the centuries the Church has been increasing the strictness of the laws, until now the average highlander is expected to fast on 165 days each year and the clergy and elders on about 250 days.*

Donald Levine states that 'the rationale commonly given for the extensive schedule of fasting is that man's nature is wicked and only by weakening himself in this manner will he be turned away from some act of aggression against others'. This reason for the imposition of such irrational laws is interesting. It hints that from the outset Ethiopian Christianity found itself incapable of effectively spreading Christ's teachings among a people temperamentally opposed to any gospel of gentleness: so a desperate remedy was adopted and the highlanders' harsh aggressiveness countered by an equally harsh code of mortification—which in time came to assume a disproportionate importance at the expense of most other aspects of Christian teaching. Yet even in the curbing of aggression the Ethiopian Church has not been very successful. It is still regarded as an honourable act to kill anyone who has given even the mildest provocation, and the lines of a popular Amharic poem say:

'Kill a man! Kill a man! It is good to kill a man!
One who has not killed a man moves around sleepily.'

Haile Mariam and his two comrades are natives of Aksum, the religious capital of Ethiopia, and all three accused the priests of living in luxury off the peasants—and of being far too numerous anyway. Whatever about the former hackneyed accusation, the latter is evidently true; in Asmara I was told that Ethiopia has an estimated 70,000 Coptic clergy—and fewer than seventy doctors.

Which reminds me—this morning we met a comparatively well-dressed man, carrying a rifle, who produced a phial of penicillin and asked me in sign language to inject him. I tried to explain that even if I had a syringe I certainly wouldn't inject anyone without knowing his medical history; but sign language

* A highlander's fast means nothing to eat or drink until midday—though he may have been working hard from sunrise—and even after midday milk, eggs, meat, animal-fat and fowl are forbidden, so he must survive on pulses and cereals. Children begin their first fast at about the age of seven, by abstaining before noon during the sixteen days of *Felsata*. After this the regular Wednesday and Friday fasts should be kept, though often this rule is not enforced until a child is ten or eleven; but from the age of fifteen the gruelling eight-week Lenten fast must be endured.

is not really up to this sort of explanation and my would-be patient went on his way looking aggrieved. The Amharic word for 'needle'—and therefore for 'injection'—is '*murfee*': so my name always causes great amusement.

Trachoma and other eye-diseases are tragically common here; also a number of men are blind in one eye—possibly as a result of injuries received while fighting.


*2 January. Adua*

I set off at 7.30 a.m. and arrived here ten hours later, having ambled along happily for eighteen miles, seeing only five adults and a few young shepherds.

All day the track climbed gradually between ridge after ridge of low hills. For miles a narrow river ran beside it, the water moving clear and green among gigantic, rounded boulders—many of them looking remarkably like Henry Moore's reclining figures—and twice the temptation of deep, wide pools proved irresistible. Saying 'Hang bilharzia!' I turned Jock loose and jumped in, clutching a bar of soap.

At 11 we stopped for brunch beneath a grove of tall, wide-spreading trees, and here I saw my first African monkeys—a troop of capuchins racing and swinging through the branches above me. Also—walking with bird-book in hand—I identified today the Lilac-breasted Roller, Bateleur, Namaqua Dove, Purple Grenadier, Red-cheeked Cordon Bleu and Black-billed Wood Hoopoe. These birds were marvellously tame; as Jock and I plodded quietly through thick dust we were often within a yard of them before they moved—and even then many only hopped or flew a few feet further away.

During the afternoon we passed a herd of over a hundred camels, all purposefully chewing the highest branches of small thorny trees and big thorny shrubs. One was pure white—a rare and beautiful animal. Probably this herd recently brought salt from the Danakil Desert and is now being rested in preparation for the journey home. Camels don't survive long in the highlands, as the British Army soon discovered when it invaded Ethiopia from the Sudan in January 1941. Out of 15,000 camels fifty reached Addis Ababa in May and an officer reported that 'a compass was not needed; one could orient the column by the stink of dead camels'. Various reasons have been suggested for the camel's allergy to the highlands—thin air, precipitous paths, the cold and wet of the rainy season, the lush grass of some areas and the fact that camels have never learned to avoid certain unfamiliar herbs which lethally inflame their stomachs. In the past this allergy has saved the highlands from sharing Egypt's fate and being repeatedly invaded by neighbouring camel-nomads.

This has been a day of deep contentment—wandering alone along a *makeena*-free track, seeing only hoof prints in the dust, with all around the healing quiet of wild places, unbroken save by bird-song. The loveliest time is from 4.30 p.m. on, when the light softens and colours glow. This afternoon, brown, red and yellow cliffs, flecked with white marble, were rising above dark green scrub, and on every side the outlines of high mountains became clearer as the heat-haze thinned.

At 5.30 we came to the crest of a hill and there, half-a-mile away, was Adua—a white-washed town at the foot of a splendidly distorted mountain-range, with lines of slim green trees between its houses. On the outskirts we were captured by the inevitable English-speaking schoolboys, who led us to this brothel, thinly disguised as a hotel. Bedrooms lead off the central courtyard on two sides, on the third are the cooking-quarters and stables, and on the fourth is an Italian-type bar, from which frightful wireless noises emanate continuously. Groups of girls lounge around the courtyard giggling and smoking—in this country cigarettes are the prostitute's hallmark—and, though no one is overtly hostile, the *faranj* is aware of being regarded with contemptuous amusement. There could be no stronger contrast to my reception at Mai Cheneta.

When we arrived a rather tiresome young teacher was in the courtyard, bargaining with one of the girls—whom he temporarily abandoned to practise his English on me. I asked him to help me buy barley for Jock, but he seemed to think that this would entail too much delay so making an evasive reply he returned to his girl. Luckily the schoolboys proved more co-operative and while I was unloading Jock—watched by grinning servants who made no attempt to assist me—they fetched the grain in my bucket. Their profits must have been considerable, judging by the meagre change they returned out of a five dollar note: yet they demanded a fifty per cent tip each. By now Adua has become semi-Westernised, being on the Asmara–Gondar motor-road.

While I was unpacking another teacher appeared and, explaining that I wished to make a telephone call, I asked him to direct me to the post office. For some quaint reason Adua's telephone lives in a chemist's shop, to which this young man kindly guided me through steep, pitch-dark laneways. Before discovering that I had governmental connections my companion was rabidly revolutionary in his political views and he got an obvious shock on hearing me ask for the Palace at Makalle. While we were waiting for the call to come through he tried awkwardly to retrieve the situation, then finally decided to be frank and begged me not to repeat anything that he had said lest he should lose his job.

Most English-speakers soon ask me why my government ordered me to come to Ethiopia and how much money was granted for my expenses; and they are bewildered when I say that my government doesn't even know I'm here and wouldn't dream of paying my expenses. The average highlander cannot imagine a country in which people are free to go where they choose when they choose, without governmental permission—not can he imagine any ordinary individual being rich enough to travel abroad.

This little room has freshly white-washed walls and the cotton sheets are spotless; yet appearances can be deceptive and the bugs are busy as I write. An electricity supply functions from 6 to 10.30 p.m., but there are no switches in the rooms and the bulbs give the dimmest possible light. However, one worthwhile local amenity is the crude and stinking loo next door; throughout the country-side the loo-problem is acute in every settlement—to my mystification, discomfort and embarrassment. (Here sign-language can always be used effectively in emergencies, but its use leads to a certain loss of dignity.) Squatting just anywhere is not customary, yet I never can find an authorised squatting-spot and sometimes wish that I were back in Nepal, where one simply goes outside the door like a dog.

*3 January. Aksum*

There was a Jock crisis when we arrived here at 4 p.m.
While unloading I noticed that the base of his tail has been
rubbed raw—so I hurried off to seek some sort of veterinary
aid. Predictably, none was available; and in a country where
pack-animals are worked mercilessly, even when covered with
suppurating saddle-sores, no one could be expected to take
much notice of my little crisis. Therefore I'm now treating the
patient with Yardley's talcum powder—presented to me in
Asmara for my feet—and the pale pink tin, embellished by
graceful floral designs, is an object of much admiration in the
hotel yard. Despite the incongruity of the treatment it should
work within a few days, the sore being so small and new.

My companion's physical state was not today's only mule-
trouble. The road from Adua to Aksum teems with traffic
(relatively speaking—one vehicle passes about every twenty
minutes) and those twelve miles shredded poor Jock's nerves.
While controlling his plunging and rearing I twice thought
that my right arm had been dislocated, and tonight my
shoulder muscles are throbbing. Yet Jock is not to blame; for
some reason Ethiopian lorries are singularly noisy, especially
when tackling steep slopes, and Ethiopian buses harbour fiendish radios and blow ear-splitting horns non-stop—so how could
any rural mule retain his self-control?

This morning I rose at 5.30, to see Adua's two most interesting churches. Ethiopian churches are locked after the daily
Mass has been celebrated, and I prefer to avoid searching for
a man who will search for a priest who will search for the key—
and only find it if he has hopes of being well paid.

When we left the hotel at 8 a.m. hundreds of children were
on their way to school—Adua being a centre for secondary
education—and one gang of about twenty boys was soon following us, shouting and laughing and teasing Jock in an
attempt to make him bolt. Jock very properly ignored all this,
and at first I merely waved at the youngsters and laughed back;
but then out of the corner of an eye I saw one boy whipping
my straw hat off the top of the load and another putting his
hand into the hanging bucket, where I keep my camera, torch

and map. I swung round and gave the nearest lad a blow across the shoulders with my *dula*, whereupon they all fled.

After some five miles we climbed a steep—but not high— pass and at the top I sat on a flat boulder under a tree to eat brunch while enjoying Adua's grotesque mountains and think- ing about Adua's significant battle—the first defeat of a European army by African warriors. Then we crossed a wide plain, where barley was ripe—though hardly more than a foot high, and dirty with five-foot thistles. (Most of the thistles I've seen so far are much smaller and have blue-green stems and large primrose-yellow flowers.) I had many fellow-walkers today, all of them curious and most of them friendly. About half-way I was joined by two men, one of whom insisted on leading Jock—until a truck approached and Jock decided otherwise. After that I led Jock.

Aksum is one of Ethiopia's main tourist attractions and out- side the town I was commandeered by two small boys, who proved to be professional parasites. Both mistook me for a man and offered to get me 'a good bad woman for to-night', as they so graphically expressed it. They were taken aback when I put them right, but unlike their Indian counterparts did not then offer to provide me with 'a good bad man'.

This hotel is shoddier than last night's Ritz, but the staff are much more agreeable. Here I must get my kit sorted out; tomorrow I'll look for cardboard boxes in which everything can be neatly packed. To load a mule securely the ropes have to be tightened to an extent that has left me with a mangled mess of ink on clothes, toothpaste on books, insecticide in dried fruit, pills mixed with broken glass, torch batteries crushed beyond redemption and films torn to shreds. Not to mention the fact that everything is permeated through and through with white dust, sacking being the least dust-resistant of materials.

*4 January*

Yardley's talcum is working well, but I've decided to stay here an extra day to give the sore time to heal completely.

I spent an exhausting morning at Police Headquarters,

having been 'picked up' after breakfast by a suspicious constable. It was bedlam in the C.O.'s little office, where eight officers were simultaneously shouting—in Tigrinya—about the impossibility of *anyone* walking through the Semien Mountains, least of all a solitary woman. After two hours I lost my temper at the stupidity of assuming a journey to be 'impossible' merely because one wouldn't care to do it oneself. I hated bothering Leilt Aida again, but at last was forced to call Makalle and ask her to soothe the maddened crowd—which she did, with difficulty.

Aksum's tourist trade is in its infancy, yet already the place reeks of commercialism. Everywhere one is furtively followed by little boys and shabby youths, each claiming out of the corner of his mouth to be 'best guide, cheapest guide for Aksum'. Ras Mangasha recently ordered the suppression of this sort of thing—which makes it easier to shake off these touts, who greatly fear the police.

This evening I had a talk with Birhana Meskel, the official tourist guide—an elderly, knowledgeable man who deplored Aksum's changing atmosphere. He assured me that ten years ago every woman here wore ankle-length skirts, but now many harlots have moved in from Adua and Asmara, wearing calf-length skirts, and generally the ancient city is fast losing its atmosphere of devotion and learning. I listened sympathetically to all this, though I couldn't help thinking that Aksum's devotion and learning must have become mummified quite some time ago: otherwise they would hardly have crumbled to dust at the first touch of tourism.

Now I must talcum Jock for the night. Since early this morning he has been enjoying the hospitality of a kind Peace Corps couple, who teach at the secondary school and live in a house surrounded by a large grassy garden.

## 5 January

Aksum is the first town on my route without a mosque; the resident Muslims wanted to build one, but the Old Testament-minded local priests said 'We're not allowed to have a church in Mecca, so you're not having a mosque here'.

The population of Aksum is about 20,000 (500 of whom are clergy), though the town is so compact that this figure seems hard to credit. All these highland towns are extraordinarily ugly, but Aksum does have a certain sad, hidden splendour, discernible when one is alone among the ruins of an empire that once was ranked with Babylon, Rome and Egypt. Yet the melancholy is great wherever a proud past is not allowed to rest in peace, but is disturbed and degraded by trippers and touts.

No women are permitted to enter even the grounds of the monastic Church of St Mary of Zion—Ethiopia's most hallowed church—but this morning I went to the Church of St Takla-haymanot, where many of the paintings have recently been renovated. Ethiopian church art is interesting, yet to me these naïve, stylized paintings are not true art, if by art one means the disciplined product of a creative imagination. The delicacy of Moghul miniatures or the richness of Hindu carvings touch me, whereas these paintings, though inspired by our common Christianity, merely interest me. It has been suggested that here, as in Tibet, the development of pictorial art was inhibited by the rigid conservatism of clerical practitioners—but the best of the Ethiopian murals that I have seen so far cannot compare with a mediocre Tibetan *thanka*.

By now the talcum has been completely victorious and Jock is full of grass and the joys of life, so tomorrow we head for the Semiens. Ever since I arrived in Aksum they have been beckoning—a vast barrier of blue chunks stretching across the southern horizon.

# 5

# Gunmen for the Guest

To-day is Christmas Eve and when we left Aksum at 8 a.m.
the holiday traffic was at its peak. For miles around I could see
groups walking or riding across the wide plain towards their
home-villages, and within half-an-hour we had been absorbed
by a cheerful party which was also going south. Its members
were a local District Governor on a mule, attended by two
gunmen, a young priest—also riding—attended by one gun-
man, the Governor's twelve-year-old son—walking sturdily—
and a ragged Muslim trader driving eight donkeys loaded with
salt-blocks. And soon we were joined by Abebe, a breathless
eighteen-year-old student who told me that he had been running for miles to catch up with a party which included 'gun-
people'. There is a certain Chaucerian quality about this sort
of travel, and in their way such casually companionable wan-
derings can be as enjoyable as solitary trekking.

A few miles south of Aksum we climbed a long, rocky ridge,
dotted with round, green bushes, and on the crest I was glad
that I had walked ahead and could enjoy this moment alone.
Below me—like a vast bowl brimming with beauty—lay a
broad, sunny valley, lined with golden grasses, and from its
floor rose a low hill, crowned by a tree-surrounded church,
and faintly, across the silence, came the solemn chanting of
many priests—a sound so sweet in its remoteness that it seemed
to belong to the soul of the mountains rather than to the rituals
of man.

As we descended to this valley Abebe told me that our party
—except for the Muslim—would here make a slight detour to
pray at the church, which is dedicated to Emmanuel and cele-
brates its patron's feast day on Christmas Eve. Now I could see

many white-clad figures passing between the trees on the hill-top, and a few graceful groups of elders had gathered on the bright meadows beneath to discuss immemorial village problems.

Within the overgrown church enclosure men were every-where, but the women—some fifty or sixty of them—stood together on one side of the main door, their off-white *shammas* covering their heads. Here I heard for the first time that eerie, melodious ululation which highland women produce on such ceremonial occasions; the trembling wave of sound, which is never sustained for more than a few moments, has an unfor-gettable purity and poignancy.

This circular church was typical of its kind—an old building, crudely constructed of stone, mud and wood, and recently re-roofed with tin. No one suggested that the *faranj* female should enter it, so I took the hint. Soon after our arrival seven priests emerged from the main door and led some twenty *debtaras* (deacons) around the church three times in a noisy procession. The chief priest held aloft a silver Coptic cross and the others waved strange little silver rattles (*sistra*) that tinkled pleasantly. Two *debtaras* walked backwards before the priests, each vigor-ously beating a three-foot oblong drum, and the other youths kept up a loud, cheerful chanting and clapping of hands. Despite the importance of the occasion no fine robes were worn. The chief priest was draped in a creased and torn black gown, but the rest were in ordinary clothes, apart from the untidy white turbans always worn by all ordained clergy.

As we left the enclosure the Governor invited me, through Abebe, to have lunch at his mother's home. (He had heard of me in Aksum and knew that I was a protégée of Leilt Aida.) Already I had become fond of Ato Gabre Mariam—a burly little man with a pompous manner but kind eyes—so I grate-fully accepted this invitation and a steep two-mile climb brought us to a tiny settlement surrounded by wild fig-trees.

The Governor had not been expected and his old mother almost wept for joy when he appeared; immediately we were all ushered into an empty hut, made of new green branches intertwined with old stakes, and while the men were gathering to embrace and kiss their distinguished relative excited children spread straw on the earth floor and laid hides on top of it for our greater comfort. Then the women brought in a huge jar of *talla* and a flat basket of roasted whole barley, and half-an-hour later black coffee was served in tiny handleless cups (made in China!). Lunch was not ready until 2.30, by which time we were well away on our second jar of *talla* and full of festive cheer. This 'Christmas *talla*' was a refined, clear brew that looked rather like English 'mild'.

For lunch countless rounds of *injara* were laid on the wicker stands—about the height and circumference of a coffee-table—which are used as communal plates. Then fast-day bean-*wat* was ladled on to the centre of the *injara*, and when a little boy had poured water over our hands we set to, pulling off strips of *injara*—beginning around the edge—and enfolding in them mouthfuls of *wat*. This *wat* was so fiercely spiced that tears were slowly running down my cheeks by the end of the meal. Luckily we also had two delicious purées; one was white and unspiced, made from ground peas, the other was brown and slightly spiced, made from ground beans—and both had been beaten to the lightness of a soufflé.

The formalities of highland social life bring much elegance into these primitive homes. When the Governor's young relatives came to greet him, they touched both his feet with their lips and forehead before being raised by him and receiving kisses on their right cheeks; and it is evident that where everyone has his established position in the hierarchy such rites have an almost religious significance. Not that they are confined to special people or special occasions—they also grace the simplest actions between equals. When one man hands another a gourd of *talla* he never holds it out unthinkingly, but presents it with both hands, bowing slightly. And the recipient accepts it with both hands, half rising if he is seated, and inclining his head. In this way each trivial human interchange pleasingly becomes a miniature ceremony; and to-day I realised that I myself have already adopted some of the less obvious highland conventions —not deliberately, to be polite, but as an unconscious response to the finding of something that was lost. My instincts could hardly be less conventional, yet to me these antique highland customs seem not mere empty gestures but symbols of an essen-

tial stability at the heart of society. Seen against the background
of our helter-skelter civilisation they would appear comical or
tiresome; seen here they are sad reminders of all that we have
discarded on our way to efficiency. It is not surprising that
when highland peasants have an opportunity to observe
Western social behaviour they imagine us to be a race of un-
feeling barbarians.

We were back on the trail uncomfortably soon after lunch,
lest darkness should fall before we reached this village—where
Ato Gabre Mariam has invited me to spend the night in his
compound. Beyond the settlement we crossed a region of black
lava rock and stony fields; then a long, precipitous descent
brought us to the Plain of Fools—so called because travellers
often fancy themselves near the end of it when many miles
remain to be covered. But personally I was not at all anxious
to reach the end of such a blissful walk—through strong, clear
sunshine, with a cool wind sweeping up from the south and an
apparent infinity of rugged glory on every side.

From this plateau our path again descended—steep as a
ladder—into a deep gorge; and then it immediately ascended,
equally steeply, to the next plateau. Here Abebe indicated a
tree-covered hill on the near horizon and explained that our
destination lay just beyond it; this landmark looked less than
a mile away, but the intervening terrain was so chaotic—there
were two more deep chasms—that it took us another hour to
reach it.

Aedat tops the highest escarpment I have yet seen and we
approached it by rounding the wooded hill above an apparently bottomless canyon. Now a brief sunset splendour—crimson, orange, bronze and lemon—was seeping through all the
sky. And as this glow touched the ochre, purple, yellow and
white of the cliffs beyond the void, our whole world seemed
caught up in a triumphant conflagration of beauty. Then we
saw the little village—built of pink stone—and it too was so
wondrously glowing that for an instant one doubted its reality.

From this high, narrow ridge the cobalt roughness of the
Semiens stood out darkly against a reddening horizon; and
to the west more distant, smoother mountains were lilac against
a primrose sky; and to the east, beyond the tawny shadows now

filling the ravine, lay a ravaged width of chasms and cliffs, bounded by Makalle's plateau—a long, grey pencil-line below the first star. As I followed the Governor's reception party through the village I felt drunk on colour and space.

This compound is at the southern extremity of the plateau, but Ato Gabre Mariam had dismounted before we turned the last corner of the hill; it would be considered a shameful thing for him to have ridden while his guest walked. Now I am happily settled in his round 'guest-room' *tukul*, beneath a thatched roof supported by a disproportionately thick and monstrously misshapen tree-trunk. I like the 'clothes-hangers' here—several cow-horns embedded in the mud walls.

As I write—sitting on the mud bed, relaxed after a thorough leg-massage—my host and eight other men are squatting on hides around the fire, drinking and talking. One of the younger men—Dawit, the Governor's nephew—was brought up in Addis Ababa, where his father is a clerk and, having been trained as a 'Medical Officer', was sent here last week to run the Health Centre for three years. Despite an Addis education his English is not as good as Abebe's, and in the circumstances his lack of intelligence seems alarming. Admittedly rural medical officers receive only a rudimentary training, but Dawit's knowledge of his subject is virtually non-existent. However, the local Health Centre is unlikely to be provided with a very demanding range of drugs, and his presence may do some good if he can persuade serious cases to go to Aksum hospital— though not many serious cases would survive that journey.

My visit is a Christmas gift from the gods for Dawit, who has reached the extreme of boredom after a week's exile from Addis—*sans* cinema, *sans* bars, *sans* night-clubs, *sans* everything. He views Aedat as an ultra-primitive hell-hole, from which his father was lucky enough to escape and to which he has been unlucky enough to return—at the command of a government whose orders he dare not disobey. He considers the local food, drink and accommodation repellent and he despises all the villagers, including his own relatives. I winced when he jeeringly referred to the rest of the company as 'savages' who were content to wear dirty clothes, sit on dirty floors and blow their noses into the fire. His whole attitude reveals a too-familiar pattern—the corruption by Western superficialities of a non-Western mind, which then quickly rejects its own traditions while remaining incapable of extracting any virtue from ours. I feel deeply sorry for Dawit and his kind, who have been seduced by a shadow and then left to rot in a cultural no-man's-land.

Today my reorganised kit caused a little bother. Neatly packed cardboard boxes may suit me, but it suited Jock much better to have everything jumbled up in the sacks, which then settled to fit the curve of his back. Twice since lunch-time the load slipped and this worries me slightly. Jock's manners on such occasions are perfect—he stops at once to await re-loading —but if I were alone when the sacks came adrift all the mulish politeness in the world wouldn't enable me to put them together again.

This evening I have several nasty cuts and scratches on my arms and legs. The local vegetation brandishes a most deleterious variety of thorns, spikes, barbs and razor-edged leaves.

*7 January*

I had hoped to be on the brink of the Takazze Gorge by this evening, but integration went so well yesterday that no one would hear of my leaving Aedat on Christmas Day. I've therefore had a riotous time boozing and feasting in the homes of Ato Gabre Mariam, Abebe, Dawit and Giorgis—the local teacher—not to mention a breakfast banquet with an endearing old priest at the famous local church of Debra Ghennet.

The Governor and I set off to Mass at 6.30 a.m., preceded by my host's eight-year-old son, proudly wearing a bandolier and carrying a rifle—from which I deduce that the 'armed guard' fetish is more a status symbol than a safety device. The path climbed through a dense wood of unfamiliar trees and on our way we overtook several men and women, all of whom exchanged elaborate greetings with the Governor—and questioned him about me, if their position allowed them that freedom.

This church has twice been partially destroyed—by Mohammed Gragn some 300 years ago and by the Italians some thirty years ago. Only one mural survives and the building looks more like a disused barn than a church. When we arrived Mass had begun and I stood just outside the south (women's) door, from where I could see a group of elderly widows receiving Communion. (Because the majority of highlanders choose civil marriages they cannot receive the sacrament during the lifetime of their spouses.) This ceremony began when two white-robed priests, carrying richly-coloured silk umbrellas, emerged from the concealed sanctuary to which only clergy are admitted and stood in front of the women. Then a third priest appeared, bearing a silver cross, and as the choir began to chant the umbrella priests shook their *sistra* and the chief priest stepped out of the sanctuary, carrying a wooden chalice in which cross-shaped pieces of bread were dipped before being given to the communicants.

Throughout the highlands only the priests make wine and they refuse to divulge their method to any layman. In 1770 James Bruce observed crushed grapes being given to communicants on a spoon, complete with seeds, but nowadays it is likely that raisins are often used to make the sacrificial wine. It seems odd that this form of alcohol has never become popular in the highlands; vines would thrive in many regions and have long been known here—I noticed representations of grapes and their leaves on an altar stone at the base of one of Aksum's monoliths. Possibly a lack of adequate containers is the snag, since highlanders have no casks, bottles, sealed skins or glazed pots—and wine would not long remain wine in their crude earthen jars.

When Mass was over the Governor summoned me into the church, the chief priest dispensed me from removing my boots and one of the *debtaras* handed me a prayer-stick—a five-foot staff, with a curved horizontal silver handle on which one can lean comfortably while taking part in the long Coptic ceremonies. We then walked around the straw-strewn outer ambulatory to a raggedly carpeted section in front of the torn sanctuary curtain, which is pulled aside at certain times during Mass so that the male congregation may see the altar. Here we paused for a few moments, because the choir—at the Governor's request—were now chanting a special prayer for my safety in the Semiens. (This Dawit explained later, and I was touched

by Ato Gabre Mariam's so nicely expressed concern—as indeed
I have often been, during the past two days, by his various
gestures of friendship. I only hope the final gesture won't be
the provision of an armed guard tomorrow morning.) Then
four priests stepped down into the ambulatory and performed
one of the traditional religious dances. Facing each other in
pairs they advanced and retreated with stylised but vigorous
movements, wielding their prayer-sticks as though they were
spears, while the congregation clapped their hands rhythmically and drums were beaten and bells rung and *sistra* shaken.
Next I was shown the few Ge'ez manuscripts—inscribed on
goatskin parchment, bound in wood and richly illustrated—
which have survived. These were thrown in a dirty chest on
the floor of the inner ambulatory and obviously no one here
deserves to have the care of such precious volumes; it is reveal-
ing to contrast the neglect of these books with the reverence
shown towards any volume of the Buddhist scriptures by even
the least educated Tibetan monk. As we left the church I
echoed Dawit's 'Savages!' under my breath. People who blow
their noses into the fire hardly qualify for this epithet, but
people who abuse centuries-old illuminated manuscripts most
certainly do.

Behind the church ramshackle buildings surround a farmyard ankle-deep in dry horse-dung and it was impossible to
distinguish the priests' quarters from the stables. The chief
priest's filthy little room is over a granary and a perilous outside
flight of loose stone steps leads up to the low doorway. When I
sat on the edge of the iron bed my host covered my bare knees
with a length of cotton—but in such a charming way that this
mark of disapproval seemed almost a compliment. He is an
old man, lean and white-bearded, with fine Semitic features
and bright, kind, humorous eyes. Whatever may be the general
level of virtue among the Ethiopian clergy, one knew that here
was a true man of God.

When Dawit had joined us we were served with a quart of
*talla* each—at 8.30 a.m., which even by my standards is a little
early. Half-an-hour later breakfast began, and continued for
two hours. Everyone ate prodigious quantities of *injara*, various
kinds of highly-spiced meat-*wat*, hunks of tough steak fried in

rancid ghee and strips of delicious raw beef dipped in *berberie* paste—the highlanders' favourite delicacy and the source of their endemic tape-worm infestations.

Christmas is not among the major Ethiopian church feasts; the main celebrations are secular and the main secular celebration is eating—I've consumed so much raw meat to-day that I should be able to bound over the Semiens like an ibex. Other delicacies included hot unleavened wholemeal bread, eaten with honey and hard-boiled eggs—an excellent combination—and a strange fruit about the size of a Swede turnip, with a skin like a lemon (but much rougher and thicker), and a smell like a lemon when cut, though the sweet, palatable flesh is hard, white and juicy. The locals eat this with salt, though I preferred it without, and the children eagerly eat the tough skin.

I have rarely seen a more gloriously situated village than this—or a more primitive one. Mercifully tin sheeting has not yet arrived and the oblong stone hovels have flat clay roofs, on which parched grass grows thickly. Apart from the central track there are no laneways. The dwellings are scattered haphazardly across this rock-strewn ridge, and even where a number have been built close together no one has bothered to clear the narrow intervening space of boulders and stones. Many are now in ruins, which gives the place a post-earthquake appearance; when houses begin to collapse their owners usually choose to construct new ones, rather than to repair the old.

During the afternoon Dawit invited me to his tiny room, and when I lit a cigarette he asked if he might have one—though yesterday, in his uncle's compound, he had given the impression of being a non-smoker. He then explained that the highlanders have such a strong religious prejudice against tobacco that when he was seen lighting a cigarette, the day after his arrival here, four youths were encouraged to stone him by their outraged elders.* However, *faranj* smokers are now tolerated—fortunately for me.

* Ethiopian Christians so detest smoking that no one may kiss the cross who is thought ever to have used tobacco—and Yohannes IV considered it his duty to have the lips of smokers cut off. Some highlanders believe that tobacco was the only plant not to wither at the hour of Christ's crucifixion and others believe that the first tobacco plant sprang from the intestines of Arius. Probably the prohibition

As Dawit and I were finishing our second round of *talla* Giorgis arrived and invited us to his home, where steak was being fried by his sixteen-year-old wife for the delectation of the already replete *faranj*. On our way we heard an uncanny noise—one prolonged, wild howl, which Giorgis said had been produced by the women of a bereaved family to inform their neighbours of a death within the compound.

Giorgis is a tall, muscular twenty-year-old, who wears thread-bare Western clothes beneath his *shamma*, to mark his position as a teacher and a native of 'urban' Makalle. His home is a recently-built, high-ceilinged, one-roomed house, with two big doors which admit lots of light—and here the impression of poverty is far greater than in the average dusky *tukul*. This family has now been living in Aedat for six months, but their possessions are so few that the big, bleak room seems less a home than a temporary lodging. While Giorgis was fondling his eighteen-months-old daughter I noticed that already she has infected eyes. The filth of all highland toddlers, even in the Governor's affluent compound, is shocking. Once old enough to look after themselves they make some attempt to clean their faces, but mothers never bother about this task and one is appalled by the sight of so many snotty, fly-covered noses and mouths, and encrusted, infected, fly-covered eyes.

There is no state school in Aedat and Giorgis is employed by the church school as a writing teacher at a monthly salary of £6—as compared with the £22 which a state school writing teacher would receive.* Yet the Church is estimated to own

---

originated in hostility to Muslims, as did similar prohibitions against eating camel-flesh and drinking coffee—though now coffee is Ethiopia's main export and has become a popular drink. Certainly the tobacco taboo did not come from Egypt, where the Copts have always smoked, and a nice story is told about one nicotine-deprived nineteenth-century Abuna who declared—ineffectually—that he would break all his pipes over the priests' heads if they prevented him from lifting the ban on tobacco.

* Until recently the highlanders have been strongly biassed against writing and Dr Levine explains that 'The act of writing was considered to be inherently shame-ful; like any manual activity other than farming and fighting, writing was regarded as degrading work, the business of scribes whose status was thereby not much higher than that of potters and metal-smiths. Only a small percentage of the clergy learned to write, and those who did were rarely adept. The products of writing, moreover, were deemed either too sacred or too nefarious to warrant

at least 15 per cent of Ethiopia's arable land, so Giorgis' bitterly anti-clerical sentiments seem understandable.

As we were walking back to the Governor's compound I was surprised to hear the alien cry of a muezzin: then Dawit pointed out an inconspicuous 'mosque' hut, with an unsteady little 'minaret' built on to one gable, and told me that Aedat has a community of native Muslim traders—known as Jabartis.

Soon after we had joined Ato Gabre Mariam and his cronies at their evening *talla* session a pretty, fair-skinned girl was escorted into the hut by two gunmen. She was wearing a white, full-skirted dress and a thick *shamma*, both with skilfully embroidered, brightly-coloured fringes, and she was carrying a bottle labelled 'Haig' but containing excellent *tej*. Dawit explained that she is the seventeen-year-old daughter-in-law of a village headman and that on hearing of my arrival in Aedat she had got her husband's permission to ride over the mountains to meet her first white woman—bringing as a gift this valuable bottle of *tej*. (In these parts the bottle itself is no less valuable than the contents.) Her enterprising curiosity must be uncommon among highland women, but when actually confronted with a *faranj* the poor girl was so overcome that she could only sit beside me staring at her toes. However, by supper-time she had relaxed somewhat (we had been co-operating well as *tej*-drinkers) and I then asked her—through Dawit—how long she had been married and how many children she had. My last question was a most unfortunate one; though married four years she is childless, and as she admitted this her smooth young face was suddenly haggard with misery.

Apart from the Italian occupation this region has never been in touch with the outside world: and I should think that after

---

giving laymen easy access to their medium. Script belonged above all else to the realm of scripture. The awe felt for holy writs was a deterrent against using that medium for other than devotional purposes. The chief private use of writing was for the magic formulas of the *debtara*, another connection with the supernatural that discouraged its lay practice. The *debtara's* art served injurious as well as beneficial purposes, and the fear that those who learned to write might stumble onto potent phrases was reason for restricting that skill to a small group of the initiated.' However, since the Liberation all legal accusations and court proceedings have to be set down in writing, so the highlanders' passion for litigation is now overcoming their aversion to the written word.

their war-time experiences the older generation cherish isola-tion. To-day Giorgis pointed out a net-work of caves in a nearby escarpment and told me that during the occupation most of the villagers had hidden in these almost inaccessible rock-chambers, which centuries ago were used as hermitages.

### 8 January. A Tukul on a Hillside

I had planned to leave Aedat at dawn, but Ato Gabre Mariam insisted on my waiting for a ceremonial farewell break-fast—and this being Sunday all the women went to church, so the feast was not served until nine o'clock. Such a waste of the day's best trekking hours irked me, yet a rejection of this final flourish of hospitality would have given great offence. A very appetising flourish it was, too—an enormous round tin tray piled with sheeps' kidneys, hearts and livers, and with huge lumps of mutton fat, all roasted on a spit over a wood-fire. Together my host and I attacked this mountain of meat, he dissecting the various organs with a sinister-looking knife—it had a razor-sharp, backward-curving tip—and then handing me the choicest tit-bits.

Half-way through the meal Dawit appeared, and to my con-sternation announced that he would be accompanying me on my way to the Takazze, as he had decided to visit his paternal grandfather—whom he had never met. However, for the mo-ment his servant could not be found, so we must wait a little. I then accepted the fact that this was One of Those Days—acceptance being made easier by such a bellyful of meat that I felt disinclined even to walk across the room. The Governor immediately ordered an early lunch for the travellers; and, in case I might feel peckish in the interval, a small tin kettle of sweet boiled milk was produced to keep me going. (Normally sugar is not used in this region, but my host had brought some with him from Aksum.)

We eventually got away at 12.30—Dawit on a borrowed mule, with his armed servant and two other youths trotting beside him, Jock following, and myself in the rear. For a couple of miles the Governor—accompanied by five attendants—rode with us, as is the custom when a guest departs.

Beyond Aedat our track ran level between low mountains and on either side cattle were grazing the richest-looking pasture that I have seen in this country. Then we came to the edge of a deep crater-like depression, thickly lined with green shrubs, and on a hill in its centre, far below the track, stood a church, surrounded by the usual trees, which is greatly revered because during Mohammed Gragn's invasion it is believed to have been miraculously made invisible, and thus saved from destruction. (The church is so improbably situated, even by highland standards, and so naturally camouflaged that I would never have noticed it had I been alone.)

Here we sat on the edge of the crater while Dawit's servant took part in a fascinating 'long-distance-call', which started when a minute figure on a hill-top far above us demanded information about the *faranj*. This figure proved to be the headman of a nearby village and, on hearing that I was a protégée of the Tigreans' beloved Leilt Aida, he at once invited us to have *talla* some miles further along the track. Then the hills and valleys began to echo and re-echo with haunting, disembodied cries, as his orders for our entertainment were relayed to the village by invisible shepherds. When using this rather public but very effective method of communication the highlanders employ a high-pitched voice and a peculiar rhythmic chant that carries for miles through the still, thin air of the mountains.

For the next hour we were crossing an arid grey-brown plateau towards a formidable *amba* of sheer red rock that overlooks a broad gorge, dark with tangled vegetation. On the edge of this gorge a score of villagers greeted us and we sat on enormous, smooth boulders beneath a huge, gnarled tree and were given hunks of *dabo* and wooden tankards brimming with *talla* that had been carried from the village in an earthen jar on a woman's back. These men were considerably agitated about my crossing of the Takazze Gorge. They affirmed that many *shifta* are now encamped there, lying in wait for Christmas traffic, and they tried hard to persuade me to turn back. I know that *shifta* do patrol the gorge, but I doubt if many of them lie in wait on this particular track, which is rarely used, even at Christmas time. (The depth of the gorge here has

always restricted traffic between the two sides.) When I declined
to turn back because of *shifta* the despairing villagers tried the
deterrent-value of snakes, leopards, malaria and extreme heat.
Then they gave up, and their gloomy farewells would have
been appropriate to a death-bed scene.

'Precipitous' is going to be an overworked adjective in this
diary; but that can't be helped, for unless a highland track is
crossing a plateau it usually *is* precipitous. Our descent after
the *talla*-halt was very precipitous indeed—a slithering scramble
on loose soil around vast rocks between thorny bushes . . .
When we finally reached the bottom Dawit remarked feelingly
that had he known what the route was like his grandfather
would have been left unvisited.

Another two miles brought us to our destination, an isolated
compound on a wide hillside that was prickly with stubble and
already cool beneath a dove-grey dusk. Half-way up its slope
this hill becomes an *amba*, and beyond the immense, regular
block of its summit lies the Takazze Gorge.

There are four *tukuls* here and we are being entertained in
the largest—a well-built stone hut about forty feet in circumference, with a high, conical thatched roof (unsupported by any
pole) and two mud double-beds. One of these is built into an
alcove in the thick wall, which is unusual. As I write, amidst
a throng of Dawit's welcoming relatives, we are almost awash
in *talla*, and outside the door three cooking fires are blazing
rosily against the dark mountain. Oddly enough no fire has
been lit in here and the only light—apart from my candle— is
an oil-wick hung high on the wall and now glinting on the
many rifles stacked beneath it.

This evening Adua and Aksum—not to mention Asmara,
Cairo and London—seem to belong to another planet.


*9 January. A Cattle Shelter on a Mountainside*

Last evening the word *shifta* recurred often in my companions' conversation and I could sense a crisis simmering.
Then this morning Dawit's grandfather—a vigorously authori-
tative old man—said bluntly that unless the last settlement in
Tigre (beyond the *amba*) would provide a bodyguard Dawit

must bring me back here. For our different reasons (laziness and pig-headedness) Dawit and I were equally opposed to this plan. But now I am a world away from visas, government permits and amenable princesses. In theory I am free to travel how and where I please, yet in practice I have become a responsibility of the locals and am caught firm in a web of centuries-old traditions. So for the moment I must accept my loss of freedom. To have defied tradition this morning would have been futile, since I can't load Jock. It would also have been ungracious, because these people were greatly inconveniencing themselves for my sake, and it might have been unwise. Instinct told me that beneath their dutiful solicitude lay a basic distrust of the unprecedented lone *faranj*, and I suspected that were I to inflame this by incomprehensible nonconformity I might see a very different aspect of the highland character. For me such a situation is new. I have never before travelled among people who inspired sufficient fear to make me abandon my aim of the moment.

The morning air was penetratingly cold as we stood in the compound while Dawit wrote—on paper provided by me—a message from his grandfather to be read to the relevant village headman. I would have thought a verbal message sufficient, but evidently my protector considered the solemnity of the written word better suited to the occasion.

At seven o'clock we set off, full of hot milk and hard *dabo*. Dawit, his attendants, a local man and myself went straight up, across and down the *amba*, but four of Dawit's armed cousins led Jock a long way round. Not even highland mules can cope with this escarpment, for which 'precipitous' is utterly inadequate.

The top of the *amba* was about a mile wide and two miles long; low scrub dotted its stony, uncultivable flatness and the slanting sunlight showed up fresh leopard spoor in the dust of our faint path. Yet near the southern edge is another 'famous church'—how inaccessible can you make your famous churches! —which, as usual, was locked. Even here the roof was of tin: but the past fortnight has inured me to this disfigurement and I have come to accept, as an integral part of the highland scene, these circles of pale grey amidst a grove of trees on a height. Around the eaves hung hundreds of bells, crudely fashioned from bits of left-over tin, and at each touch of the wind these sent gentle, lonely little melodies far across the plateau. Here I also saw a stone bell, such as was noticed by Francisco Alvarez, the Portugese priest who visited the highlands for six years from 1520. This slim granite slab, some four feet by one and a half, was suspended at waist-level between two stunted wild fig-trees—and when I struck it with my *dula*, on the dent worn by centuries of strikings, it produced what Alvarez well described as 'a sound like cracked bells heard at a distance'.

Near the church a gigantic wedge of rock has split away from the *amba* and stands alone, with surprisingly green vegetation covering its boat-shaped top. Such wedges are not uncommon in the highlands, but legend says that a miracle caused this split. Once a saintly monk was accused by malicious villagers of keeping a mistress, so he announced that he would pray to the Virgin Mary to prove his innocence by splitting the *amba*—and next morning this wedge was seen to have broken away.

There were a few stone hovels between the church and the escarpment, but we saw no one as we passed; on these exposed heights people prefer not to get up until the sun has warmed the air. Now I was overlooking the Takazze Gorge, though it was still invisible—lying 5,500 feet below, lost amidst an intricate convulsion of mountains through which the river has been carving a deeper and deeper channel during aeons of time. Before we descended Dawit pointed to another *amba*, level with ours, that rose beyond the gorge and was almost overshadowed by the Semiens. He said that there I would spend the night, in the first settlement of the province of Begemdir and Semien. But as it happened he was wrong.

The last Tigrean settlement is huddled on a sloping natural terrace immediately below the *amba*. Its women and children fled the moment they saw me, but a score of grim-faced men soon gathered round us and for the next forty-five minutes I sat on a pile of smooth rocks enjoying the morning sun while watching for Jock, but not enjoying Dawit's angry argument with the locals. His grandfather's message made no impression whatever—in spite of being written—and he was obviously aggravating things by adopting an officious 'urban' attitude towards these benighted savages who had never before seen a white woman. To me this attitude seemed as reckless as it was tactless, for the slim Dawit is about five foot three and any of his muscular opponents could have picked him up between two fingers and dropped him over the nearest precipice—which at a certain point I thought someone would do. By then his attitude had antagonised me too, and perhaps this was an advantage. I intervened to point out that no one was under any obligation to endure a gruelling two-day trek on behalf of a wandering stranger: and, as I spoke, the locals seemed to realise that I was on their side. Then Dawit changed his tactics and I heard frequent mentions of Leilt Aida and Ras Mangasha, followed by repeated references to the Emperor and gestures in my direction which made me suspect that I was now being presented as a close personal friend of Haile Selassie. At all events this litany of Imperial names worked, and when Jock's green bucket appeared in the distance I was being entertained with cow-warm milk, and a surly bodyguard had begun reluctantly to assemble. Considering this surliness and reluctance I wondered if there was much to choose between being escorted by these men and being waylaid by *shifta*.

Dawit was now suffering from conflict—feeling both relieved at having rid himself of responsibility and doleful at the thought of snapping his last link with Western civilisation. (For me it was indeed a novelty to be regarded as a link with any form of civilisation.) However, two people amongst us were completely happy—the small sons (aged twelve and ten) of an Aedat Muslim trader. For six days these boys had been camping on the terrace, with three donkey-loads of salt, hoping for the arrival of an armed party to protect them during their crossing of the gorge.

I was conscience-stricken on seeing the size of my escort—fourteen men, eight of them armed—but Dawit said that this was considered the minimum force for a safe passage through *shifta* territory. My would-be-unpretentious one-woman expedition had now got completely out of hand, and it seemed iniquitous to drag so many men into the dreaded depths of the Takazze Gorge. The malaria that I am protected against could bring endless misery to people who are beyond reach of medical aid, so before we left I asked Dawit to instruct my companions in the use of malaria tablets, which I promised to distribute at the end of the day when Jock was unloaded.

At 9.30 we set off—accompanied by the local priest—towards the terrace from which the descent begins. To me our path was indistinguishable from the rest of the rough mountainside so, looking ahead to the time when I will have eluded all guides, I tried to learn how to detect such trails.

On the level starting-point terrace—which was about forty yards wide and scattered with boulders and old, twisted, creeper-hung trees—the men paused and began what sounded like (but may not have been) a serious quarrel. Apparently some of them were trying to back out, now that the influence of the Imperial litany had waned, and two were glancing at me rather nastily. One of these was the priest, an elderly man with a hard mouth and cunning eyes, and the other was a youth whom I had noticed speculatively feeling Jock's load before we left the village. Amidst the mountain stillness angry shouts were soon reverberating like a series of explosions, and then the two factions began to threaten each other with *dulas* and rifle-butts. I felt that it would merely heighten the tension were I to show any impatience, suspicion or fear—all of which I was feeling in varying degrees—so I sat impassively on a rock, while the animals grazed nearby on long, burnt-up grass. Then the two little boys joined me, looking apprehensive; and—despite their adult task and hitherto manly demeanour—when the shouting became more enraged they moved closer to the presumably soothing female presence. Luckily I have an irrational faith in the fundamental goodness of human nature. I can never take the badness very seriously until it is operating, so throughout such crises as this my fear remains embryonic.

Then, suddenly and inexplicably, the quarrel was over, the priest turned back to the village—irritably twitching his horsehair fly-whisk—and the rest of us walked silently towards the gorge.

This was the toughest descent I have ever experienced. I tend to accuse the highlanders of exaggerating the difficulties of my trek, but they certainly have not exaggerated the difficulty of crossing the Takazze Gorge here; if it were even a degree more difficult it would be impassable to humans. The best way to describe our progress is to say that for the next two and a half hours we were slowly falling down a mountain. Even my nimble companions frequently slipped, and over some stretches I had to toboggan on my behind, while all the time clouds of yellow dust were filling my mouth, eyes and nostrils and becoming mud on my sweat-drenched body.

The upper slopes of this mountain are forested, but the lower are naked and desert-hot and have been deeply scored by torrents cascading to the Takazze, which rises about fifteen feet during the wet season. We followed one of these water-courses for the last few hundred yards—and then were within the gorge, on almost level ground. But still the river remained hidden.

For the next half-hour our track wound through low hills covered in high, burnt-gold grass and dotted with baobab trees. These monstrous growths have smooth grey trunks some ten yards in circumference—though they are no more than twenty feet tall—and short, thick, leafless branches sprout from their tops only, making them look like repulsive prehistoric beasts. After three weeks at 8,000 feet the thick, hot air of the gorge oppressed me like an invisible substance as I tottered along amidst my little forest of rifles, vaguely noticing many birds and shrubs that one never sees on the highlands.

We had a moment of mild drama at the point where our path went through a narrow gap between two hills and brought us at last within sight of the river. Here the leader stopped abruptly and yelled '*Shifta!*' as he bent to pick up a ragged *shamma* from the side of the path. The cotton cloak was stained with dried blood and had been torn by three bullet holes, and the stony ground nearby was also blood-stained. However, in a region where guns are so common, and many men are excessively prone to quarrelling, a little blood and a few bullet holes seem inconclusive evidence of *shifta* activity.

At this season the sluggish Takazze is only two feet deep and twenty yards wide, though from bank to bank across its sandy bed is a 200-yards' walk. On the southern side we rested for half-an-hour, beneath an enormous wild fig-tree, and the men washed all over—in two shifts, lest the Enemy should take us unawares. Meanwhile the unfortunate animals, having drunk deep, were pathetically seeking non-existent food amidst a cruelly hot wilderness of boulders. Each of their loads had slipped forward on to their necks at least twice during the descent, and by now they must have been fancying themselves in some sort of equine Hades.

As I sat smoking irreligiously, with my feet in the river, I became aware that this silent, motionless gorge has a curiously unquiet atmosphere. It is wide and bright and full of colour—green river, red-gold grasslands, silver sand, blue sky—yet such a strange uneasiness pervades it that I no longer wondered at the highlanders' aversion to the place.

The second half of the marathon began with an enervating two-mile walk up a dry, rocky, sun-stricken river bed. Then we started our four-hour climb—a relentless ascent up slopes of scorched turf as slippery as ice, leading to slopes of shale so steep that for every three steps forward one slid two steps back, leading to a thousand-foot stairway of black lava rock on which one's leg-muscles seemed to burn with exhaustion while one's lungs ached at every breath. But all the time it was getting cooler, and the incomparable joy of 'going higher' was sustaining me.

At this stage all the barriers went down between my escort and myself. In the gorge they had been perceptibly less surly—even showing concern for my new crop of foot blisters—and now they were displaying a touchingly affectionate respect. The explanation was obvious. When tackling such a climb one has to go at one's natural pace—to go either more quickly or more slowly adds to the strain—and, since my natural pace was somewhat faster than their own, my companions imagined me to be a superwoman of sorts. To the highlanders physical courage, or skill, or endurance are such important qualities that by inadvertently beating them to a mountain-top I had become an honoured guest instead of a damn nuisance.

When at last we reached level ground I almost wept with relief to see our path continuing level for a mile or so, curving around the mountain beneath a 300-foot wall of rock. This escarpment was so sheer that I decided we must have got to the end of the day's climb, as not even a highlander would

attempt it; so I went striding ahead—tiredness forgotten—
thinking thirstily of *talla*. Then an urgent shout checked me—
and I saw my companions going up the escarpment like flies.
For a moment I considered accompanying the boys, who were
taking Jock and their donkeys a long way round; but not knowing how long that way might be I chose the short cut and
eventually pulled myself on to the *amba* feeling proud of my
new-found ability to rock-climb.

By now my escort were being far too zealous about their
reluctantly-assumed responsibility. Four gunmen followed me
when I hurried elatedly to the tip of an 'aerial peninsula', from
which I could gaze down on the vast panorama that spread
south and east beneath a still vaster sunset glow. Here I wanted
to sit alone, and gaze and gaze—but soon I was being hustled
towards the settlement. Yet I had had time to feel both awed
and triumphant as I traced the faint thread of our path leading
out of the again invisible gorge and ascending from mountain-
top to mountain-top—with never a descent, for these mountains
form a giant's stairway to the *amba*.

This plateau is littered with stones the size of a man's head
and I noticed that *teff* had recently been harvested between
them; perhaps the ground is not cleared on these exposed
heights because large stones curtail erosion. Archaeologists
might find something of interest here, as the *amba* is also littered
with small stones of every conceivable texture, colour and
shape; when the last horizontal shafts of light fell across the
flatness it seemed that we were walking through some fabulous
treasure-trove.

The boys, Jock and the donkeys rejoined us near the settlement, where there was a meagre straggle of two-foot high
bushes. I was needing the hospitality of some bushes, but again
my obsessively loyal quartet of gunmen followed me, and stood
no more than a yard away with their backs discreetly turned
and their rifles at the ready—an apparently absurd precaution
on this domesticated plateau.

However, I began to see the point a moment later, when
four armed men emerged from the settlement and came towards
us through the bronze afterglow, shouting suspicious enquiries.
Undoubtedly 'the natives were hostile'—not to me in particular,

but to all of us. Our leader quickly produced Dawit's grandfather's chit—which he had been carrying wrapped in a rag in his pocket—and pretended to read it, though he is illiterate. But this achieved nothing and I realised that the situation was not being helped by neither side knowing the other's language. (Though Tigrinya and Amharinya both derive from Ge'ez they are as different as Italian and Spanish.) Then the gallant little Muslim traders, who are bilingual, attempted to act as interpreters—and for some reason the effect was disastrous. Suddenly one of the villagers picked up a sharp stone, held it threateningly and said '*Hid!*'—an insulting expletive universally understood in the highlands and usually heard when dogs are being driven out of *tukuls*. Our leader was standing beside me and at this I saw his hands tighten angrily on his rifle. But either regard for my safety or an untypical prudence restrained him, and turning abruptly away he led us off across the plateau towards the south.

At once the boys hurried to his side and pointed ahead to a dark mountain mass that rose from the edge of the *amba*. I couldn't guess what was being planned, but later it transpired that we had been invited to accompany them to the safety of this compound, where they have now delivered their loads of salt. We began to climb the steep, newly-ploughed mountainside in starry darkness, and when I switched on my torch its miraculous brilliance caused much delighted astonishment. It was strange to remember that less than twelve hours ago these men and I had been so mutually distrustful.

This family is Tigrean and—though I would have thought the arrival of fifteen unexpected guests a little disconcerting—our host has given us the warmest of welcomes. Perhaps he is glad to be again among a gathering of his own people. There are five stone huts in the compound, so primitively built that one could easily pass them by and never suspect that humans dwelt within. The flat mud roofs are on a level with my head, but I haven't seen the interiors because highlanders prefer not to admit guests to the family huts, if any alternative accommodation is available, and on arrival we were led to this cattle-shelter. The shelter's inner wall is part of a hut wall and the outer is a row of stakes interwoven with brushwood; there are no gable walls and the roof is also of stakes, on which fodder straw is stored. The enclosure measures about twenty yards by ten and soon two fires had been lit on the earthen floor—despite the proximity of so much brushwood and straw. Then came *talla*, and in my honour the chief family heirloom was brought forth—a large, green, cut-glass tumbler, thick with the *talla*-scum of decades. Our host is a lively, lovable old man, unusually fluent in sign-language, and he conveyed that he had killed many Italians in his day, incidentally securing this tumbler as loot. Fortunately for his susceptibilities I am too thirsty this evening to be deterred by any degree of filth.

By nine o'clock all fifteen of us—and our host and his two eldest sons—were being served with a massive meal of *injara* and mutton-*wat*; and the *faranj* was also given a bowl of curds. While we were eating, a tall, slim youth stood motionless in the centre of the floor, draped in a knee-length garment and holding aloft a flaming brand; he looked movingly handsome, his expression grave and his shapely head silhouetted against the night. But the illumination he provided was a little too strong, for it is always preferable to eat highland meals in a detail-obscuring gloom. Here there are no tin ladles, so *wat* is served by soaking pieces of *injara* in the soup, quickly slopping them down on the *injara*-table and adding a few fistfuls of chopped meat; and our hostess blew her nose through her fingers before breaking the *injara* for our second helping—which rather counteracted my earlier observation that all highlanders wash their hands before meals.

*10 January. Another Cattle Shelter on a Mountainside*

This has been a completely crazy day, during which I only covered eight miles and never knew from hour to hour who was deciding what about the *faranj*. To a normally decisiveEuropean life seems oddly unreal when all one's actions are being circumscribed by the inexplicable whims of people with whom no communication is possible.

Last night my escort solemnly handed over to our host the chit dictated by Dawit's grandfather. This scruffy scrap of paper has by now acquired tremendous significance; apparently acceptance of it symbolises the assumption of all responsibility for my safety. Then, at 5 a.m., the Tigreans left for home, to escape the noon heat of the gorge. (Highlanders detest tropical heat even more than I do.) I heard them preparing to depart and longed to be able to show gratitude effectively; but money has little value in this region, where most goods are bartered, so last evening I distributed matches, combs, mirrors and the promised malaria tablets—which were instantly and gleefully swallowed, despite Dawit's lecture on using them as cures rather than as prophylactics. These seemingly inadequate gifts gave immense pleasure to the men, who sat gazing entranced at their own reflections and soon broke most of the combs in their fuzzy hair.

At 6.30 I heard the family stirring, crawled out of my fleabag, packed up rapidly and, when my host appeared, asked him to have Jock loaded. But he shook his head emphatically, sighed heavily, smiled reassuringly, indicated that I was to seat myself on the pack-saddle and left the compound to attend to his morning duties at a hygienically remote point on the mountainside.

For the next two hours I wandered around nearby, enjoying the swiftly changing morning colours, or sat in the shelter fraternising wordlessly with innumerable children and adolescents. Last night these youngsters were too scared to approach within yards of me, but this morning, overcoming their timidity, they edged closer and closer to the Strange Being—and eventually one little girl summoned enough courage to determine the creature's sex by poking at its chest. On discovering that breasts existed beneath my loose shirt this brave explorer rushed off to find her mother, screaming 'Set nat! Set nat!' (It's a woman!) However, her companions could not easily credit this improbability so now, emboldened by her example, they proceeded to remove my shirt—which led to further exclamations of wonder when they saw the colour of untanned *faranj* skin.

At 8.30 my host and I breakfasted together off smoke-flavoured curds and fresh, pale *injara*—which is without the bitterness of the darker variety that goes with *wat*. Then, an hour later, I saw to my relief that Jock was being loaded, and at 9.45 he was led out of the compound by a little boy and I was escorted by my host, and two other greybeards, on to the path for the Semiens. A short, steep climb brought us to a narrow, level ridge—with profound chasms on either side—that led to an extraordinary square mountain immediately ahead. At the foot of this obstacle, hardly two miles from the compound, we stopped suddenly, and everyone sat beneath a tree in a pleasantly cool breeze, and a lengthy discussion took place between the grey-beards. Meanwhile nine other men, including a fourth grey-beard with a rifle, were converging upon the tree from various unlikely directions; and when all had assembled the momentous chit was passed from hand to hand and looked at every way up and feelingly discussed—the only snag was that nobody could actually *read* it. Then a tall, handsome young man emerged from the depths of the eastern gorge. His alert manner distinguished him from the average peasant and he *could* read, if slowly and unsurely, so he declaimed the contents of the chit to the assembly. Another vigorous and verbose debate followed, after which my host eloquently dictated his own chit to the young man—who used the *faranj's* pen and paper, watched by an assembly now awed to breathlessness. (As I should know, few things fascinate these highlanders as much as the act of writing.)

All this took one and a half hours, during which time I sat philosophically contemplating the everlasting hills and Jock munched elevenses amongst the scrub. Our positions were very similar today—neither of us knowing the reason why, and both of us waiting patiently to be escorted or driven over an indefinite distance to an uncertain destination.

At midday the party broke up, after elaborate farewells all round. The armed grey-beard turned south, leading Jock; I followed meekly and the rest of the grey-beard corps brought up the rear. Our path soon swung around to the golden-grassed eastern flank of the square mountain and ran level for a mile or so, with a spectacular thousand-foot rock wall directly above us and a fearsome drop directly below. Though this path is much used no one does anything to maintain it; at present it is merely dangerous, but during the rains it must be impassable.

Not the least exciting thing about these highlands is their

unpredictability: suddenly our path vanished on the brink of a valley, leaving us to make our own way down a steep slope of loose grey soil, scattered with deceptive boulders that looked firm but shifted nerve-rackingly when stepped on. Then we followed a dried-up water-course for half-an-hour, climbed a slight rise and saw a compound in the near distance, solitary amidst a flat, arid waste. Despite the altitude it was brutally hot in this enclosed valley and already my companions were wilting. When we reached the compound they collapsed, groaning with relief, in the shade of a cattle-shelter—and called loudly for the man of the house, who was evidently a friend. He at once spread cow-hide seats, shouted to his wife to bring *talla* and unloaded Jock—to my dismay and Jock's delight. It was now 2 p.m. and there we sat for the next two and a half hours, being served with very gritty *injara* and very hot bean-*wat* at 3.15—by which time I had drunk so much *talla* that I was half-asleep. Our youngish host, who looked ominously emaciated, coughed and spat continually and to honour the guest insisted on always refilling my wooden tankard from his own, instead of direct from the jar. Luckily T.B. was endemic among Irish cattle during my childhood, so I probably have a fair immunity. Our kindly, haggard hostess seemed equally tubercular, as did the coughing adolescent girls who peeped at me around corners from time to time and then hastily withdrew, giggling nervously, if I caught their eye. This was the poorest compound I have yet visited; everyone looked seriously undernourished.

At 4.30, when the men returned from their work in the fields, another chit-palaver began and by the time it had ended shadows were cooling the valley. Then Jock was reloaded, the two precious chits were entrusted to four young men—one of whom borrowed our host's rifle—the grey-beards gave me their blessing and I set wonderingly off down the valley with my new escort.

A brisk forty-minute walk over level ploughland and a tough twenty-minute climb brought us within sight of this settlement —and within sound of the giant curs who were snarling a savage unwelcome. My companions signed me to sit on a boulder, while they negotiated with the headman, and soon several men had collected to stare at me expressionlessly, and a few little children had come surprisingly close—but when I stood up to fetch my jacket they fled in real terror, the tiniest ones bursting into tears. Just so might European children have behaved fifty years ago had an African appeared in their village.

From where I was sitting—quarter-way up a slope at the narrow western end of the valley—royal-blue mountain masses seemed almost within touching distance on three sides. And the long, angular mass to the south, beyond the hidden ravine of the Ataba, was the northernmost fortification of the Semiens.

Stars were burning above the heights when the headman came to welcome me; like so many of his race and generation he is splendidly handsome—iron-grey hair goes well with mahogany skin, clean-cut nostrils and deep-set eyes. As he conducted me into his cattle-shelter-cum-guest-room I reflected that one of the strangest paradoxes of highland life is the extraordinary assurance and dignity—of a particular quality not found at all levels in European societies—which distinguishes so many of these peasants. Even in such a remote region as this, and when confronted with such a disquieting phenomenon as myself, their innate courtesy rarely fails them. Yet in many ways they are ignorant, treacherous and cruel to a degree—which has led some foreigners to dismiss their more attractive aspect as a form of deceit, or at best a meaningless routine of etiquette. But to me the two aspects, however contradictory, seem equally genuine.

This shelter is much like last night's, and the supper ritual was as usual—except that our host broke off some pieces of *injara* before we started and said a prayer commemorating the Last Supper while presenting them to his guests. As always children stood silently in the background, waiting for the adults to finish. Sometimes boys join the circle around the fire while food is being prepared, though they never speak and are required to remain standing in the presence of guests. When the meal is served they withdraw and after the adults have eaten the left-overs are heaped on one wicker tray and passed back—and occasionally, as a mark of affection, an adult will push a handful of food into a favourite child's mouth, receiving a low bow as thanks.

Highland babies and toddlers are pampered and lovingly fondled by all the family—but from about the age of three respect for their elders, instant obedience and complete silence in the presence of adults are rigidly enforced. No child, when speaking to an unrelated elder, will raise his voice above a whisper, and any boy who is careless about his shepherding duties can expect a severe beating. Dr Levine remarks that the effect of all this repression is 'to inhibit rather than to stimulate the development of individuality'. Yet most boys seem happy and high-spirited, as they scamper about on the sunny mountainsides and their sisters seem no less contented, as they work with mother around the compound acquiring the essential domestic skills. Doubtless such unreasonably harsh discipline stunts the mental and spiritual growth of a race, and one can see it as both cause and effect of the static state of highland culture; but it also has the stabilizing merit of consistency, and I know a number of Western children who would benefit greatly if only someone were primitive enough to inhibit the development of their personalities.

To-night I must choose my sleeping-place with caution; last night Jock was tethered so close to me that during the small hours he trod on my left shin-bone—a painful occurrence. Now another chit-palaver is being held, but I am determined to break loose tomorrow. Today I rather enjoyed the odd sensation of being totally without responsibility for my own movements, but I don't want a repetition of the experience. As yet it is impossible to plan my breaking loose; certainly Jock must be loaded before I rebel, and then I'll have to devise an escape technique suitable to the particular personalities involved and the circumstances of the moment.

# 4

# On the Roof

*11 January. A Camp on a Mountainside*

My escape this morning was so easy that one could call it a release. At dawn yesterday's escort returned to their compound, and for some reason my host appeared not to take *faranj*-protection very seriously. By seven o'clock Jock had been loaded and the chits given, with many admonitions, to a disgruntled, unarmed, puny youth, who looked quite scared at the idea of taking off into the wilds with a *faranj*; and, on realising that he alone was to accompany me, I felt already free.

Beyond the compound I firmly deprived my companion of Jock's halter, set a fast pace up a high hill, increased the pace across a level two miles and, as the sun was getting hot, almost sprinted up another higher and steeper hill—at the top of which I paused, breathless and streaming sweat, to gaze sadistically back at my distant victim, now desperately signalling me to wait. When I began to slither quickly down the steep shale slope Jock looked at me reproachfully, seeming to ask if I had taken leave of my senses. However, the sure-footed highlanders can always beat me on such descents and soon my escort was waving the chits in my face, while indicating a compound some half-an-hour's climb up the northern mountain. But for three hours we had seen no one and the youth was now thoroughly demoralised. Pointing ahead I repeated '*Bicha!*' ('Alone!') several times, in a threatening voice. Then, to ease things for him when he had to confess his failure, I went into the chit business myself and inscribed a long message in my most flourishing hand on impressively-headed ship's writing paper; and when he had accepted this I said good-bye and went full speed ahead towards the next hill. Once I glanced back, to see the poor lad sitting beneath an acacia tree,

89

looking bewildered. I hope he wasn't beaten on his return home.

It was blissful to be on my own again—alone in a region that looked more grandly wild and felt more utterly remote than anywhere else I have ever been. For the next two hours we ambled up and down the low grey hills that here run parallel to the Ataba ravine—which was close below, with its fast, shallow river running clear and green beneath a southern wall of fissured red rock. This area is so barren that until one o'clock I saw no *tukuls* and few traces of cultivation.

Then a small settlement appeared ahead, and three snarling dogs came racing down the steep slope. Shouting '*Hid!*' I stoned them in the approved fashion, as their noise brought a few cautiously curious men to the edge of the settlement. Had we not been observed I would have passed by, preferring to avoid the locals until dusk, but now I decided to attempt some foraging for Jock. As we approached the nearest compound the women fled indoors and the men uneasily moved to a little distance before questioning me in Amharinya. I replied '*Amharinya yellum*', indicating my tongue and shaking my head— and then I pointed to Jock and asked hopefully, '*Buccolo injara?*' (Mule food?). At once the tension slackened, either because this request was so reassuringly normal, or because it was already obvious that however inexplicable my presence might be I hardly constituted a menace to the community. Two men stepped forward and led Jock into the compound, beckoning me to follow; and as he was being unloaded, and given an armful of un-nourishing straw, the women peered from their *tukuls* to ask if I were '*set*' or '*saw*'. I replied '*set*,' but everyone looked disbelieving; so a man 'sexed' me in the usual way—and when he had confirmed my femininity the women relaxed and shyly invited me into a *tukul*.

Within this tiny hut I sat near the door, on a mud bed, while men from all over the settlement came crowding round to stare. No *talla* was produced—evidence of extreme poverty—but two women immediately set about preparing a meal, first pointing to a mysterious substance hanging from the ceiling and enquiring if I approved of it. I was hungry enough to approve of anything chewable so I nodded enthusiastically and said '*Thuru!*

*Thuru!*' (Good!). The substance proved to be strips of dried beef—a precious delicacy—and when it had been chopped up and simmered with salt and cinnamon (two other delicacies) the tasty stew was served on a round of stale, inferior *injara*.

Meanwhile some men were questioning me about my route —one question that I can always answer, merely by reciting a list of names—while others were examining my body as though it belonged to a circus freak. My feet were picked up and my boots gazed at in wonder, my hair was felt and exclaimed over, the golden down an my tanned forearms was gently pulled to see if it was in fact *growing* there, my shirt was opened and the whiteness of my torso marvelled at, and my rather conspicuous calf-muscles were prodded respectfully—and then the men looked at me and laughed, while prodding them again and saying, 'Addis Ababa—*thuru!*' Which I took to mean that they considered the muscles well-suited to the journey.

This interlude reinforced my theory that in remote regions it is best to show a total dependence on the locals. Within fifteen minutes I had been accepted by that settlement—as a most puzzling phenomenon, it is true, but also as someone to be fed, and joked with on terms of essential equality. The particular kind of communication established there would have been impossible had I arrived protected by armed men flourishing chits. In this country, as elsewhere, the best currency for purchasing kindness is trust.

Yet in certain circumstances trust must be tempered with prudence. While I was eating the men had turned their attention to my kit, which was no less a source of wonder than my body. Every object not in the sacks was scrutinized eagerly, and I could see that some objects were being coveted. To possess so many marvellous things bespoke a wealth beyond imagining, and soon a group of men began to beg insistently for a comb (they had seen mine), for the heavy rubber torch (they mistook it for a weapon), for the bird book (its brilliant illustrations delighted them), for the bucket, the water-bottle, Jock's rarely-used bridle and my map. It was not unpleasant begging, but wistful as a child pleading for the moon; their intelligence failed to tell them that most of these possessions were supremely important to me—and at present irreplaceable, even were I a millionaire. I had intended getting my gift-box out of its sack and distributing a few combs and mirrors among the family who had entertained me; but now I realised that it could be tempting these men unfairly—and possibly dangerously—to let them see how many enviable articles are contained in my sacks. So I left having given them nothing. In future I must remember always to carry a day's supply of gifts in Jock's bucket.

For three hours we continued west along the valley floor, seeing no one, though occasional patches of stubble proved that the lower slopes of the northern mountain wall are inhabited. By now my map has rather lost its grip. It is lavish with lines of little red dots, marking 'tracks'—one of which is alleged to accompany the Ataba up this valley—but any track there may be is invisible to the naked European eye. Not that this matters, for one has to go west, between these gigantic ranges, and the terrain is easy enough. All day no break appeared in the massive fortifications to the south; but there must be a break somewhere, and doubtless we'll come to it eventually.

Soon after five o'clock a brief stretch of visible track led us down to river-level, and on the opposite bank 'steps' of high hills seemed to lead to the Semiens. Having crossed the Ataba (here a narrow stream) the track again vanished, but it was not too difficult to find a way up the forested hills and we climbed gradually—because diagonally—for the next forty minutes, rising to 8,400 feet. Here there were no signs of cultivation, so when we came to this natural terrace I decided to stop and unload Jock before dark. (How to re-load him to-morrow morning is to-morrow's problem!) Very likely a settlement lies not far off—I think the next hill is ploughed—but it would be lunacy to attempt these forested, friable, tractless inclines by torchlight.

Now poor Jock is fending for himself; I can hear him munching nearby, so evidently he's making the best of tough, scorched grass. His owner guiltily enjoyed an excellent supper—six ounces of tinned cheese with half a pound of raw prunes, eaten by brilliant starlight. Here the sky arches like some exotically decorated Emperor's tent above all those square *ambas*, curving crests, triangular spires and jagged ridges that tonight form the boundaries of my world. Level with this ledge, on the other side of the valley, I can see a few little fires—companionable red dots in the darkness—and occasionally I hear the distant howling of dogs. At least I hope it is the howling of dogs, and not of hyenas; undoubtedly this is hyena country, which worries me slightly. Yet the lighting of a fire might attract human marauders, so instead I'll tether Jock near me—a precaution that will restrict his grazing. Fortunately hypothetical hyenas cannot destroy my pleasure in this superbly beautiful 'Night on the Bare Mountain'—where the air feels like cool velvet and cicadas are serenading me from the valley and the still majesty of the mountains looms all around.

*12 January. A Shepherd's Camp in the Ataba Valley*

I slept deeply last night—with no hyena troubles, even in a nightmare—and woke just as morning 'flung the Stone that puts the Stars to Flight'. It was 5.50, and for moments only a silver pallor hung in the east. Then quickly a faint pink flowed up from the hidden horizon—giving mountains and valley a new, soft, shadowed beauty—and soon this had deepened to a red-gold glow which seemed briefly to hold all the splendour of all the dawns that ever were. To lie beneath such a sky, surrounded by such peaks, brings an almost intolerably intense awareness of the duality of our nature. We belong so intimately and joyously and tragically to this physical world, and by its own laws we soon must leave it. Yet during these moments one knows, too, with humility and certainty, that each human spirit is immortal—for time cannot destroy whatever element within us reverences the glory of a dawn in the mountains.

While breakfasting off more cheese and prunes I considered our load problem, and finally improvised a variation on the pannier theme. This ingenuity boosted my self-esteem considerably, but only temporarily. If necessity is the mother of invention she proved a very bad mother in this case and after precisely thirty-five minutes the whole invention fell asunder. Luckily we were then within twenty minutes' walk of a settlement, so tethering Jock beside the shambles I went for help —and succeeded in obtaining it, after a long, patience-sapping session with two men whose natural slow-wittedness was accentuated by astonishment and suspicion.

Jock has a chill today. Last evening he was in a lather when we stopped and, though I rubbed him down hard, it is clear that Nights on Bare Mountains don't suit him as well as they do me. He has been in wretched form since morning—sneezing repeatedly, looking hard-done-by when going uphill and refusing to eat. So we took it easy all day and only covered twelve miles.

The landscape changed completely within two miles of our camp. Suddenly the valley broadened, the dark soil was extensively cultivated and many hillsides were covered in freshly green shrubs, through which scores of birds darted brightly. During the forenoon I counted six settlements and the people were unexpectedly friendly—several men pursued me to present raw eggs or gourds of fresh milk or curds. Then would follow a long delay, while I sat on a stone enjoying these refreshments and explaining where I was coming from and going to.

The local dogs, however, were far from friendly. These enormous curs are the most dangerous animals in Ethiopia and twice today they really scared me. Once a pair followed us for about a mile, slavering and snarling ferociously. They seemed impervious to stones and only retreated when I'd knocked one of them half-unconscious with my *dula*, to deter him from leaping at my arm. Then, an hour later, a pack of five surrounded us in a paroxysm of aggressive fury, but Jock reacted by lashing out intelligently at the three who were closing in behind us and then swinging around to aim at the others. It was the first time I've seen him kicking and the implications of a mule-kick were not lost on the curs. At once they retreated to a safe distance —from everybody's point of view.

Today's direction-finding was much more taxing than yesterday's. The inhabited foothills were criss-crossed with many faint paths and it was impossible to determine which path might ultimately turn south. Then from one o'clock, when all the settlements had been left behind, we were crossing trackless hills (now arid again) by whatever route looked easiest. This morning I attempted to find out the approximate point at which one can enter the Semiens; but in answer to my careful sign questions everyone merely pointed to the colossal massif towering immediately above us and repeated 'Semien! Semien!', while going through a pantomime of being exhausted to the point of collapse—which was neither illuminating nor consoling. However, at three o'clock the head of the valley came in sight—another gigantic mountain wall, obscuring the western sky—and I decided to descend to river level, since the Ataba seemed likely to be my most reliable guide to the heights.

Half-an-hour later we were beside a deep pool of cold, green, ice-clean water, so Jock had a long rest while my filthy body was being scrubbed. Then we meandered along an intermittent path just above the river, often having to force our way through thick groves of aromatic shrubs. Here a few cow-pats and goat droppings appeared though no settlements were visible; but at six o'clock, as I was looking around for a camping-site, smoke rose ahead—and five minutes later I saw this shepherds' camp, where three young men and three boys were preparing for their nightly vigil.

Having given everyone time to appreciate my harmlessness I invited myself to stay the night, feeling relieved that here were Jock-loaders. After a moment's hesitation the men welcomed me, by pointing to a stone near the fire, and then came the already familiar process of investigation and acceptance—which here is being more protracted than usual, for in this confrontation with the unknown these shepherds are without the reassuring support of their community.

As I unloaded Jock and rubbed him down the herds were being rounded up—scores of goats, eighteen cattle, four donkeys and twenty-six kids. The kids give most trouble, for they have to be caught—much against their will—and then secured in quartets by means of leather thongs knotted around their kicking forelegs. The other stock, who have sense enough not to wander after dark, are simply driven on to the open space between the high-blazing fire and the cliff above the river. When the two cows had been milked into gourds the milk was shared with me and I was offered *dabo* and roasted barley, but as both were in short supply I feasted instead on tinned mackerel and raisins.

At present I'm not well-informed about world events, but I

do know that some space-craft is in orbit. I saw it rise above the northern mountains at 7.15 and it disappeared below the southern mountains ten minutes later. The shepherds saw it too, as it slowly traversed the sky—looking just like a small golden star, apart from its weirdly purposeful movement. Then they glanced at me uneasily, perhaps imagining some sinister link between the appearance of a *faranj* and this derangement in the heavens. I had wondered, as I watched it, if it were manned; and I also felt uneasy, thinking of the ominous contrast between the life of an astronaut and the life of my companions—which is now as it was when 'there were . . . shepherds abiding in the field, keeping watch over their flock by night. And, lo, the angel of the Lord came upon them, and the glory of the Lord shone round about them . . .'

*13 January. A Settlement in the Semiens*

Last night my sleep was disturbed by armies of small black ants who seemed to relish insecticide. Also I was lying on an incline, with my feet braced against a boulder, and I tended to unbrace them every time I dozed off in defiance of the ants—which meant wakening abruptly to find myself sliding towards the fire.

However, I enjoyed being awake in that camp. The shepherds kept watch in pairs, a man and a boy always sitting by the fire, and as they sat they chanted an interminable monotone duet. Judging by the names mentioned this must have been a saga of all the bravest warriors of highland history; and the singers put such feeling into their voices that often I could guess which were the words of the victorious Emperor, or the conquered chieftain, or the scheming traitor. It was splendid to hear the ring of these proud, sharp phrases against the dark silence of the valley. For highlanders history is not of the past, seen down an orderly vista of dates and events: it lives within them, as inspiring memories of courageous or cunning individuals who may have lived—for all they know—a hundred or a thousand years ago.

As I lay listening smoke streamed past me, in a grey-blue horizontal column, laden with rosy sparks; and this movement of insubstantial loveliness was background to a motionless tangle of tall grasses—growing between me and the fire—which formed a design of such intricate delicacy that for hours I gazed up at it in endless delight. I felt grateful then for having been born in time to know this world of simplicity and peace, which may soon be annihilated by the Age of the Astronauts.

This morning Jock seemed quite recovered. Good grazing had been available all night and his performance today has proved that he took full advantage of it. At 6.15 we left the shepherds, who had been singularly unhelpful when questioned about our route. Whichever direction I pointed in, saying 'Semien?', they nodded vaguely and replied '*Mado*' (Yonder). So I decided simply to follow the Ataba. But when we came to the head of the valley following the Ataba was no longer simple; at the junction of the three massifs lay a confusion of rocky, rushing rivers, sheer precipices and ancient forests of giant, creeper-hung trees. However, somewhere amidst this wilderness there had to be an upward path, and after struggling around in circles for some twenty minutes I noticed a narrow tunnel through the forest, on the far bank of one river. And that was it. From there a track climbed south up a cleft in that mountain-wall which for two days had been unbroken.

At first we were amidst the chill gloom of the forest, where many rotten trees have been caught as they fell by networks of tough creepers which now support the dead giants at strange angles. Then the path was overhung by green and gold shrubs, between which the emerald flashings of the river could be glimpsed far below. An unexpected descent took us down to river level, and having crossed to the eastern wall of the ravine we were again climbing steeply on an open, grassy slope where the path was of slithery earth. (On the west wall it had been rocky, and therefore easy to climb.)

By nine o'clock the sun was reaching into the ravine, yet the air was getting colder every moment—though this didn't prevent Jock and me from lathering sweat. Half-an-hour later we at last reached level ground, and fifty yards ahead three men were threshing barley. They seemed mesmerised by our appearance, but when I had unloaded Jock and collapsed on a pile of straw they quickly recovered and shared their *talla* with me.

An uneven shoulder of the mountain formed this ledge (some three miles by two), where a few settlements—perched on hillsides amidst stubble fields—were overhung by rough grey crags rising from green forests. Now I really was in the Semiens, at 10,300 feet, and for the next hour I rested here, being revived by timid but generous locals who filled me with *talla* while I gazed joyfully at the heights and the depths all around me.

When Jock was being reloaded I had the ropes tied extra-tight—a regrettable but necessary precaution. Earlier the load had been slipping slightly and on the isolated heights ahead I dared not risk it falling off.

From this ledge the path climbed steeply for half-an-hour before levelling out in a cool green world of tall, aromatic shrubs. Then it curved around the mountain, overhanging an apparently bottomless abyss, and soon was climbing again to the 11,500-foot crest of a ridge of black soil. Here only a few clumps of heather grew between smooth boulders and it was so cold that I stopped sweating.

A short stretch of flat, bleak moorland brought us abruptly into a new world, where on every side the immense slopes, sweeping above and below the path for thousands of feet, were so thickly covered with golden grass that the very air seemed golden too. From here we climbed gradually, rounding one grassy spur after another, while to the east, south and west jagged rock summits rose far above us, severe against an intense blue sky. As we penetrated deeper and deeper into the mountains I realised that our track would have to go *over* one of those summits, improbable as that might seem, for there could be no other exit from this colossal amphitheatre.

I was scanning the various peaks, wondering which escarpment we were fated to tackle, when my eye was caught by a violent disturbance in the long grass on the next spur. At first I thought it must be a herd of alarmed goats—though this seemed unlikely—but an instant later shrieks and screams of an uncanny stridency shockingly ravaged the stillness. We were then rounding the spur—and I stopped, accusing myself of having an hallucination, for the slope ahead was apparently swarming with misshapen lions. It took me half a minute to realise my privilege. This was a herd of some two hundred Gelada

(Bleeding Heart) baboons—one of the rarest of animals, which is found only in Ethiopia, and in Ethiopia only on the highest mountains. So my hallucination was understandable, for the magnificent male Gelada has a thick lionesque mane—a waist-length cape of dark fur—and to strengthen the illusion his tail is handsomely tufted.

Our presence was provoking hysterically raucous protests. The Geladas swarmed across the whole slope—above, below and on the path—and the nearest were hardly ten yards away, giving me a clear view of the heart-sized patch of crimson skin on each chest and of their long, powerful fangs gleaming in the sun at every shriek. In the circumstances, I could have done with a less clear view of these fangs. All baboons are reputed to be cowards but apparently Jock and I look unusually innocuous, for this troop was showing not the slightest inclination to move off the path. Then my memory perversely produced what is doubtless an old wives' tale about human bones having been found among others in the Geladas' boneyards. At which point I decided to take action—and a few stones immediately cleared the path, though none of the males moved far away and their hideous peals of rage almost deafened me as we slowly passed through the herd. Luckily Jock had maintained his customary stoicism during this encounter, merely looking relieved at having a chance to stand still.

On the next spur I paused to watch the Geladas' antics. Their many human gestures have the chastening fascination of all monkey-behaviour and in their social life they seem to be aggressive and irritable and to expend a great deal of energy on squabbling, male with male and female with female. But this does nothing to distinguish them from their more advanced cousins—and anyway our intrusion may have upset everyone's nervous system.

Soon after, we were on the western mountain, where our struggle began. Green forest covered the shadowed precipice, icy streams formed miniature waterfalls and whenever I stopped, to quieten my pounding heart, I began to shiver. From here it was impossible to see the summit—or indeed to see any distance ahead, through this dark tangle of trees—and poor Jock had to be urged on with vehement shouts, for which I had little breath to spare, and with occasional whacks across the hindquarters that almost reduced me to tears of remorse. Again the track had become elusive and sometimes we didn't know which way to turn—though at least I realised that our general principle must be to move *upwards*, whereas Jock felt that whenever possible it would be much more rational to move *across*.

As the air thinned each step became a pain. Now Jock's jumps from ledge to ledge would have taxed a steeple-chaser, and often he had to clamber up long slabs of table-smooth rock that lay at dreadful angles, or to leap across deep, narrow gullies, or to keep his balance on inclines where every boulder shifted beneath his hoofs. But, oddly enough, he went ahead willingly at this stage, as though aware that I had become too exhausted either to shout or to whack, and that our climb was now a crisis in which he must not fail me. He was magnificent, yet here I found suspense on his account a far worse agony than aching muscles or lungs. To my inexperienced eye it seemed that at any moment he might break a leg, which would have been much more serious than my doing so; at an extremity he could carry me, but with the best will in the world I could not carry him. I was beginning to wonder which of us would collapse first when suddenly we were out of the trees, on a narrow ledge of yellowed turf—and looking up I saw the summit two hundred feet above. Inspired by this sight, I was about to take the lead—but apparently Jock had been inspired too, for he made an heroic final effort and got there first, to stand with head hanging and sides heaving. Poor fellow!—as I pulled myself on to the top I longed to be able to unload him.

However, on seeing what we had conquered I forgot everything else. We were now at 13,800 feet, and directly beneath the northern verge of this plateau lay a fierce, sombre scene of geological anarchy. One fancied that at the time of creation some basic law had here been forgotten—and nothing grew or moved amidst the grotesque desolation of these riven mountains. Then, looking north-east, I saw beneath me the countless strangely-eroded peaks and ridges that from the Ataba valley had looked so high; and beyond them I could recognise the mountains of Adua and Aksum, amongst scores of other ranges. In three directions I was gazing over hundreds of miles th.ough crystal air—away and away to far, far horizons, where deserts and the sea are 'as a moat defensive. . . .' No wonder I felt like a mini-Hilary, with all Northern Ethiopia lying at my feet.

While devouring a pound of dried apricots I sat on a sweep of burnt-gold, springy turf, where low bushes covered with daisy flowers grew between sheets of pale grey rock, and scores of two-foot giant lobelias looked incongruously like dwarf palms. Their long, shiny, pale green leaves glinted in the sun, making sparks of silver light all over the summit, and through the enormous silence came the faint, fairy-like chiming of the wind in those leaves. There is an overwhelming integrity about the silence of such places; in its purity and power it differs utterly from the noiselessness of even the remotest inhabited regions. This afternoon's silence seemed no less tangible than the crags around us.

My proudly-conquered 'summit' is in fact the extreme edge of that immense Semien plateau which tilts gradually south-ward to the ridges above Gondar; so now we were able to walk effortlessly down an almost imperceptible incline. New crags rose nearby to the east, but ahead and to the west golden turf stretched illimitably, its flatness emphasised by a scattering of six-foot lobelias—like so many sentinels posted on the plain—and its only boundary the infinite arc of a cloudless sky. In the simplicity of its colours and contours this was a landscape of liberation; here one could indeed be 'forgetful of the world', since now nothing had meaning but the spaciousness, radiance and silence that briefly set one free from everything.

Half-an-hour later we were on broken moorland where bushes of giant heath had graceful streamers of wispy moss floating from their branches. Many of these bushes were dead, and here the instinct of self-preservation prompted me to re-member the world and to consider the less romantic aspects of being on an uninhabited 13,000-foot plateau at 4 p.m. So I paused to collect firewood, fixing one bundle on top of Jock's sacks and tying my own bundle with a spare length of rope, However, this tiring precaution proved unnecessary, as the next five miles were thinly wooded with heath, juniper and lobelia.

At 5.40 we seemed doomed to a night out—but then I saw goat droppings on the turf and a moment later I noticed that the upper slopes of a valley to the west had recently been ploughed. A brisk five-minute trot brought us to the edge of this deep, circular depression beneath sheer, smoky-blue mountains. Ripe barley lined the valley, creating a lake of golden light in the evening sun, and far below were three tiny settlements, each sheltered by a few blue-gums. Harvesting had begun on the slopes and as I stood there, luxuriating in relief, I could hear the distant whip-cracking and chanting of threshers who were driving muzzled oxen round and round through knee-high piles of barley.

The steep descent on loose clay was difficult for me, but Jock seemed pleased by the change. For him smooth, dry turf is very trying, and to my dismay those hoofs which had taken him so unerringly up that nightmare escarpment often slipped treacherously on our way across the plateau.

As we approached the main settlement three little boys excitedly yelled, 'Faranj! Faranj'!, so I realised that here for-eigners are not unknown. Yet the score of men who at once gathered silently around us were obviously suspicious—no doubt because I lacked an escort and had come from the 'wrong' direction. (Faranj trekkers usually hire mules at Debarak and enter the Semiens from the west.) However, after travelling hard for ten of the previous twelve hours I felt too tired and hungry to care about anyone's reactions, so I quickly unloaded Jock, getting no assistance from the men, and sat in the stubble on a sack, signing my need for shelter. But this only increased the general uneasiness, since faranjs normally have tents, and without addressing me the men began a vehement discussion.

Ten minutes later a youngish man came striding across the field with a rifle over his shoulder and a truculent expression on his face. He wore western clothes beneath his shamma and immediately demanded my permit, by making a stamping gesture with his right fist on his left palm; but as he was illiterate my Ethiopian visa meant nothing to him. What he wanted was a familiar-looking chit, issued by some local governor, and there followed a few unpleasant moments while he shouted angrily at me and slapped my passport contemptuously. I could sense that he was unpopular with the other men and now some of them began to speak up for me, referring to the fact that I was a lone woman, and one of them invited me into his compound. Emboldened by this support I took back my despised passport and indicated to the company that the visa was Ras Mangasha's chit—a deception which satisfied even the official, though in theory Ras Mangasha's authority does not extend beyond the Takazze.

Once their initial suspicions have been allayed these highlanders are consistently hospitable and soon I was being given a place of honour near the fire in this tiny *tukul*. My altimeter shows 12,400 feet and within moments of the sun's setting it began to freeze; at present my hands are so numb that I can hardly hold the pen. It seems odd that in Tigre, where the climate is comparatively equable, most dwellings are solidly built of stone, yet at this altitude one finds only wretched wattle hovels. Cakes of mud or dung are usually plastered over the stakes, but here I can see stars twinkling frostily in every direction and at intervals a blast of icy wind comes whistling through, making my candle gutter and sending wood-smoke swirling into everyone's face. Such huts are common throughout Negro Africa, but with the example of Tigre so close their construction in the Semiens is extraordinary. Perhaps it is relevant that the Aksumite Empire—which introduced Semitic building techniques to the highlands—corresponded almost exactly to the modern Tigrinya-speaking regions and had as its southern boundary the Takazze Gorge. However, the Aksumite Empire flourished quite some time ago, and the failure of the Amharas to learn from their Tigrean cousins hints at an abnormal mental inflexibility.

For supper—after my host had devoutly said grace—crisp, hot barley bread was served with our *injara* and vegetable-*wat*; this bread contained so much foreign matter that I lost half a tooth while enthusiastically masticating. The Man of the House had wanted to kill a chicken for me, but as I could not permit such extreme generosity he presented me instead with four tiny eggs.

I notice a few slight differences in the customs of this household. For our hand-washings a wooden bowl of water was passed around—an apparently unnecessary economy in an area of many springs. Also, one empties one's *talla* vessel before having it refilled, and at each refill a burning twig is held briefly over the gourd to allow drinkers beyond the firelight to see what quality of *talla* they are getting. But here, as elsewhere, the server always pours a little of the guest's drink into her own hand and tastes it, to prove that the brew is not poisoned. Evidently it suits some highlanders to poison certain guests.

This is one of the filthiest hovels I have ever been in—which is saying quite a lot. Yet here filth never seems intolerable, as it might in a European slum. One finds no stale food, dirty clothes, scraps of paper, empty tins or unwashed utensils—only manure, wood-ash, leaves, straw and chicken-droppings on a never-swept floor, completed by the smell of humans who are no smellier that I am at present.

I enjoy this neolithic world where money is unimportant and all the objects in daily use have been made of mud, wood, stone, hides or horn. However, in one respect life may prove a trifle too neolithic tonight. Eight adults and three children live in this hut, which has a diameter of about eighteen feet, and as the twelfth inhabitant I'll have to roll up like a hedgehog. In such a confined space my meagre kit seems to occupy an inordinate area, but when I suggested dumping it outside consternation ensued. So many people can live in one minute *tukul* only because they have no personal possessions, apart from their land, its products and their livestock. Every object here is communal—for storing and grinding grain, or for cooking and serving food. Despite the savage frost, there is not even any extra bedding; yet these people do suffer from the cold, which may be why they sleep in a crowd. I felt guilty about needing to sit near the fire, though wearing everything I've got, so after supper I moved away and wriggled into my flea-bag—a procedure which causes much astonished amusement in every compound.

This family is most endearing—generous, considerate, friendly and gay. Within a few hours they have made me feel that I belong to them, and in defiance of the language barrier we seem to have spent a lot of time laughing at each other's jokes. I am learning that the quickest way to come to terms with the highlanders is by appealing to their sense of humour.

Two hours ago everyone else curled up in their threadbare *shammas* under their stiff cow-hides; but my sleeping prospects are so poor at this temperature that I've kept on writing, hoping that eventually extreme exhaustion will cancel out the cold—which, unhappily, does not affect the bed-bug population. Just inside the crude plank 'door' is a 'two-tiered bunk' type of bed which I haven't seen elsewhere. It is made of wood and hide thongs, on the charpoy principle—but without anything approaching the skill of Indian craftsmanship—and as my torch-light caught it, when I was going out a moment ago, bed-bugs were swarming all over the wood. No wonder the occupants are muttering miserably in their cold-bedevilled, verminous sleep.

Now I think I'll read a chapter or two of *Pain and Providence*.

*14 January. A Tent in the Semiens*

After a few hours of shivery dozing it was a relief this morning to hear the harsh crow of a nearby cock. Everyone else must have felt the same, for my hostess was up in the dark, vigorously blowing on the embers—which had been covered with ash—and as the first light seeped through the wall the other adults rose and crouched around the blazing sticks, so closely wrapped in their *shammas* that only their eyes were visible and each voice was muffled. Many of the poorer highlanders never eat before midday and as no one seemed to be thinking of breakfast I opened a tin of tuna fish and ate it with my pale pink plastic spoon, watched by a fascinated family who accepted the empty tin as though it were a golden goblet. Everyone disapproved of my leaving so early—they shook their heads and rubbed their hands together while repeating '*Birr! Birr!*' ('Cold! Cold!') But I reckoned that I would feel a lot less cold if moving and we started out at seven o'clock.

Strangely, none of these men was an efficient mule-loader, and this worried me as we walked down a sloping stubble-field that felt iron-hard under black frost. On being asked about the path to Derasghie my host had vaguely indicated the summit of a sheer mountain to the south-west and I had no idea how populated—or unpopulated—the route might be.

Our path—having skirted one end of a canyon that lies

hidden at the edge of the valley—expired at the foot of a steep, newly-ploughed slope. So we simply went straight up, and even during this strenuous climb I was being seared by the frosty air. We paused on the crest, and looking back over the valley I noticed how few compounds there are in relation to the area of cultivated land and to the livestock population. Yesterday evening big herds of cattle, sheep and horses were grazing on all the stubble fields—here barley is cut half-way down the stalk—so, however primitive their homes may appear, the locals cannot be really poor. These fat-tailed sheep and small horses were almost the first of either species that I've seen in the highlands; sheep can survive in most regions, but are commonest at this altitude, and horses are nowhere as popular as mules, whose sure-footedness makes them much more valuable, both for riding and pack-carrying.

From this ridge the general view to the south-west was of a baffling array of seemingly unlinked escarpments and ledges. Directly below us lay a gorge of fearsome depth, overshadowed on three sides by perpendicular mountains of black rock on whose darkly forested lower slopes I could detect no sign of a track. Yet without a track it would be impossible to cross this formidable massif, so leaving Jock I began to quarter the ridge. Eventually a series of donkey hoof-prints leading south gave me hope—by following them we might find the track which I knew must exist somewhere. However, I'm no Red Indian, and as the hard, wind-swept ground had taken prints only between boulders, where the dust lay sheltered, we progressed hesitantly, climbing a shoulder of the southern mountain before turning north to descend a steep incline sparsely covered with withered grass. Then we came to the tree-line—and ten minutes later were on a wide, rocky path which was obviously the local M1.

For an hour we continued west, climbing gradually through a hushed, twilit forest of giant heath; eerily, most of the trees seemed dead, and all were elaborately draped in fine, pale green, ghostly moss. Immediately above us yard-long icicles hung in hundreds from the eternally-shadowed cliffs, like an armoury of glass daggers; and all the time it got colder as the path became rockier and steeper.

I no longer expect these highland tracks to stop climbing until they have reached the top of an escarpment—however much against nature such behaviour may seem. And sure enough, in due course our path took a deep breath, as it were, and soared straight up—providing a new danger for Jock, since thick black ice now lay between the stones. But the invincible creature made it somehow—bless his stout heart!

This final climb taxed my own body to the limit. Scanty sleep on two consecutive nights and a recently rather frugal diet—in relation to energy expended—have so diminished my stamina that I reached the top of the 14,400 foot escarpment feeling like death not warmed up. For a few moments I shared Jock's disinterest in the panorama and simply sat beside him with my head on my knees. Then, having recovered enough breath to smoke, I began to appreciate a view that was more confined than yesterday's but no less dramatic in its own way. This indeed was the heart of the Semiens—a jagged, dark, cold, cruel rock-world—and to have 'won' it was reward enough for any degree of painful fatigue.

Here the path vanished amidst lava slabs and when it re-appeared, on a long turf slope, it had multiplied confusingly into half-a-dozen pathlets, which rambled off inconsequentially towards various points of the compass. A low, grassy ridge stretched nearby on our right, and on our left the plateau swept gradually up to a rough rock crest which I later discovered was the summit of Buahit (14,796 feet)—Ethiopia's second highest mountain. At this point I had no notion whether the Derasghie track went south or east, but I emphatically favoured walking down rather than up. So we proceeded south.

It was now half-past eleven and the sun had some warmth, though a steady breeze was blowing coldly across this roof of Ethiopia. Jock's load had come loose on the ascent and my desperate attempts to straighten the sacks and tighten the ropes had not been very successful. However, this worry was banished —temporarily—when two men appeared over the horizon, driving four donkeys in our direction. It took these knights a little time to overcome their incredulity but then they willingly rescued the distressed damsel—though their eagerness to help was more impressive than their skill at mule-loading.

Before saying good-bye I pointed south and enquired, 'Deras-ghie?'—whereupon one man caught my arm, nodded vehe-mently, jabbed the southward air and shouted 'Derasghie! Derasghie! *Thuru! Thuru!*' But the other man caught *his* arm and jabbed the eastward air, shouting, '*Yellum! Yellum! Buzzy! Buzzy!*' (No! No! There! There!) From all of which I astutely deduced that both paths led to Derasghie, and that opinions differed as to the better route for a lone female with a mule; but since it was not possible to discuss the relative merits of the two paths I decided to continue lazily downhill.

Fifteen minutes later I was astounded to hear myself being hailed in English by an Ethiopian on the far bank of a nearby stream; and I was even more astounded to see a tall young white man crossing the stream and to hear him greeting me with a strong Welsh accent. I stared at him as though he were a spectre—and indeed the poor boy looked alarmingly like one, for he had spent the night lost on the slopes of Buahit. When we were joined by a haggard young Englishman, I learned from the boys' guide-cum-interpreter, Afeworq, that I had come upon the last scene of a painful drama, which mercifully was having a happy ending. Yesterday Ian and Richard had left their camp, near Ras Dashan, to explore the Buahit area, and during the afternoon they somehow got separated and thoroughly lost, so both had spent the night wandering around alone without light, food or adequate clothing. Early this morn-ing Afeworq left the camp to search for them, and just before I appeared the three had been reunited.

Ian, the Welshman, explained that two other Englishmen were at the camp and that all four are Addis school-teachers on a ten-day Semien trek. He added that tomorrow he hoped to climb Ras Dashan (15,158 feet), Ethiopia's highest mountain, and at this a certain fanatic gleam must have shown in my eye, for he asked if I would care to accompany him. Inevitably I said, 'Yes, *please!*'—forgetting both Derasghie and my dilapi-dation at the thought of a 'highest mountain'.

It took us five hours to walk the next eight miles. Richard was suffering from mountain-sickness and no one had much spring in their step as we climbed the long slope to the top of Buahit. From the summit we could see a tremendous chasm to the north, half-full of colossal wedges of broken rock—but my attention was soon diverted to the practical aspects of this landscape. Here we were on the verge of a 300-foot cliff which I wouldn't have dared to attempt with a pack-animal had I been alone, but as Afeworq knew a possible zig-zag route he led Jock down.

At the foot of this escarpment the load came off, having been loosened by Jock's gallant jumping. Afeworq tried to cope—but he is a Gondar-born youth, who knows no more than I do about mule-loading. He then nobly offered to carry one sack on his head, and I carried the other over my shoulder, and thus encumbered we struggled on down steep paths of loose soil on which I frequently fell, being unable to keep my balance beneath the weight of the swaying sack. Richard was now almost collapsing and seemed unaware of our crisis, but Ian soon began to suffer from frustrated gentlemanly instincts—which had to remain frustrated, as he was clearly in no condition to assume the White Woman's Burden.

We must have looked a pathetic sight as we staggered towards the camp, where Alan and Mike welcomed us with hot tinned soup and Ryvita.

This is a high-powered expedition, equipped with an enormous tent, a Primus stove, cooking utensils, crockery and cutlery, boxes of *faranj* food, a riding-mule, a muleteer and three pack-horses. Here we are down to 12,400 feet, in a wide, turf-lined hollow with running water nearby and a neighbouring settlement from which men come to exchange fresh eggs for empty tins.

Now early to bed, in preparation for Ras Dashan.


*15 January. The Same Tent in the Semiens*

A long sleep in a warm tent is good medicine. At seven o'clock this morning everyone looked ten years younger and half-an-hour later we set off—leaving behind Alan, Afeworq and the pack-animals.

Descending to river-level we followed the stream for about a mile, before climbing for two hours through stubble-fields and ploughland, where the boys took it in turn to ride their mule. This region seems to be thickly populated and we passed several groups of surly-looking locals.

At 10.30 a short, steep climb brought us to a wide pass from which Ras Dashan was visible. It is a most unassuming mountain—merely a long ridge of rock on which one point is slightly higher than the rest—and without a guide one could never pick it out from amongst the many other mountains that here sprawl gloriously against the sky.

Now Richard's mountain-sickness reasserted itslf, so he reluctantly decided to return to camp. Mike was also looking ill, but he doggedly tackled the next lap—a long walk around spur after spur, across sunny slopes of golden turf dotted with two-foot lobelias. (The higher the altitude the lower the lobelia.) Between these level stretches there were a few muscle- and lung-straining climbs and by midday thirst was tormenting me, though the boys seemed immune to altitude dehydration. Foolishly, I had left my water-bottle in camp, not realising that above river-level all streams would be frozen. (They were a very beautiful sight—gleaming tongues of ice hanging from the mouths of dark caverns near the summit of every mountain.)

By one o'clock an exhausting climb had taken us on to the Ras Dashan plateau, where the path skirts the western flank of the summit ridge and swings around to run parallel with the ridge on its southern side, across a wide, bleak plain littered with chunks of rough volcanic rocks.

Half-an-hour later the mule was tethered to a stone and we were led off the track towards the established route to the summit. The incline was easy, yet at this height our clamberings over rock-slabs and massive boulders felt strenuous enough, and we spent twenty minutes covering that last half-mile. Then a real climb of some fifty feet took us to the highest point in Ethiopia—and five minutes after Ian and the muleteer I crawled on to the summit, feeling very like a fly that has just been sprayed with D.D.T.

Our moment of triumph was somewhat marred by Mike's disappearance. I had assumed that he was just behind me, but in fact he had vanished, and our shouts and whistles brought no reply. Then, concluding that he had simply stopped to rest, and would soon catch us up, we settled down to eat *dabo*, dates, nuts and raisins, while surveying the magnificence that lay below us.

Twenty minutes later, when we had decided that Mike must have turned back, Ian suddenly glimpsed him in the distance, wandering away both from us and the mule. No one in a normal state could possibly go astray on that plain, with Ras Dashan to guide them, and as we scrambled down from the summit Mike's gait changed to a wavering stumble—so while Ian went straight to him the muleteer hurried to his animal and was soon riding recklessly towards the 'patient'. I continued south-west to the pass—unable to repress a selfish joy at being briefly alone with Ras Dashan—and half-an-hour later Mike appeared over the horizon, looking like a highland chieftain with his two attendants trotting beside him.

As we lost height Mike recovered rapidly, and told us that while wandering on the plain he had 'seen things' and heard voices calling from the wrong direction. I hadn't known that these classic symptoms of mountain-sickness could develop at such a comparatively low altitude.

We got back here soon after dark, fell upon the lavish stew which Alan had ready for us and then sat around the fire talking books. One appreciates the occasional contact with one's own civilisation, and this particular contact is to be maintained for another day, because to-morrow my route to Derasghie will also be the boys' route to Debarak.

## 16 January. The Same Tent on Another Site in the Semiens

The business of camping makes life very complicated. If I get up at 6.30 I can be on the track half-an-hour later, but though we all got up at 6.30 this morning it was 9.45 by the time the boys had cooked a hot breakfast, packed their equipment, dismantled their tent, washed themselves in the river and supervised the loading of their pack-animals. I should have thought that one treks in the Semiens partly to get away from complications, and it seems rather peculiar deliberately to bring them with one. But then my way of travelling seems something worse than peculiar to the boys, so no doubt it's all a matter of taste, as the lion said to the antelope.

We climbed for three hours, to cross Buahit again at a point slightly lower than our route of two days' ago. This track is a 'main road' and our fellow-travellers warned us about the presence of *shifta* on the route to Derasghie. Consequently Afeworq has been trying to persuade me to by-pass Derasghie and come to Debarak instead.

From the pass we descended gradually for seven miles, across springy turf, between frequent outcrops of rock and low hills covered with stunted shrubs—and always the lobelia were standing rigid against the sky.

Before finding this site, in a stubble-field near a settlement, we were walking through flat brown ploughland that stretched away to the horizon on every side. Above 12,000 feet barley is the only crop that does well and the locals bring their surplus grain to the markets at Debarak and Derasghie, to exchange it for teff, rye and wheat.

The Semien shepherd boys wear brown and white sheepskin capes and round, high sheepskin or woollen caps—the first variation in dress I've seen in the highlands.

Fuel is scarce here. On arrival we bartered empty tins for lobelia trunks, which burn badly, and for dried dung, which cooks food slowly. This site is without any shelter and at dusk the icy wind rose to gale-force; but nearby is a circular, stone-walled cattle enclosure and the kindly locals have said that our animals may use it too.

From here we are overlooking a deep valley, beyond which another long 'twin' ridge slopes gradually down from the heights, and Afeworq has indicated that my path to Derasghie runs west for a few miles along the flank of this ridge, before turning south-east.

During supper the boys and I argued amiably about travel. They said that they couldn't understand anyone voluntarily living a *tukul*-life—and I said that I couldn't understand anyone trekking through a country in splendid isolation from the humans who inhabit it. One has no opportunity to establish normal relations with the locals when living in a strange little tent-world of portable mod. cons, where the *faranjs* converse in their own language while the 'natives' stare from a distance, being 'observed' with detachment and resented if they come too close. Travelling in a group has been an interesting experience, but it is not one that I would wish to extend or repeat, grateful as I am for the boys' very generous hospitality.

# 5

# *Timkat and Traffic*

The piercing cold kept us all in our flea-bags until 7.30 this morning, and it was 8.30 before Jock and I left the camp, led by a local who was also going to Derasghie. Last evening, as an anti-*shifta* precaution, Afeworq had contacted this taciturn little man—whose fair skin went curiously with Negroid features.

Remarkably, there were no steep climbs in today's twenty-two miles and there was only one steep descent, from the camp-site to river-level. Then our path ascended the ploughed ridge diagonally, passing many giant thistles—twenty feet tall, with enormous balls hanging from their upper stalks like toys on a Christmas tree—and sometimes crossing uncultivated stretches where clumps of thyme and heather grew between outcrops of rock, or the now familiar Semien shrubs shed their small green leaves into Jock's bucket. From the crest of this ridge we walked for hours down a slightly broken, sloping plateau, seeing occa-sional conspicuous groups of twisted pines. Here I got a close-up view of two magnificent Lanner Falcons, with red-brown heads, dark-grey backs and black wings; both had perched on boulders and neither moved until we were almost beside them. Apart from these the only birds I've noticed in the Semiens are Thick-billed Ravens—natives of Ethiopia—but the Lam-mergeyer (Bearded Vulture), which has a wing-span of eight to nine feet, is also quite common here.

At about 10,000 feet the vegetation became more colourful and many yellow-flowered shrubs and enormous pinkish-purple cacti lined the path. Over the last five miles several settlements were visible in the distance and we passed one church, where my companion paused to perform the usual ritual of kissing

the enclosure wall. This enclosure contained some fine trees—
junipers higher than the church itself, wild fig-trees and
oleasters. The practice of preserving trees only within church
compounds is probably a relic of pre-Christian feeling, for
trees are sacred to many of Ethiopia's other ethnic groups—as
they were in pagan Ireland.

Foreigners seem popular in this region and everyone we met
was exceptionally friendly. The normal greeting is an unsmiling bow, and should a man's *shamma* be covering his head
he will lower it while bowing; but here the men also shook
hands and smiled warmly, including three mule-riders who
respectfully dismounted to salute me in proper fashion. Today,
too, I saw for the first time a highland woman on a mule—
riding astride, wearing tight, ankle-length, velvet trousers beneath her skirt, and carrying a white silk umbrella. She herself
didn't greet me, but ordered her servant to do so, whereupon
he prostrated himself before the bedraggled *faranj* and touched
my battered boots with his fingertips, which he then kissed.
Here umbrellas are more common than rifles and presumably
they too are status symbols, since at this season there is neither
rain nor heat to justify them.

A month ago I would have laughed at my map for calling
Derasghie a 'town', but now it seems just that to me. Amidst
the straggle of *tukuls* and oblong mud huts there are two Muslim
traders' stalls, in which one can buy Chinese torches and
batteries, Indian cotton, Polish soap, Czechoslovakian pocket-
combs, kerosene and salt. There are also a primary school,
a Governor's office, a Health Centre and a Police Post—all
these institutions being housed in extremely primitive
buildings.

Hoards of children greeted us by shouting '*Faranj! Faranj!
Faranj!*'—a reception which brought the law on me, so that
within moments I was being marched off to the Governor's
office. When we appeared in his compound the Big Man was
about to leave for Debarak, but he postponed his departure
to cope with this disconcerting problem, for which conven-
tion provided no set answer. Immediately a twenty-year-old
'Dresser' from the Health Centre was summoned as interpreter;
but unfortunately Asmare speaks minimal English and his

Amharic pride led him to confuse various issues by pretending
to understand much more than he did.

The Governor demanded my non-existent travel permit and
when I produced my visa instead he scrutinised it suspiciously,
complained that he couldn't read the signature and asked who
had signed it. I replied 'The Ethiopian Consul in London',
but I had to admit to not knowing the Consul's name and my
ignorance of this elementary fact seemed to confirm whatever
his worst suspicions were. Yet he was not being at all unpleasant and I sensed that he was merely making a formal show
of his power, as much to impress his subordinates as to awe
me. However, we were now at an impasse, for, having expressed
such strong disapproval of my 'papers', and reacted so sceptic-
ally to my improbable tale about walking from Tigre through
the Semiens, he could hardly relent with dignity. I therefore
decided that the moment had come for me to claim unblush-
ingly that Leilt Aida was one of my closest friends—and at
once the atmosphere changed completely and *talla* was brought
forth.

Inevitably, the Governor wanted to provide me with an
escort, but I successfully argued that the walk to Debarak would
be an Old Ladies' Outing compared with trekking in the High
Semiens. Then, as both Jock and I are in need of rest, I asked
if we might have lodgings for three nights—which will give
me an opportunity to see the Timkat ceremonies here on the
nineteenth—and the Governor immediately told Asmare to
show me to the 'guest-room' beside his office.

This guest-room is more weather-proof than the average hut,
as the inner walls have been well plastered with cow-dung.
The builders evidently felt a feeble impulse to be 'Western',
because two spaces have been left unplastered, to serve as
windows—though these admit little light, since the roof-stakes
project far out and down to form a verandah. (This common
device can be a danger to the unwary, especially after dark, as
the sharp stakes are often at eye-level.) There is no furniture, the tin door won't shut and when I arrived the uneven
mud floor was thinly covered with straw: but before his departure the Governor ordered a 'carpet' of freshly-cut blue-gum
branches.

*18 January*

I slept well last night. We are still in the Semiens, at 10,200 feet, but the penetrating frosts of the High Semiens have been left behind.

At 7.30 Asmare guided me to Derasghie Mariam, the most important of the local churches. It is, of course, famous—by now I've realised that to the locals every highland parish church is famous—and Asmare proudly informed me that the Emperor Theodore was crowned within its sanctuary. Its murals are the finest I've yet seen, but circumstances were against any leisurely enjoyment of them. Protective sheets of dirty cotton hang from ceiling to floor and these had to be lifted aside, with difficulty, by Asmare—using a long pole—while a group of priests and *debtaras* lurked in the background, looking predatory. The light was poor, too, though *debtaras* opened various twenty-foot-high doors; but for all that I greatly appreciated what I could see of these gay or bloodthirsty saints. It is clear that at some period Derasghie produced—or attracted—artists whose imagination and sense of humour could not be repressed by ecclesiastical conventions.

The clergy here are not very amiable. At the enclosure gatehouse, where a score of blind and maimed were patiently awaiting alms, three priests objected to my entering (though I was decently attired) and they only relented on hearing Asmare mention the magic name of Leilt Aida. Then, when we were leaving, I gave the chief priest a dollar—but he looked at it with angry disdain and aggressively demanded five dollars. So I snatched the note off his open palm and gave it to the beggars instead. Later this morning a Muslim trader invited me into his stall for a glass of tea, and as I was enjoying this rare luxury another Muslim politely asked if I would sell him a cigarette for twopence. It was difficult to persuade him to accept one as a gift, and I couldn't help contrasting his attitude with that of the local priests.

Here one gets a most exhilarating sense of space, for Derasghie is on a plateau so vast that mountains are visible only in the far distance to east and west—where their crests appear just above the edges of the plain.

I spent the afternoon wandering through nearby fields, tenaciously attended by children. Everywhere barley was being harvested and I noticed that wild oats were also being threshed and then winnowed from the barley for storage in separate containers.*

This evening the Timkat ceremonies began at sunset. Timkat commemorates the baptism of Christ—the word Timkat means baptism—and it is one of the three most important Ethiopian church festivals. (The other two are Easter and Maskal, which is held in September to commemorate the finding of the true Cross by Empress Helena.) At this time are baptised the children of syphilitic mothers, and when the priests have blessed a pool convenient to the church the devout bathe in this sanctified water. The ceremonies begin on the eve of the festival, when the Tabot, representing the Ark of the Covenant, is carried to a tent—preferably near a stream—where Mass will be celebrated early next morning.†

Perhaps because of my disagreement with the clergy at Derasghie Mariam, Asmare brought me this evening to a smaller church nearer the town. We were accompanied on our way by scores of men, women and children—most of the children in new clothes and all the adults in clean *shammas*. Soon after our arrival within the enclosure a procession left the church, preceded by a gun-man and led by an elderly priest draped in tattered, gaily-coloured silken robes and bearing

---

* Oats are never cultivated in the highlands, despite the enormous livestock population, and in most areas the common wild oats are weeded out of a grain crop before it ripens—or, if the farmer hasn't had time to weed, they are thrown away after winnowing. But in this area they are sometimes mixed with barley to make *talla* or *injara*, though no one uses them alone as a food.

† Reverence for the Tabot is one of the main emotional links between Ethiopian Christianity and Judaism. A solemnly revered tradition says that when the Emperor Menelik I—son of King Solomon and the Queen of Sheba—was returning to his mother's country from Israel his father ordered the first-born son of the High Priest of the Temple in Jerusalem to accompany him. Then the High Priest's son decided to steal the Ark of the Covenant, containing the original Tables of the Law which Moses received on Mount Sinai, and to bring it to Ethiopia—where it is still preserved at Aksum. The young man's reason for taking such a curious decision is obscure. Possibly we are meant to infer that he had a vision of Ethiopia's future glory as a Christian country and felt that the Ark might most suitably be deposited on the holy highland soil. At all events a Tabot, representing the Ark, has always been cherished on the altar within the sanctuary of every Ethiopian church.

on his head the Tabot, hidden beneath a grubby, gold-embroidered, waist-length cloak. Beside him walked another priest, holding over the Tabot a variously-coloured, silver-spangled silk umbrella, and close behind walked two more priests, also draped in gay silken rags. The procession was completed by two drummer *debtaras*, dressed in lay clothes, and as it wound its dishevelled way down a steep slope it was followed by scores of chanting men, ululating women and silent children—who were more interested in the *faranj* than in the Tabot.

At first the men had been chanting slowly, but soon their rhythm quickened and they broke up into three groups, forming circles of wild dancers who leaped high in the air every other moment while brandishing their *dulas* as though they were spears. Frequent whoopings and hand-clappings accompanied the leapings and *dula*-wavings and clearly everyone was having a wonderful time. Meanwhile the ululating women remained close to the Tabot, and when the procession reached the tent everyone was quiet for a moment, and all *dulas* were thrown to the ground as the Chief Priest prayed and the men bent forward, eyes cast down, while chanting their responses.

After the Tabot had disappeared a strip of matting was laid on the ploughed earth for the local V.I.P.s and a *debtara* invited me to take a seat. Then a priest came from the tent, carrying a basket of hot, blessed *dabo*, and having given the first piece to the *faranj* he distributed the rest amongst the general public—who each reverently kissed their hunk before eating it.

By now the air was cold and as we hurried home the trees on the church hill were standing out blackly against a blood-orange western sky, and the distant mountain crests to the east were a delicate pink-mauve-blue, and all around us the last of the sunset lay on the crackling barley stubble in a strange, faint, red-gold haze.

*19 January*

I spent the early morning at the scene of yesterday's ceremonies, watching the faithful being sprinkled with blessed water as the sun rose. Then Asmare reappeared to accompany me to today's main festivities, in a long, level field some two miles from Derasghie Mariam. As we arrived white-clad crowds were converging on the Tabot tent and scores of shouting horsemen could be seen galloping to and fro across the wide grasslands—including many little boys riding bareback at top speed with great skill. Today the women looked particularly animated, for Timkat frees them of all domestic responsibilities. Many young wives were eyeing the horsemen boldly, and by now both they and their husbands are probably enjoying temporary changes of partners.

Timkat is also one of the occasions when unmarried girls dress in their finest clothes and groom their hair meticulously, for unmarried youths often avail themselves of this appearance of virgins in public to choose an attractive mate. The youth will then ask his father to begin negotiations with the girl's father—though he can never be sure either of his father's cooperation or of the negotiations proceeding satisfactorily. There can be no question of marrying without paternal consent. To do so would invite a solemn cursing and permanent disinheritance, since marriages are arranged to link families rather than individuals. However, if a young couple find each other incompatible discreet unfaithfulness is overlooked and divorce is easy. Yet an unmarried girl is constantly chaperoned, and in some homes she is even forbidden to do strenuous jobs lest her hymen should be accidentally ruptured. On the other hand, a boy who is still virgin at eighteen or nineteen will be jeered at by his contemporaries and called 'silb' ('castrated one'); so dissatisfied young wives have a wide choice of lovers.

At eleven o'clock a tiny boy in a spotless white tunic left the tent ringing a large bronze bell and followed by the inevitable gun-man. Then appeared a handsome young priest, robed in black and scarlet silk and wearing a golden crown surmounted by a silver cross. He was followed by the Tabot itself, invisible beneath red velvet on the head of an elderly priest clad in gold, purple and crimson vestments and walking beneath the shade of a silver-spangled blue, yellow, red and green silk umbrella— borne by a young priest. Next came a second crowned priest, two *debtaras* beating enormous gold and silver drums and an old priest swinging an empty silver censer and holding aloft a large, crudely-worked silver and gold cross. The procession was completed by seventeen priests from other churches, carrying prayer-sticks and *sistra* and wearing heavy black, white or navy-blue woollen cloaks.

The laity's progress was less orderly. To-day the young men were in fine 'war-dance' form and many leaping, whooping groups preceded, accompanied and followed the procession. Shouting horsemen cantered up and down, scores of middle-aged men walked beside the priests, continuously singing 'haaa-hooo, haaa-hooo' in low-pitched voices, the ululating women kept abreast of the Tabot, and small boys rode their ponies like gay demons—racing to the front, then skilfully wheeling round and racing to the back, proudly flourishing their miniature *dulas* as though they were spears.

Half-way to the church the procession halted beside a small tent, and the Tabot-laden priest disappeared to drink *talla*. Then another priest recited a long prayer and all the cloaked clergy chanted happily, some of them performing a slow, graceful dance while others—laying aside their prayer-sticks and *sistra*—clapped rhythmically and the women ululated non-stop and the young men bounded joyously.

During this pause the horsemen began to race seriously, providing an exciting spectacle as they frenziedly urged their fast, light mounts over the smooth turf.* A 'spear'-throwing competition with long, pointed sticks was part of the game, and one could see that this warrior-art is still very much alive, even among the younger, rifle-nurtured generation.

Sitting on a boulder—watching the dancing priests and the leaping laymen and the galloping spear-throwers, and listening to drums, bells, sistra, chantings, ululations and pounding hoofs—I felt, not for the first time, an uncomfortable reaction to Ethiopian Christianity. To me there is something false about it, and by now this feeling has given me a guilt-complex, since ignorance of the Ethiopian Church should prevent me from passing judgement on it. Yet I have observed other incomprehensible religious rites—Muslim, Buddhist and Hindu—without

---

* Despite the greater popularity of mules highlanders have always used horses in battle, because of their superior speed, and many of Ethiopia's most famous warriors were known by their horses' names rather than by their own, since the foot-soldiers usually adopted the name of their leader's horse as a war cry.

ever experiencing this sense of something dead, or atrophied, or unborn: I don't quite know which word fits. My reaction has nothing to do with the display of outward reverence—which may be governed by the superficial customs and racial temperament of a particular crowd—but it has everything to do with the atmosphere that a crowd evokes at a religious ceremony. Here I am aware of no spiritual vitality. It seems that a sacred ceremony is simply providing an excuse for colourful processing, prolonged singing and dancing, a day off work and lots of extra food, alchohol and love-making. All of which is good for the morale of a hard-working community, and might well be a means of expressing sincere religious feeling; but in this context both the genuine gaiety and the ritual gestures of devotion seem quite unrelated to true worship.

The midday sun was very hot as we started to climb the rock-strewn church hill, yet within the enclosure the tireless young men resumed their leapings and whoopings, which contrasted curiously with the formal, stately movements of the nearby dancing priests. Half-an-hour later the Tabot was carried once around the church, before being accompanied into the sanctuary by the clergy; but the lay dancers remained without, bounding up as though on springs, then squatting for an instant—leaning on their *dulas*—then bounding again and re-bounding, while their shouts grew louder and wilder and sweat glistened on their tense faces and their eyes gleamed with some mass emotion that may possibly have been religious fervour.

I was invited to lunch by a relative of Asmare's, whose spacious *tukul* was crowded with guests. When we arrived my host's mother sent a granddaughter to her own *tukul* to fetch *araki* in honour of the *faranj*, and soon the girl returned with six clean liqueur glasses and a decanter of colourless spirit. *Araki* is much the same as Nepalese *rakshi* and Tibetan *arak* (this Arabic word has travelled far!), but it has a peculiar flavour of its own, rather like smoky anice. It also has a peculiar potency of its own and as I returned to my room the fields seemed much more uneven than they had been earlier.

By nine o'clock this evening the whole of Derasghie was *en fête*. In most compounds drums were being beaten strongly beside huge bonfires around which dancers were still bounding high, keeping up their monotonous, self-hypnotic chanting. Also much song and laughter issued from *tukuls*, where women, children and older men were sitting drinking around smaller fires; and between compounds bands of young men, accompanied by drummers, were singing and swaggering, followed by groups of cheering, giggling young women—whose virtue is, I assume, uncertain. As I write the sounds of gaiety are becoming louder on every side: but this is a happy, friendly noise and it won't keep me awake.

*20 January. A Compound on a Plateau*

Usually highlanders rise at dawn, but this morning I could find no one to load Jock until 8.30. A small boy accompanied us to the edge of the town and pointed out the track to Dabat—which expired within a mile, amidst acres of volcanic rock. So all day we've been going north-west instead of due west.

After crossing several low, grey-brown hills we came to broad, bright grasslands where boys were herding sheep and cattle. Here another track appeared, and thinking that it might be the right one I optimistically appealed to the boys for guidance, but at the sound of my voice they fled to the shelter of a forested hillock and then peered fearfully at me through the bushes.

Ten minutes later we were on the brink of a valley whose floor looked so remote that one might have been viewing it from an aeroplane. The descent took two and a quarter hours, on a *very* precipitous path of loose clay, scattered with round pebbles on which my feet slithered uncontrollably. I fell eight times, acquired three open cuts and twice had to go tobogganing on my behind—a slightly painful procedure, when one is wearing thin shorts. Meanwhile Jock was methodically picking his way down—though even he stumbled occasionally—and at intervals he paused to graze while waiting for me to catch up. Luckily there were a few narrow ledges, on which the path ran level for thirty or forty yards, and I stopped on these to apply nicotine to my nerves while enjoying the spectacular view and admiring the most varied selection of shrubs and wildflowers that I have yet seen in the highlands. Dense growth covers this mountain and though it is now Autumn here a glorious array of blossoms remain—blue, yellow, white and pink.

Soon after reaching comparatively level ground a few compounds appeared and our path degenerated into a criss-cross of faint pathlets. The descent had loosened Jock's load, so when we came near a compound I reluctantly decided to look for help. (As husbands and wives are left alone in their *tukuls* only during the day-time, unexpected callers can be a nuisance.) I shouted from a tactful distance and a young man appeared, looking rather grumpy, but he securely re-roped Jock and we were soon on our undecided way—my enquiries about the route having elicited the inevitable vague '*Mado*'.

This region was bewildering. Here I could see that what had seemed to be the valley floor was merely a gigantic, sloping ledge, which hid the true, narrow valley—now about 600 feet below us. The descent to river-level was gradual, but I doubted if we should descend at this point, for no track could possibly climb the tremendous north–south barrier beyond the river. Our faint path also ran north–south, and logically we should here have turned south, but an intimidating chaos of massive mountains and (presumably) deep gorges lay in that direction, so I decided to follow the northern line of least resistance.

After about a mile our pathlet became a clear, level track, which for two hours wound round a succession of golden-grassed spurs. We passed a few women—carrying enormous loads of fire-wood—who greeted me with shy friendliness.

When the track suddenly dropped to river-level I saw four vividly green fields lying by the water's edge like displaced scraps of Ireland. This was an unfamiliar crop, and only then did I realise how much one misses fresh growth. While Jock was drinking I stood entranced—to gaze on that tender, bright greenness felt like the quenching of a visual thirst.

On the opposite bank our track faded away amidst plough-land, but I continued north, towards a break in the mountain-wall, hoping that it would reappear—which it did, and took us from 7,800 feet to this plateau at 10,600 feet.

I felt dazed by beauty during the ascent. Four uninhabited

mountains led up one from another, with short, level walks over each summit but never a downward step; and as we climbed through dark green forests, or across red-gold, rock-strewn grasslands, or up rough black escarpments, every turn of the path revealed new, immeasurable heights and depths. By 6.30 we were at 10,500 feet and the deep valley on our right was full of dusk and shrieking baboons. From here I could see the path going over yet another escarpment, some 200 yards ahead, and that final climb brought us on to a wide plateau, where a settlement lay only fifteen minutes' walk away.

Already the sun had set and two minute pink cloudlets were poised above the south-western horizon. I would have hugged them had they been a little nearer; cloudless skies are delightful in theory, but after living beneath their perfection for five weeks an Irishwoman feels that something is missing.

Apparently Timkat is still operating here. As we approached the settlement, through a chilly, grey-blue twilight, I heard sounds of revelry and saw scores of men and youths sitting on the hillside drinking *talla* as they watched ten men dancing to the music of an *azmari* (wandering minstrel). Our arrival astonished everyone, but I was warmly welcomed and pre-sented with two gourds of *talla* simultaneously—and after that climb I emptied them almost simultaneously. Then a laughing woman fed me with unfamiliar, delicious bread—wafer-thin, toasted crisp and faintly seasoned with salt and spices. As I sat on a boulder, devouring this delicacy, the *azmari* came to stand before me, playing his *mazenka* (a one-stringed fiddle) while improvising a song in my honour. (I could distinguish the words for 'mule', 'high mountains', '*shifta*', 'woman', 'cold', 'alone' and I regretted my inability to understand it fully.) By now a golden half-moon had risen and was shining more brightly than a full moon at home; and it seemed to me that a day's trek could have no happier ending than to sit in moon-light on a high mountain drinking with a friendly crowd and being serenaded by a wandering minstrel.

However, a day's trek could quite easily have a more com-fortable ending. This tiny, smoky *tukul* is totally unplastered and already my marrow feels frozen. The colossal local fleas seem preternaturally resistant to insecticide and my bed-to-be is a heap of large stones which serves as a fireside seat during the day and doesn't even have the merit of adequate length. Nor can I lie on the floor, which will be sardined with children. (Here the adults sleep on wooden shelves attached hammock-wise to the support poles and spread with straw instead of hides—possibly because straw is warmer, or cheaper.) The one consolation is a lean and amiable ginger cat, who has decided that I am a twin soul and is weaving around my legs as I write. Highlanders treat their few domestic cats far better than their many dogs—though this is not saying much. Perhaps the principle is that the more savagely dogs are treated the more savagely will they treat intruders.

And so to bed—with dyspepsia, because this evening's vege-table-*wat* was so excruciatingly spicy.


*21 January. Debarak*

Being at Debarak instead of Dabat means that we have joined the Asmara–Gondar motor-road twenty miles further north from Gondar than I had intended; but if one insists on travelling alone in this country one can't reasonably complain about getting lost.

Even my insensitive body jibs at a heap of stones as a bed. I slept badly last night and was glad of an early, circulation-restoring start. To-day's track was both clear and easy; for fifteen miles it rose and fell over a succession of yellow-green or grey-brown ridges that were like the immobilised waves of some mighty ocean. After walking for a few hours through this sort of terrain one's whole being seems soothingly involved in the gentle rhythm of regular climbs and descents.

On the crest of one ridge I saw my first highland funeral—two men carrying a *shamma*-wrapped corpse on a simple bier, followed at a little distance by half-a-dozen women keening professionally. Tears were streaming down their cheeks, but when they saw Jock and me their weeping and wailing stopped and for ten minutes they stood excitedly speculating, while the corpse went on its way unmourned.

Over the last four or five miles the track seemed crowded, after my fortnight of unpeopled remoteness—and one could see that the 'civilisation' of mass-production was at hand. Some men were wearing khaki bush-shirts and blue cotton shorts, instead of home-spun tunics and jodhpurs, a few with-it youths had Wellington boots in their hands—to be put on before reaching the town—and the donkeys were loaded with kerosene tins, or were carrying grain in jute rather than in hide sacks. It seemed inevitable when little boys ran towards me on the outskirts of the town with hands extended, crying 'Cents! Cents! Gimme cents!'

Debarak looks attractive at first sight. From the crest of a distant ridge the majority of its tin roofs are concealed by a thick wood of blue-gums, and this wealth of trees is pleasing on the naked plain. However, the reality is a hideous child of the engine-age—a shanty-town born to soothe drivers' nerves before they begin the northward descent from the Semiens or after they have completed the southward ascent. It is not marked on my map—though it must have been conceived during the Italian occupation—and one wishes that in this case the map were accurate. Recently Debarak was made capital of the Semiens (one of the six districts of the province of Begemdir and Semien) and it has a governor, a police-station, a telephone, a petrol-pump, a Health Centre, several bars and as many brothels, a secondary school—and an American Peace Corps teacher. Some of the houses off the road are square, two-storey wooden buildings—like overgrown log-cabins— which look well beneath the tall blue-gums; but the Piccadilly of this capital is a large market-place, furnished with mechanical weighing-scales and surrounded by *talla-beits* and scruffy stalls, selling cloth, salt, kerosene, saddlery, rope, kettles, saucepans, glasses, coffee-cups, torches, batteries, gaudy nylon head-scarfs and a few very rusty tins of imported fruit which look as though the Italians had left them behind.

Jock has apparently forgotten his baptism of diesel fumes. When we reached the main street and saw a moving truck he promptly reared in protest—whereupon the load conveniently fell off on to a hotel doorstep. 'Hotel' is of course a courtesy title. This sleazy Italian-built doss-house is blatantly a brothel, where harlots (to use the favourite term of English-speaking highlanders) may be observed partially undressing truck-drivers in the bar. I am now installed in an adjacent bedroom, amidst extreme squalor. The once-blue walls are nastily smeared, the floor tiles are stained with food and candle grease and littered with cigarette ends and dead matches, the broken window is patched with cardboard and the three iron beds are spread with revolting blankets. I intend to sleep on the floor; bed-bugs are an occupational hazard, but the likely result of using these foul beds is not.

Tonight I am suffering from what the Americans call 'Cultural Shock'. This road runs like an infected scratch down the tough, rough, healthy body of the unprogressive highlands and on coming to these towns one knows that they are sick. Contact with our world seems to suppress the best and encourage the worst in the highland character; here it is evident that already the locals have degenerated from an integrated, respect-worthy peasantry into a community of coarse and crafty primitives. Walking around Debarak—or sitting in its bars, watching highlanders in dirty jeans and T-shirts drinking 'Chianti' and smoking cigarettes—one sees a much cruder aspect of the highland culture than one would ever see in an isolated settlement. At the foundation of this culture certain indigenous Hamitic-Negroid influences are being forever delicately balanced by Asian–Hebrew–Christian influences; and apparently the lightest touch of Westernisation can tip the balance in favour of the less advanced tradition.

The High Semiens have left my lips so badly cracked that if I absent-mindedly smile little trickles of blood run down my chin—an inhibiting affliction, when one's only means of communication is a smile or a frown.

Since we arrived here at 2 p.m. the sky has been refreshingly obscured by slowly-drifting pale grey cloud.

*22 January. Ciarveta*

Today's twenty-three miles were unexpectedly enjoyable. For much of the way our track ran close to the motor-road and Jock staged a minor crisis every time a vehicle passed; but sixteen vehicles in eleven hours don't constitute an intolerable volume of traffic, even for me.

All day we were crossing what in this context is an undulating plain, though at home one would describe it as 'hilly country'. In every direction, to the blue ridges along the horizon, charming patterns harmonised with calm contours. Side by side lay sloping expanses of ripe barley, green emmer wheat, brown ploughland, yellow-green *atar* and pale gold *teff*; and on level sweeps of golden-brown pasture-land grazed herds of sturdy horses, brown and white fat-tailed sheep, piebald goats and lean cattle. Many thatched settlements looked cosy amidst groves of blue-gums and the landscape was lively with singing shepherd-boys, chattering women bent double under earthenware water-pots, and chanting, whip-cracking harvesters.

A fresh breeze had been blowing all morning and at midday clouds again drifted up from the south, adding wonderfully to the beauty of the scene as their shadows slowly passed over these vast widths, gently fading the colours—which then seemed all the brighter as the sun restored them.

Ciarveta is a recently-built village on the bleak crest of a 9,000 foot ridge and, despite this being the main road, our arrival caused quite a sensation. To the locals *faranjs* are curious creatures who quickly drive past in Land Rovers, motorcars or—more rarely—buses.

I was given a friendly welcome in this square, two-roomed shack, where an icy wind cuts through the 'chimney-gap' between the tin roof and the tops of the mud walls. There is one iron bed, equipped with two filthy blankets, but most of the family sleep in hides on the floor. For the *faranj's* supper my hostess scrambled six tiny eggs—a sophisticated addition to the menu. Her method, however, was not so sophisticated. The eggs were broken into a dirty enamel bowl and beaten thoroughly with very dirty fingers before being slopped into a probably dirty saucepan containing rancid butter and salt. Yet the result was excellent, though having stupidly lost my spoon I soon discovered that it is not easy to eat greasy scrambled eggs with one's fingers.

The women of this area are more elaborately tattooed than most, mainly on their necks. Among highlanders a long neck is regarded as a sign of great beauty and attractively designed tattooed 'necklaces' are thought to accentuate the length.

Jock is now amongst those present, because everyone affirmed that if left outside he would probably be stolen. Such a possibility has never been considered elsewhere, so this suggests that mule-stealing proclivities are among the fringe benefits of a motor-road.

### 23 January. A Compound on a Mountainside

Today's twenty-seven miles took us through placid pastoral country until 3 p.m. Then abruptly we were again amidst rough mountains and the road went curving around high, forested spurs, with shrub-grown cliffs rising sheer above us and deep, broad valleys below.

Soon after midday I heard market-noises coming from a big plantation of blue-gums above the road so I made a *talla*-questing détour up the steep slope, past hundreds of animals and through a crowded square surrounded by tin-roofed shacks —where our progress caused some consternation, since Jock found it difficult to avoid the piles of merchandise that lay all over the ground.

Having refuelled I took a stroll around the square, leaving Jock in the charge of a boy who had politely appointed himself my temporary servant. These weekly markets are the corner-stone of highland trade, and are regularly attended by people who may have come twenty miles to exchange home-produced goods and acquire the imported goods made available by Muslim traders. (Trading as an occupation is despised by the highlanders, who only recognise two honourable ways of life— soldiering and farming. Therefore they never attempt to compete with the Muslims, many of whom are Yemeni Arabs.) The rural markets have also become centres for the collection, by big-town merchants, of surplus grain, hides and wool, which could not be bought economically from individuals in scattered settlements. This is one reason why I find it so difficult to buy fodder for Jock: highlanders are not used to doing business outside the market-place and are slow to adapt to the unfamiliar.

Going to market is among the chief pleasures of highland life. Most highlanders can walk tirelessly from dawn to dusk, so these long, leisurely treks are not a hardship, but a welcome break in the routine labours around field or compound and an occasion for meeting relations and friends, and for collecting such news as may be percolating through from the outside world to the market-town.

As we left the village many others were leaving too and I could see lines of trotting donkeys moving across the plain in every direction, some of them followed by whole families, down to the newest member on mother's back. Then, looking up, I saw other groups making their way along the crest of a nearby ridge—the women draped in simple, chiton-like dresses, carrying high loads on their heads, the men striding behind pack-animals, their *dulas* held across their shoulders, supporting both hands, and a rich man cantering proudly on a gaily-saddled mule—all silhouetted against the grey sky.

Two hours later a break in the cliff-wall on our right revealed how high we still were, for below us lay the weirdly wind-sculptured summits of a range of blue mountains that spread far away to the western horizon.

We then climbed slightly to cross a pass, before beginning the final, gradual descent from the Semiens. By sunset we had reached 8,400 feet and were rounding a steep mountain which towered above us on the right and fell away below us on the left. To the south-east I could see our serpentine road diving through a narrow gap that leads to Gondar—only fifteen miles further on—but here no settlements were visible, and I only noticed this tiny compound when surveying the mountainside for a camping-site. (If not marked by blue-gums *tukuls* are inconspicuous to the point of invisibility.)

It is unusual to find a solitary compound amidst such rough territory and these people are really poor—a rare phenomenon in the highlands. Their only animals are a broken-down donkey and two ferocious curs and they have no grain, which means no *talla* or *injara*. At first I wondered if they were semi-outcasts from some non-Christian tribe, but then I noticed that they all wear the *Matab*—a neck-cord which signifies membership of the Ethiopian Orthodox Church. A young couple live in one *tukul* and their hunger-dulled expressions remind me of Indian peasants in Bihar. They have three children, none of whom look likely to live much longer.

As I approached the compound the wife was filling her water-jar, and when she saw me coming through the bushes she screamed and fled, though every day *faranjs* drive along the road a hundred yards above.

I am being entertained in the smaller *tukul* by three old men who mistake me for a boy. A small saucepan of boiled haricot beans appeared for supper, but peasant hospitality is rarely daunted by poverty and my hosts insisted on sharing with me. I was so ravenously hungry that the nutty-flavoured beans seemed a food of the gods. However, conscience doth make martyrs of us all and I controlled myself after a fistful—though the grey-beards repeatedly urged, '*Tegabazu!*' (Help yourself!) and '*Mokar!*' (Try!). Unfortunately my emergency rations are at an end and as I write I rumble.

Here the night air is almost warm, so I'm going to sleep unverminously beneath a sky of moon-bright clouds.

*24 January. Fasil Hotel, Gondar*

I woke early, after my first bugless sleep since leaving Derasghie. All around it was night and overhead stars still glittered between dark shreds of cloud—but in the east, above the mountains, a long strip of clear sky glowed like copper in firelight. Always that immediate moment of wakening after a night in the open has a very special quality, compounded of freedom and peace.

The morning air was chilly, so while watching the dawn I remained in my flea-bag, being driven by a desperation of hunger to drinking dire Ethiopian brandy for breakfast. By 6.30 we were on our way and half-an-hour later I saw a group of men and boys driving laden donkeys off the road on to a steep, rocky track. Obviously they were going to Gondar market, so I followed them—and this short cut reduced the road's fifteen miles by three. Apart from that first descent it was an easy track, and after four and a half hours' slow walking across pastures, stubble-fields and ploughland we rejoined the main road, turned the shoulder of a mountain—and saw Gondar below us, cloaked in trees.

Then an odd thing happened. All the morning I had been

aware of the extreme tiredness of hunger and every slight climb had felt like an escarpment, but I hadn't been conscious of making any extraordinary effort to keep going. Yet here I was suddenly stricken by what cyclists call 'the knocks', and for ten minutes I had to sit on the roadside, struggling to summon the strength to walk *down* that final slope. The extent to which those knocks may have been fostered by Ethiopian brandy in a vacuum remains a moot point; but the psychology of the incident is curious, for had Gondar been ten miles further away my knocks would probably not have developed until another ten miles had been covered.

I had planned to stop first at the Post Office, but now even letters mattered less than food. Wobbling into the respectable Fasil Hotel I sat in the bar-restaurant, on a blue tin chair at a blue tin table, begged the startled barman to give me something—anything—edible, and within half-an-hour had put away a mound of pasta and *wat*, five large rolls, an eight-ounce tin of Australian cheese and six cups of heavily-sugared tea.

Standing up from this banquet I saw a fearsomely repulsive figure behind the bar; it is a strange experience to stare at one's own reflection for some moments without recognising it. When I did recognise myself I no longer wondered at that unfortunate woman fleeing last evening. If I saw any such apparition coming through bushes in the dusk I too would flee, fast and far. The combination of ingrained dirt, sun-blackened skin, dust-reddened eyes, sweat-matted hair, height-stiffened lips, blood-caked chin and sunken cheeks really did have an unnerving effect. I had been aware of losing weight, but I hadn't realised just how emaciated my body was. At once I booked in here for a week, to fatten up before the next lap.

When Jock had been stabled I went up to my room—preceded by a pair of servants solemnly bearing my dusty sacks—and the next two hours were spent in three successive hot baths. I had no clean clothes to put on, but as I went downstairs the mere fact of having clean skin made me feel positively chic.

The news of our arrival had already spread and quite a crowd was awaiting me in the bar—which embarrassment became understandable when I learned that Leilt Aida has recently been telephoning the Chief of Police every evening, to enquire if we have yet arrived in Gondar. One member of my 'Reception Committee' was the Director of the Gondar Bank, who kindly offered Jock the hospitality of his back garden during our stay here; and he also promised to organise a daily supply of grain.

When I went to the Post Office to telephone Makalle I collected a belated Christmas mail; so the rest of the day was spent 'attending to my correspondence'.

# 6

# *Gondar*

This respectable Italian-built hotel is good value at twelve-and-sixpence a night. Now owned by a rich Gondare, it is a meeting-place for neatly-dressed students and civil servants who gamble with dice or cards, play billiards, or talk by the hour while drinking bottled beer. None of the good-humoured, slow-witted staff speaks English, but they all try—rather unsuccessfully—to be helpful. My room is about the size of the average *tukul* and has running cold—and sometimes hot—water, a large window that opens wide, a disconcertingly soft bed with fresh linen, a bed-side lamp, table, chair, chest of drawers and wardrobe. It was spotless until the arrival of my lamentable sacks, from which showers of fleas at once sprayed on to the floor and bed in search of pastures new.

After a large breakfast of coffee, rolls and Israeli jam I set out to do a 'preliminary survey' of Gondar. The Italians had planned to make this city the capital of their African Empire and many large, featureless buildings remain as monuments to Mussolini's ambitions. The Post Office, bank, Army Headquarters, Police Headquarters, government offices, provincial court-house, spacious private houses, shops, hospital and cinema are all the sweets of occupation; without these Gondar would only have the ruins of its Royal Compound to distinguish it from Debarak. Even now the major—though not the most obvious—part of the town is the usual conglomeration of small shacks lining dusty, stony laneways.

Within the past few years the number of Gondar motor-vehicles has increased considerably, though horse-gharries are still used as taxis. The electricity operates all night, as in Asmara and Addis, but Ethiopian time is kept. This means that 12 a.m. is our 6 a.m.—a logical system, since the new day does begin at dawn, rather than when one is going to bed. Weeks ago I changed my watch, for mental arithmetic was never my forte and in some areas all passers-by ask the time. (This questioning is a game to be played with *faranjs*; no highlander cares whether it is three o'clock or four o'clock, and the sun keeps him informed about the main events of the day.)

The Fasil Hotel restaurant serves only pasta and *wat*, so at lunch time I went to the Tourist Hotel to continue my camel-campaign of feeding up in preparation for the next lap. The Ethiopian Tourist Organisation's newly-published guide-book had informed me that 'the Itegue Menen Hotel in Gondar has a fairly good restaurant and tennis-courts as well as a swimming pool, though the latter is usually empty. Rates are rather high.' However, I thought ten shillings reasonable for a four-course, Italian-cooked lunch that included unlimited green salad* and tomatoes, fresh butter (made near Asmara) and Port Salut that was not at all travel-weary.

The Itegue Menen Hotel is large, comfortable, attractively decorated and efficiently run by Italians: yet somehow it seems pathetic. Ethiopians frequently complain about their lack of accommodation for tourists, but today there were only four other visitors in the enormous restaurant—Americans who had flown from Addis and who provided me with much free entertainment. To them the Itegue Menen is such a primitive hostelry that they recoiled with yelps of horror from the salad, and before the meal one woman asked for soda-water in which to wash her forks and spoons.

After lunch I returned to my room—borrowing some books and visiting Jock on the way—and since then I have been diligently reading up the history of Gondar.

---

* Wherever Western settlers create a demand for green vegetables, root vegetables and fruit, these can be grown successfully in the highlands, but the locals consider all such foods inferior and never cultivate them for home consumption. Yet the highland diet is healthier than ours in some respects. It is rich in calcium—as anyone can see by looking at the people's teeth—and *teff* alone compensates for many deficiencies. This unique cereal is extraordinarily rich in iron, which explains why highlanders don't show the usual symptoms of worm-infestation; their systems contain enough surplus iron to nourish parasites without any great ill-effects.

*26 January*

This morning I 'did' Gondar's Royal Compound—for two hundred years the centre of the Imperial Court of Ethiopia.

In 1632 the Emperor Susenyos was forced to abdicate, having antagonised his subjects by allowing Portuguese Jesuits to convert him and by authorising the conversion of the Empire. He had already founded a capital at Gorgora, after his armies had been driven north by invading Galla tribes; but Gorgora is on the malarial north shore of Lake Tana, so his son Fasilidas moved the 'city' to the foothills of the Semien plateau, called it Gondar, forbade any foreigners to live in it and built himself a square, two-storey, Portuguese-inspired castle with a round tower at each corner.

Fasilidas died exactly three hundred years ago and was succeeded by his son, Yohannes I (The Just), who is described by my government-sponsored guide-book as 'a deeply religious person. . . . He gave all Catholics the choice of renouncing their faith or being expelled to wander the deserts of the Sudan.' During his reign Muslims were also banished from Gondar and the people's feeling for the sacredness of the Emperor, which had been weakened by Susenyos' defection, was fully restored.

Yohannes was succeeded in 1682 by his twenty-year-old son Iyasu I, known as The Great. Iyasu was a learned scriptural scholar, the finest horseman of his day, a lover of ceremony, a collector of jewels, a champion of the rights of the exiled princes on Amba Wahni and a reformer of corrupt customs collections. He also diluted the official xenophobia, made two unsuccessful attempts to establish diplomatic relations with the French court and firmly reasserted the authority of the Crown over the Church.

However, Iyasu was too great for the good of his own line. Ethiopia in the late seventeenth and early eighteenth centuries was not yet ready for a ruler who sat in a castle studying the scriptures, fingering jewels, reforming the administration and expressing a reluctance to shed blood. Gondar was the Empire's first city since the decline of ancient Aksum and by the time of Iyasu's accession the capital had become dangerously ecclesiastical and detached from the realities of highland life, which were no less harsh then than they had always been. The nobles used Iyasu's peaceful twenty-five-year reign to build up strong armies and high ambitions; and then the Emperor's son, Takla Haimanot, joined them in a conspiracy to depose his father, who was compelled to become a monk in a Lake Tana island monastery—but was murdered a few months later, lest he should attempt to regain his throne.

Fifteen years of anarchy followed. After a two-year reign Takla Haimanot I was murdered and succeeded by his fifty-year-old uncle, Theophilos, a brother of Iyasu I, who lived long enough to kill the nobles involved in the assassinations of his brother and nephew. These included Iyasu's widow, Queen Malakotawit, who was hanged with one of her brothers and their chopped-up bodies thrown outside the palace gates to the hyenas. Three years later Theophilos died—tamely, of a fever—and the throne was seized by a provincial noble named Yostos, whose mother had been a daughter of Yohannes I and who is said to have been poisoned in 1717, after a six-year reign. Yostos was succeeded by a twenty-year-old son of Iyasu I, Dawit III, who was certainly poisoned in 1719, though he had endeared himself to the people by ordering the stoning to death of three Capuchin missionaries who somehow infiltrated into Gondar. Dawit III was a fanatical adherent to the Eustathian sect of Ethiopian Christianity, which believed that the Unction of the Holy Spirit which Christ received at his baptism united his human and divine natures; and this view was opposed by the monks of Debra Libanos, Ethiopia's most revered monastery, who maintained that the Unction was the grace of the Holy Spirit given to the human nature of Christ at the moment of the union of his two natures, and having as its effect the restoration of human dignity lost by the fall of Adam. One wouldn't expect such a rarified debate to provoke the baser—or indeed any—human emotions; but shortly before he was poisoned the young Emperor took umbrage at the monks' impertinent arguing with their ruler and sent a contingent of his ferocious Galla troops to massacre the lot. Controversies of this kind still enliven Ethiopia's theological scene, though they no longer lead to massacres.

The next Emperor, 'Asma Giorgis, was yet another son of the

virile Iyasu I. (It was not necessary to be a legitimate son to succeed to the throne; acknowledged royal blood sufficed. Neither primogeniture nor legitimacy counted for anything and all the numerous sons of an Emperor shared in the privileges of their descent.) 'Asma Giorgis is always known as Bakaffa (The Inexorable) and during his ten-year reign he ruthlessly subdued the nobles and kept them down by filling all important governorships and offices with men whom he could trust because they were dependent on him. (The present Emperor follows a not dissimilar policy for much the same reasons.) Yet Bakaffa's severity did not prevent him from becoming one of the favourite heroes of highland folk-history: his name recurred often in the chantings of the shepherds I camped with and many are the tales told of his courage and cunning. He had a habit of travelling in disguise—to gauge popular feeling and use this special knowledge against the nobles—and on one of those journeys he fell ill in a Galla village and was nursed by the beautiful daughter of a local chieftain. Her name was Glory of Grace, and she became the famous Empress Mentuab.

Unlike most Ethiopian emperors Bakaffa remained faithful to his wife and produced no wide selection of heirs. He died in 1729, leaving an infant son as the Emperor Iyasu II, and Mentuab as Regent. Then came the final phase of dissolution. Mentuab's nepotism enraged the nobles and she was too weak to control their many rebellions and conspiracies. Iyasu II, when he grew up, was mockingly known as 'The Little', in contrast to his grandfather 'The Great', and the people despised him for his expensive artistic tastes. Eventually he was taunted into leading a campaign against Sennar and almost the entire Imperial army was massacred.

Meanwhile Ras Mikael Sehul of Tigre was becoming the strongest man in Ethiopia. He ruled the whole country north of the Takazze, and even dominated the port of Massawah, through his influence over the Muslim Naib. He grew immensely rich on customs dues, and could control the importing of firearms and see to it that his own army was better equipped than anyone else's. When Iyasu II died in 1753 Ras Mikael was ready to spring.

Mentuab had married Iyasu to a Galla princess disarmingly

named Wobit; and now Wobit elbowed the old Dowager Empress aside and took it upon herself to rule in the name of her young son Joas. Soon the Court had been virtually taken over by Galla officials, and the Galla tribesmen who had accompanied these chieftains to Gondar were camping nearby in their thousands. Chaos followed, and by the time Joas had come of age the highlanders were in such a state of anti-Galla rebellion that the desperate young Emperor was driven to appealing to Ras Mikael for help. The seventy-year-old Tigrean at once occupied Gondar, defeated but failed to annihilate the Gallas, married Mentuab's daughter by her second husband, murdered Joas, brought another (septuagenarian) son of Iyasu the Great to the throne, found him too ineffectual and poisoned him, enthroned his son Takla Haimanot II instead and had so many dismembered corpses of traitors thrown on the streets that protein-emboldened hyenas became a danger to the public. (It is difficult to determine what constituted treason at this stage, but doubtless Ras Mikael knew.)

Takla Haimanot II was murdered in 1779 and succeeded by his brother Takla Giorgis, who was forcibly exiled to Ambasal in 1784. By 1800 there were said to be six puppet emperors alive and already the royal buildings of Gondar were disintegrating in sympathy with the imperial power. Until the mid-nineteenth century the highlands ran blood as warring nobles strained to manœuvre themselves closer and closer to the throne. These gentlemen were dominated by the rulers of Tigre, Shoa, Amhara and Gojam; but after the last two had been simultaneously killed in battle it was a newcomer to the struggle who won through—and Kassa, the ex-*shifta*, was crowned as the Emperor Theodore II. (His father, a minor chieftain, was reputed to be of the royal line. Nor is this incredible, for by then a considerable proportion of the population must have been thus privileged.)

Theodore moved the capital to Magdala, where he was so soon to commit suicide after his defeat by Lord Napier. And my guidebook—remembering that Theodore is an obligatory hero in modern Ethiopia—tactfully explains that he 'furthered the decline of Gondar with several punitive attacks on the city, damaging the castles'. In fact Gondar was not at that time in

need of punishment, but Theodore was in need of treasure—
and had always disliked the city—so on 2 December, 1866, he
led his army into the ex-capital, plundered all the churches,
drove ten thousand people from their homes and set fire to the
whole place. Four out of forty-four churches escaped the blaze
and the more solid castles survived. But these were again
damaged by the Dervishes in 1888, by the Italians during the
Occupation, and by British bombers during the Liberation. So
it is surprising that the Royal Compound remains Gondar's
most conspicuous feature.

It took me half-an-hour to stroll round outside the high,
crenellated compound wall, past the twelve ceremonial gate-
ways, which have such evocative names as 'The Gate of the
Judges', 'The Gate of the Funeral Commemorations', 'The
Gate of the Spinners', 'The Gate of the Pigeons', 'The Gate of
the Chiefs', 'The Gate of the Secret Chamber', 'The Gate of
the Treasury of the House of Mary'. Then I entered the compound—buying a three and fourpenny ticket from a nice young
man who made no attempt to 'guide' me—and for the next
two hours I was disturbed by neither *faranjs* nor locals.

Most of the Gondarine emperors built elaborately within this
enclosure and, while walking through the long, burnt grass
from ruin to silent ruin, one is touched by the element of make-
believe that permeated those two centuries. Here a library was
built, and a chancery, a 'House of Song' and a 'Pavilion of
Delight'. Banqueting-halls and palaces were decorated with
silks, carpets, ivory, mosaics, porcelain, Venetian glass and
China dishes. But all this was as far from the truth of the highlands as Addis Ababa is today. Beyond Gondar, in every direction, hard-riding, hard-fighting noblemen were living in hide
tents, tearing at hunks of warm, raw beef, drinking mead out
of horn-cups and not being at all impressed by the novel refinements of their static capital. Now these frail though fortified
materialisations of kingly dreams lie deserted and despoiled,
their irrelevance proven by history.

This evening the Bank Director and the provincial Chief of
Telecommunications took me to a *tej-beit* beyond the town
centre. On our way we passed the market-place, where a public

gallows dominates the scene. It is still used regularly and my companions pointed it out with pride, as an indication of how efficiently Law and Order are maintained in modern Ethiopia.

## 27 January

Today I met a compatriot, Nancy O'Brien, who is in charge of the Maternity Department at Gondar's W.H.O.-run Public Health College. We lunched together, and I spent the afternoon at her clinic, later visiting the hospital—which is not free, or adequately equipped, but is much less dirty and appears to be more efficiently run than a comparable institution would be in India. Mothers are allowed to stay with their sick children, as they wouldn't bring them otherwise.

Unlike most peasant communities the highlanders have no traditional village midwives. Instead a woman-friend comes in to deliver the baby, as a neighbourly act of kindness, and even in Gondar, where medical aid is so close, it will be sought, during difficult confinements, only after the sun had set three times since the labour-pains began—if it is sought at all.

In Asmara and here I have been told, both by Western medical workers and educated Ethiopians, that almost 100 per cent of highland peasant girls have their clitoris excised at the age of eight or nine. The operation is performed by an elderly woman 'expert', who uses some crude cutting instrument, but strangely enough complications rarely follow. Highland men are convinced that excision helps to keep women faithful, though a U.N. seminar on the subject, held in Addis Ababa in December 1960, pronounced that the operation does not diminish a woman's sexual pleasure, but can cause severe pain during intercourse. The Western-educated Ethiopians with whom I have discussed the subject were agreed that highland women are much less responsive than European or American women. As one of them put it—'Ethiopian men don't know the difference, but in fact they're biting off their noses to spite their faces.' Which observation tempted me to amend the old saying, but since it seemed best to keep the conversation on a scientific level I resisted the temptation.

Ethiopia's foreign modernisers hope eventually to establish a network of rural Health Centres, staffed by young Ethiopians, which will provide not only treatment for minor ailments but elementary instruction on the isolation of contagious diseases, sanitation and personal hygiene. It would be ridiculous for me to judge the progress made so far on the basis of the Health Centres I've seen; but unfortunately none of the Public Health College students with whom I've spoken during the past three days gives me any reason to think that either Dawit or Asmare is exceptional. In addition to the difficulty of recruiting intelligent young men, this project is hampered by the highlanders' resistance to change and by the influence of the *debtaras*, whose income would decrease if Western-trained medical advisers gained the people's confidence.*

*28 January*

   This evening I dined at the home of the Bank Director, a thirty-six-year-old native of Manz who has eight handsome, high-spirited children between the ages of eleven and two—though his wife looks like a young bride. In Persia, Pakistan or India his counterpart would live in Western style, but here the impact of the West is so recent that most homes remain

---

* However, Donald Levine points out that 'The public health worker is in a position to inherit some of the awe felt for the learned *debtara*, especially since the health teams operate out of centres which provide therapy as well as instruction, which gives them the benefit of association with the quasi-magical powers attributed to one who performs successful treatment. In addition, he can be aided by the Amhara peasant's personal devotion to someone who has helped him and won his confidence. Whether this devotion can be stimulated depends, in the last analysis, on the character and resourcefulness of the public health workers themselves. Those who are able to communicate in a dignified manner with the peasants, who avoid dealing with them as an inferior and backward people, who refrain from flaunting the most important norms, and who are on good terms with local authorities and public men, have a substantial chance of being accepted after an initial period of suspicion and alienation... Despite his idyllic conception of paradise and his frequent contention that life on earth is something of little value, the Amhara wants to avoid death... The expressions for greeting and farewell stress health. Most of the prayers and vows offered have to do with achieving health. Long, painful pilgrimages are made for cures, and much money is spent for the remedies of native practitioners and for amulets to ward off illness. This powerful desire for health and life operates as a lever to overcome the resistance to change... [and]... the view of the Amhara peasantry as incorrigibly recalcitrant and reactionary is a rather shallow one. Amhara peasant culture contains potentialities for change that are as real as its most rigid beliefs and its substantial antipathy to change.'

essentially traditional. This Italian-built house is furnished—sparsely—with European couches and chairs, and at first a highland family gathering in a large, brilliantly-lit room seemed somewhat unnatural. However, I soon realised that the feeling was 'true', and our meal was a *tukul*-supper with all the refinements added, including some of the best *tej* I've yet tasted. Before and after a servant brought a jug of warm water, a tin basin, soap and a spotless towel for handwashings; and the very beautiful *injara*-stand of coloured wickerwork had a high conical lid, tied with leather thongs. When my host had said grace, *wat* of various kinds—meat, chicken and vegetables—were ladled on to the *injara* and we all drew close and set to. The second course consisted of huge lumps of grilled steak on the bone, to be picked up and dissected with one's teeth, and for the third course large, square hunks of raw beef were laid before each person—with one of those razor-sharp meat-knives which are the only pieces of cutlery ever seen in highland households. To 'carve' raw beef experts hold one end of the hunk between their teeth and cut off a mouthful with a swift upward stroke of the knife, which skims their noses by a fraction of an inch. This skill I have made no attempt to acquire.

During our conversation I again observed that goodwill towards the Italians which seems to be universal among educated Ethiopians. It is based partly on gratitude; as my host said, 'We would have needed a century to construct the roads and buildings and establish the telephone communications that were provided by the Italians within five years.' I find it pleasing that people rarely refer to the Italians' ungenerous motives for thus benefiting Ethiopia; having got rid of their conquerors, the highlanders amiably choose to view the occupation as an unmixed blessing. But then, those Italian atrocities which so horrified liberal Europeans were, to many highlanders, merely normal war-time behaviour; and it may be that the cruelty of the occupation forces made the Italians seem less alien than other *faranjs*. Among English-speakers I frequently hear Italians being spoken of almost as adopted cousins, Americans being derided for the usual reasons and Englishmen being praised for their trustworthiness but resented for their aloofness. No one, naturally, has ever heard of the Irish; so by now I have become a fluent lecturer on the history, geography, religion, language, agriculture and government of Ireland.

## 29 January

Today I celebrated the Sabbath by visiting a series of churches, beginning with Debre Berhan Selassie, which lies east of Gondar and escaped Theodore's holocaust. This small rectangular church was built by Iyasu the Great; Theodore made off with all its portable treasures, but its murals remain—and are even finer than those of Derasghie Mariam.

Most churches within reach of the road now proudly possess repellent Italian oleographs, beside which the clumsiest local painting looks like a Giotto. These abominations usually represent the Blessed Virgin and are much revered, being protectively shrouded in lengths of dirty cloth.

In each church compound begging boy-deacons surrounded me. Normally I discourage begging, as the majority of highland children have no need thus to degrade themselves, but I did 'give cents' today since these boys are expected to keep themselves, while away from home, partly by begging and partly by making the fibre parasols popular among highland women. Most of them spoke a little English and I asked if they were going to become priests. Only one said 'yes'; the others hope to attend the state school and apparently no one becomes a priest after receiving a lay-education—not because this disqualifies him, but because the state schools are so enlightening that ex-pupils could not possibly revert to following a priestly path.

It is interesting that so many Gondare boys still go to church schools before entering the state school. During Gondar's centuries as capital the static court, with its numerous clerical entourage, did achieve something positive by providing a centre for learning such as the highlands had never known before. This gave the Gondares a special place in the cultural hierarchy —and a reputation for snobbery, physical cowardice and an exceptionally dignified bearing. They also became renowned for their polished and subtle use of the complex Amharic language, and for the fact that an uniquely high proportion of their children learned to read the Psalms of David—which means that they completed the elementary course at the church schools. During this period so many young artists were attracted to Gondar's schools of religious painting that a large section of the market was reserved for the sale of parchments and pigments. And, though Gondar's sun has now set, an afterglow remains.

*30 January*

During the past week I have spent hours talking to the local representatives of Ethiopia's new middle class, who use this hotel as their chief meeting-place. Many of them are very young for the positions they hold, since few Ethiopians over the age of thirty-five have had a modern education; some were trained abroad, but the majority are country-born graduates of Addis colleges, who now deplore their exile to Gondar. As individuals they are likeable enough, yet as a type they are unimpressive. When one sees them sitting at the bar, in their smart suits and pointed shoes, ordering espresso coffee and passing around packets of Craven A, it is startling to remember that a visit to their families usually means a return to a *tukul* in a compound on a mountainside—where it could as well be 1067 as 1967.

The majority of students seem emotionally unstable and they admit to living in a state of guilty conflict. Frequently they are mocked, rejected—even whipped—if they return to their homes wearing *faranj* clothes, imprudently smoking a cigarette to emphasise their emancipation, and voicing outrageous, sinful *faranj* ideas. Yet enthusiastic—if unimaginative—*faranj* teachers tell them that it is their duty to preach to their people the gospels of personal liberty, scientific farming, hygiene and community development.

The nature of the individual's conflict depends on how deeply he has been influenced by his Western teachers. Some young men have said to me that they feel hypocritical when visiting their families, because fear drives them to simulate a loyalty to tradition which they no longer feel. Then, on returning to the city, they despise themselves for not having upheld their new beliefs, while simultaneously they are saddened to realise that they no longer 'belong' at home. Others have said that on holidays they feel relieved to be back in an orderly, comprehensible environment, though the material privations irk them; but these feel doubly guilty when again with *faranjs*, whom they have betrayed, and while living in an environment where every day they are conscious of defying their inheritance.

There are countless distressing permutations and combinations of these fundamental emotions; never before have I seen the battle between Old and New leaving so many young people so seriously maimed to such little purpose. Granted this educated minority has been handed the key to Europe's cultural treasure-chest but few will ever be able to discriminate between coloured pebbles and diamonds. Granted, too, these highlanders now wash regularly, and many can buy watches, transistor radios and television sets, and some can buy cars, and all can buy beer instead of *talla*. So they are being civilised. And when their numbers have increased their influence will bring the peasantry up to date, into the rat-race and down the drain like the rest of us. Nuclear weapons seem no more terrifying than the zeal with which we are chasing everyone else towards our own materialistic sewer.

Unfortunately it is not difficult to chase young highlanders in this direction. Their craving for educational opportunities —preferably abroad—rarely signifies a love of knowledge; it usually means that education is seen to be the only possible route towards an improvement in their material and social positions. Always one of their first questions is 'What degree do you have?'—and they are astounded to hear that I left school at fourteen. How, in that case, can I afford to travel? Then they ask what my job is, and on hearing that I write books the whole thing becomes preposterous—for how could anybody write *books* without a degree? Many conclude that I must be a nobleman's daughter (heavily disguised), or the child of some very learned *debtara*.

Most of these young men are violently patriotic, and super-sensitive to criticism of anything Ethiopian. However, too often their patriotism is based on illusions—such as Ethiopia being the leader of modern Africa, the most advanced African state, or the only truly Christian country in the world. This dream-image of the Empire's greatness contents them, and they seem unwilling to deflect any particle of their energies towards the betterment of Ethiopian agriculture or public health.* (Agriculture is in any case neglected by the Government, which prefers to 'get with it' and encourage industry—a basic error not unknown in Ireland.)

This afternoon I went on a shopping-spree, which is quite possible in Gondar, where the Arab-owned stores surrounding the piazza display goods ranging from German lanterns and Japanese tennis shoes to resin and cowrie-shells. I restocked on tinned emergency rations, dried fruit, matches, candles, insecticide, Biros and duplicate books—made in Britain. From the chemist I cadged a large-empty pill-box to hold my coinage, for I have been advised that in the regions ahead paper money will not be accepted.

One of my Gondar benefactors—Colonel Aziz, second in command at the Provincial Police Headquarters—has gone to a lot of trouble to find an old Italian pack-saddle which, in theory, will solve my loading problem. The heavy contraption looks appallingly complicated; but at least these complications are European-devised, so by straining my intelligence to its limits I may eventually come to terms with them.

* This egoism is consistent with highland traditions. Dr Levine writes that 'the Amhara have virtually no sense of "community" at all, for the concept can scarcely be rendered in idiomatic Amharic. . . In virtually every instance of a consideration of communal projects or needs that the author observed or heard of, the dominant characteristic of the discussion was a vigorous and uncompromising assertion of individual claims.'

# 7

# *Tribulations around Lake Tana*

*31 January. A Compound on a Plain*

Our departure from Gondar was delayed by Jock's new saddle. Slowly I sorted out the tangle of straps, buckles and chains and got it securely in place, but the loading defeated me. My struggle was being watched by a score of men, and eventually I sent one of them to fetch help from Police Headquarters. An hour later an elderly sergeant came sauntering down the road. Once upon a time the Italians had taught him how to load their mules—but his technique had gone rusty, so another hour passed before we were on our way. However, this last hour was well spent, because now I, too, have learned the technique.

Beyond Gondar our track ran for eight miles between gentle hills on which royal ruins could occasionally be glimpsed amidst blue-gums. Then we rejoined the motor-road, passed an ugly village and came to a junction beside Gondar's airstrip. There was no signpost, but according to my map the secondary road led to Gorgora.

Now, for the first time since leaving Massawah, I was walking through an undramatic landscape that might have been in Europe. To the west lay homely wooded ridges: to the east and north low hills and a heat haze concealed the mighty mountains: and to the south our road ran level between fields of *atar, teff*, barley, wheat, millet and maize. Small settlements were numerous and hundreds of thin cattle grazed in the charge of shepherd-boys who wore blue cotton-shorts—for we are still in a 'civilised' area. There were no horses or mules, since for them the Lake Tana region is notoriously unhealthy, but I saw two tall, strong Sudanese donkeys grazing with the cattle. To improve the local breed of diminutive donkeys and mules, highlanders sometimes buy sires from Sennar and these are used only as stud-animals. They cost five or six times as much as the best native donkeys, so their owners charge high stud fees, which may be paid in cash or grain.

Many of the men we met were carrying rifles, and several expressed strong disapproval of a *faranj* travelling alone around Lake Tana. Towards sunset we were joined by a skinny young man who was driving a donkey loaded with *atar*. The *faranj* with the *buccolo* fascinated him, so he invited me to his settlement for *talla*—and soon found that he had a guest for the night. He and his family seemed delighted, though astonished, when I settled down in their compound; and now—despite the proximity of Gondar's foreign colony—I am surrounded by dozens of interested men, women and children.

This fertile region should be prosperous, yet nowhere else have I seen such poverty and disease. Most of the children are pot-bellied, covered with infected scabies and suffering from either conjunctivitis or trachoma, and many of the adults are coughing tubercularly or trembling malariously. Six people have shown me festering wounds because everyone imagines that *faranjs* carry unlimited medical supplies.

When I unpacked my insecticide spray one mother begged me to use it on her half-blind daughter, and unhappily she refused to believe that it was not a medicine. While my back was turned she sprayed the infected eyes and the child's screams of agony might have been heard in Khartoum.

No doubt much of this ill-health is caused by the comparatively low altitude and the nearness of Lake Tana. Today, for the first time since leaving Tembien, I found the noon sun a little too hot; but at least one can sleep out here, so now I'm going to spread my flea-bag on silky *teff* straw beneath the stars. I notice that some of the family also intend to sleep out, rolled in their *shammas*.


*1 February. Gorgora*

When I woke this morning I lay still for a moment, feeling absurdly surprised to think that by evening I should be on the shores of Lake Tana. At school geography bored me numb, but I had a list of places I longed to go to because of their names—

and Lake Tana followed on Roncesvalles and the Kara Korum.

An hour after leaving the settlement we turned off the motor-road on to an animal track that went due south through ploughland, and fields of ripe grain, and mile after mile of long, yellow, tough grass. Sometimes patches of scarlet peppers lay like blood-stains among the usual crops, and I saw a few new birds and a variety of unfamiliar trees. Often the track multiplied confusingly or disappeared completely, but Lake Tana covers an area of 2,000 square miles, so it seemed unlikely that we would miss it. Then, at 4.15, came the first distant shimmer of a sheet of blue, wide as the sea—and an hour later Jock was drinking from the lake.

Here we were alone, and an immense peace enfolded this placid expanse of water—now colourless beneath a pale evening sky. Broad pastures and stubble-fields sloped quietly down to the flat, marshy shore, a holy, wooded islet rose nearby from the calmness, and away to the hazy east there were faint, high shadows—the mere ghosts of mountains. All the beauty of this place was subtle and tranquil. Nothing could have been further from my childhood vision of a remote, sullen lake, hidden at the heart of Abyssinia amidst darkly tangled jungle.

My bilharzia-minded guide-book says 'Caution: Lake Tana is not safe for swimming. The visitor should only admire—not swim, wade, drink or fall in.' But it was plain that on our way to Bahar Dar this visitor would at least have to wade, sooner or later, so as Jock greedily cropped the moist grass I stripped and paddled through warm ooze and then was swimming joyously in deep, tepid water. A flock of startled Egyptian geese flew honking from a reed-bed and I floated to watch their pattern of loveliness against the sky. Further out I glimpsed Gorgora in its cove, and beyond stretched rough, forested cliffs —but the west shore remained invisible. Turning back I saw two men driving a donkey in the distance; luckily they were not coming in our direction, so there were no witnesses to a rather aged Venus rising from the lake.

Walking along the shore I counted six extravagantly-coloured varieties of water-birds, but my book only listed one of them— the Goliath Heron, which is nearly five feet tall. A couple of High-Crested Cranes were so engrossed in an intricate mating-dance that I might have captured them had I tried. Less pleasing were the clouds of mosquitoes and other tiresome flies that rose from the sour-smelling marsh as we squelched through.

On the outskirts of Gorgora schoolboys rushed to greet the *faranj* and led us to this doss-house. It is owned by a handsome, friendly young couple and behind the bar, across a narrow yard, are the bedrooms—converted Italian-built stables. I'm now sitting in the earth-floored bar, writing on a rough table by the light of a petrol-lamp. As the owners pride themselves on being urbanised only bottled beer is sold here, so I sent out for a kettle of *talla*. A brand-new transistor radio stands screaming on the counter and every few minutes my host self-consciously twiddles the knobs, glancing sideways at me to make sure that his mechanical skill is being observed. Five minutes ago his wife came from the kitchen and sat in a corner to chat with the customers while feeding her baby out of a filthy plastic bottle. She is a plump, vibrantly healthy young woman who could probably nurse triplets with ease, but recently feeding-bottles—introduced by Arab traders—have become status-symbols. These are rarely washed, much less sterilised, so their use is a form of infanticide and W.H.O. workers are trying to persuade Gondar merchants not to sell them.

My plans are causing some consternation here. Two English-speaking teachers have been helping me to empty the *talla* kettle and they insist that it is impossible to reach the west shore unless one follows the track from Gondar to Delghie. In this country, as in India, people frequently inflate difficulties into impossibilities.

*2 & 3 February. Dengel*

Yesterday I discovered that the shores of Lake Tana are not as tranquil as they seem, and last night conditions were against diary-writing.

This country often gives one an Orlando-like illusion of living through different centuries and within an hour of leaving Gorgora the 'motor-road world' seemed a thousand years away. North of the town I found a path that took us west over steep hills, where a few fields lay between acres of high, aromatic shrubs and the compounds were guarded by curs whose owners made no attempt to restrain them for our benefit. Then all cultivation was left behind, the path vanished, and I began to feel slightly like an Intrepid Traveller as we forced our way through a dark, dense forest where thorny scrub pulled persistently at my shirt and tore long scratches on my bare limbs. Jock, too, was in trouble, for powerful, pliable branches repeatedly gripped his protruding-on-each-side load and I had to free him several times. Once he became firmly wedged between two trees and a sack had to be removed. Without our new pack-saddle Lake Tana's north shore certainly would have been 'impossible'.

Until noon we were going steeply up or down hill, making no progress in the required direction. This was not unlike the 'tangled jungle' of my childhood dreams and I soon decided that dream jungles are preferable to the real thing. When at last we escaped on to sunny grasslands every attempt to go west was thwarted by deep, narrow gullies. So I went towards the lake, hoping to find a way along the water's edge, but treacherous swamps soon forced us north again—at a lucky spot, for ten minutes later a faint, westward path appeared. Eagerly I followed it across level grassland between towering wild fig-trees, and it led to a surprising pocket of cultivated land where a family was harvesting *teff*. Their compound must have been far away, because a woman was cooking *injara* beneath a straw shelter while her menfolk urged a yoke of oxen round the threshing circle. Everyone stopped work when we appeared and gathered about us in astonishment—which soon changed to friendly concern when they saw my deep scratches, now marked by lines of flies. Several *talla*-jars lay under a tree and I was given as much as I could drink and fed with roasted *atar* while the woman tried to persuade me to return to Gorgora and the men argued amongst themselves about the route to Dengel.

Finally they indicated that we must go north for some distance before turning west, so we followed a shallow valley, making our own path through high, tawny grass and flowering shrubs, with gold-tinted, wooded ridges on either side. Here the hot silence was broken only by an incessant, plaintive bird-call, and the only movement was an occasional flash of jewelled feathers amidst the bushes. Some strange, soothing melancholy hung over this bright valley: it seemed a secret, special place, lost between mountains and lake.

An hour later we met a vague east-west track which climbed to a narrow plateau, dotted with thorny scrub, and then expired. Now the lake was hidden by a long, forested ridge and, having investigated the impossible west side of the plateau, I realised that we must turn south again and descend into the ravine between plateau and ridge. Eventually I found a path that plunged through a gloom of gnarled trees and led us—after more load-trouble—on to the floor of the ravine. Here steep, wooded cliffs created a premature twilight and giant grey rocks thrust jaggedly through the jungle grass and sometimes ancient trees writhed beside the path. But soon we were again in sunlight, and I saw that the level land to the west was patchily cultivated.

Ten minutes later seven or eight *tukuls* appeared to the left of the path, in one big compound at the base of a cliff, and as we walked towards them I began to think hopefully about *talla*. Then a group of men, who had been watching our approach, came to the edge of the compound and invited me to stop for a drink. They were led by a priest—a small, slender man of perhaps thirty-five, with remarkably regular Semitic features, an effeminate voice, intelligent eyes and the cruellest mouth I have ever seen. This face so unnerved me that I declined the insistently repeated invitations and quickened my pace past the compound, hardly knowing whether to try to look friendly or formidable. For a few moments I could hear voices raised in excited argument behind us; then we rounded an outcrop of rock and were beyond sight and sound of the *tukuls*.

Topographical worries occupied the next twenty minutes. (*See sketch.*) Lake Tana was again stretching ahead, beyond a sweep of jungle grass and a grove of wild fig-trees, and it seemed that one could easily walk round by the shore to the north side of a high ridge that rose from the plain half-a-mile away on our right. But when we got to the water's edge I discovered two barriers—a muddy inlet, thick with reeds, and a narrow channel that made what had appeared to be a walkable part of the shore into a low, rocky islet.

It was now four o'clock and I felt tired, hungry and rather inclined to agree that the north shore of Lake Tana is impossible. As the bank was three feet above the still depths of the

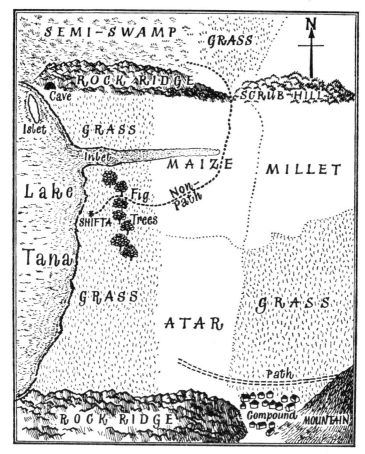

lake I watered Jock from his bucket before sitting down to eat dried apricots and contemplate this impasse.

A few moments later I heard voices and looked around to see four men approaching through the long grass. It didn't greatly surprise me to recognise the priest in the lead, nonchalantly twirling his white horse-hair fly-whisk and reverently carrying his Coptic cross. His companions carried heavy *dulas*. One of them was an older man, with a narrow, sun-blackened face, restless eyes and a habit of nervously licking his lips. The other two were youths of eighteen or nineteen—one stocky, with unusually coarse features for a highlander, the other slim, mean-looking and clearly apprehensive.

The quartet sat beside me and for the next ten minutes we chatted as civilly as the language barrier allowed. I handed round my dried apricots, but they were not appreciated. The stocky youth tasted one gingerly, then spat it out with a grimace; the others felt and smelt theirs, before politely returning them to me. Meanwhile I was listening to the remarks being exchanged by the priest and the older man; the words for mule, money, medicine and clothes were disturbingly comprehensible. The priest then declared that I must spend the night in their compound, and his expression was tense as he watched for my reaction. I smiled, bowed gratefully and declined the invitation—which was perhaps a foolish thing to do, but at that stage my nerve was going and I only wanted to get away.

Standing up, I started to move towards Jock—and at once the four surrounded me. The laymen were holding their *dulas* rather obviously, no one was smiling any more and I could feel myself going white. As he spoke shrilly to his companions, the priest's eyes were bright with greed; he used his cross to gesture towards me—and then towards the lake. Immediately an argument started, the stocky youth supporting the priest, the slim youth siding with the older man. I lit a cigarette.

During those brief, long moments I was reacting on two levels, for beneath the seething terror was a strange, indifferent acceptance—a feeling that gamblers can't always win and that if this was it, it was it.

The argument only lasted for the length of a nervously smoked cigarette, but before it ended I had an odd experience —so unfamiliar that it is difficult to describe, yet so real that it cannot honestly be omitted. While the priest was shaking his fly-whisk angrily in the older man's face, and before it was possible to judge who was winning, I suddenly knew that I was safe—as surely as if a platoon of police had appeared to rescue me. For an instant I was aware of being protected by some mysterious power; and to a person without definite religious convictions this was almost as great a shock as the unpleasant encounter itself.

A moment later the argument was over. The older man ran to Jock, took up the halter and turned towards the compound. The priest caught me by the arm—he was smiling again, though his eyes remained angry—and pointed after Jock, while the youths stood close behind us. But now I, too, was getting angry. Eluding the priest's grasp I pursued Jock, grabbed the halter and waved my *dula* threateningly. At this stage my fear was of being injured, which is quite a different sensation to the fear of death and doesn't deter one from trying to defend one's possessions. However, my ridiculous *dula*-waving was ignored. Within seconds the four were around us again, the youths had seized my arms and the men were unloading Jock.

They took my sleeping-bag, torch, spare Biros, matches, camera, insecticides, medicines (including a packet of Tampax, which amused me even at the time), two books (*Ethiopian Birds* and W. E. Carr's *Poetry of the Middle Ages*), Jock's bridle and a hundred and twenty Ethiopian dollars—about eighteen pounds sterling. My Huskies went unnoticed, being wrapped in the old pack-saddle, and neither cigarettes nor *faranj* food interested them, though these must be saleable commodities in Gondar. However, their oddest omissions were my watch (which I wear on my wrist, though in Makalle I was advised to carry it in my pocket lest it should tempt thieves) and Jock himself, who is worth another hundred dollars. Possibly they considered that in this region, where mules are uncommon, he would be an imprudently conspicious acquisition if his owner were still alive.

When the quartet left us my knees suddenly went soggy, and as I began to reload Jock my hands were so shaky that I could scarcely tie the ropes. However, this was no time or place for indulging in the tremors—I wanted to be far away from that priest by sunset.

My topographical problem was still unsolved, but now I gave up bothering about the finer points of the compass and turned north. We climbed a high hill, pushing through leafless grey scrub, and from the crest I was overlooking a plain that appeared to be covered in tall jungle grass. It extended north for an indefinite distance, but was bounded to the west by a long, low ridge that looked no more than three miles away. On this ridge clumps of trees stood out against the sky, promising settlements and, presumably, safety.

Twenty minutes later I had discovered that the 'grassy plain' was a peculiarly hellish semi-swamp. Apart from patches of black mud, in which we occasionally sank to our knees, the vegetation was diabolical. Thick, wiry grass grew shoulder-high, the stiff, dense reeds were seven to nine feet tall, and a slim, five-foot growth, which looked dead, had such powerfully resilient thorny branches that I soon began to imagine it was deliberately thwarting me. From amidst these mingled horrors I could no longer see the ridge—or anything but an infinity of reed-tops and a darkening sky. Nor was it possible to steer straight, for we had to go where the ground was least swampy and the growth least obstructive—though whichever way I turned I was lacerated again and again by that nightmare thorny plant, and by a weird kind of thistle that now appeared to complete my demoralisation. As the light faded I cursed myself for not having turned back. This inferno was a real danger that could have been avoided, whereas murderous humans were merely contingent dangers.

By seven o'clock it was dark. I remembered that pythons are reputed to live here and was suitably depressed; this seemed my day for meeting a python. Then the vegetation ahead thinned—usually a sign of a swampy patch—and I poked cautiously at the ground with my *dula*. As there wasn't any ground, swampy or otherwise, I stepped aside into the reeds on my left. Unfortunately there wasn't any ground there either, so I fell into a hole six or seven feet deep. It contained glutinous black mud, too thin to stand on and too thick to swim in, and its vertical, slippery sides were unclimbable; but for Jock's intelligent reaction I would not now be reporting the occurrence. Instinctively I had held on to the halter and steadfastly Jock stood braced on the brink of the hole—instead of bolting, as many a lesser mule would have done when their owner abruptly vanished. So I felt only a momentary panic, for I quickly realised that all would be well if the halter didn't snap. Luckily mules are tough and the incomparable Jock showed no resentment as I hauled myself on to dry ground—though his ears and jawbones must have been taking at least half my weight.

I then decided that enough was enough and fumblingly unloaded Jock. A cautious starlight survey of our immediate surroundings revealed a bewildering number of deep, narrow channels, filled with mud or water—so if I lit an anti-animal fire amidst this density of dry growth we might soon have to choose between roasting and drowning.

Sitting dismally on a spot that I had partly cleared of the more dire vegetation I ate immoderately to cheer myself up. Apart from the advisability of guarding Jock I was too cold to sleep without my flea-bag, for a chill breeze had been blowing off the lake since sunset. In this situation there was an extraordinary incongruity about the prosaic little evening routine of winding my watch.

At 2.15 the waning moon rose—but by then I had been in misery for so long that the beauty of moonlight didn't help. Reeds shaken by the wind now looked as though they were being shaken by advancing hyenas or leopards, and this new, calm lustre seemed to emphasise the lifeless silence of the marsh. Jock had at last stopped munching the short grass that flourished beneath the other growths, and there were no cicadas, or bird-stirrings, or distant dog-barks—nothing but the whispering rustle of the reeds. To pass the time I began to scrape the dried mud off my body, but when I realised that it was keeping me warm I desisted.

Three and a half hours later the first light released us. I then saw that in the darkness we had crossed a natural bridge of solid ground and become trapped on what was almost an islet. Retracing our steps we resumed the struggle and, after sitting tensely for nine and a half hours, to be moving again was such bliss that neither slime nor thorns seemed to matter any more.

An hour later the vegetation began to thin and soon we were on ploughland at the foot of the ridge. A broad path led down towards the lake and as we followed it a young man came towards us, driving a few cattle. He took one look at me, yelled in terror and fled. No doubt I've now given birth to a myth— the Dawn Devil of Tana.

It took fifty minutes to wash the adhesive black mud out of my clothes and hair and off my body, and innumerable scratches began to bleed afresh as I removed their mud plaster. When we had climbed the ridge I found a clear westward track which we followed for four hours across hilly farmland, with the lake sparkling below on our left. There were many settlements, but the locals seemed unfriendly. One little man of about fifty—dressed in a ragged bush-shirt and cotton shorts—made a miscalculation when he saw the lone *faranj*. Standing before me on the path he grabbed my *dula* and tried swiftly to pick my pockets—in full view of three leering youths who were sitting under a tree. However, in populated areas one can afford to be aggressive and this morning my mood was not sunny: I punched him in the eye, wrested my *dula* from him and brought it down hard on his skull. As he reeled away I further relieved my feelings by throwing a stone at the youths and shouting '*Hid!*'

By midday my body and mind were limp with exhaustion. Ahead I could see blue-gums and soon we were in Delghie, a market town of many tin roofs on the west shore of the lake. I rested in a *talla-beit* for two hours and had a large meal of *injara* and *wat* and five pints. As we set off again, through the hot afternoon glare, I felt slightly drunk and much restored.

Our track ran close to the lake for three miles; vast herds of sleek cattle were grazing on the lush pastures of the shore and for a time we joined a dour family going home from the market. Then the track turned inland, became a faint path and switch-backed for three hours over a series of steep, thinly-forested hills where I saw only two distant settlements and a few small fields.

By sunset we had covered twenty-two miles, and though the lake was invisible all afternoon we are now overlooking it again, for these compounds stand on a cliff-top high above the water. The locals welcomed me kindly, but the poverty and ill-health of this family are most depressing. My skinny, sunken eyed hostess has recently had malaria, her haggard husband coughs incessantly, their five pot-bellied children have trachoma and boils, and a young man lying in a corner by the door has a gruesomely injured eye into which he frequently squeezes drops from a phial of penicillin marked 'For Intra-muscular

Injection Only'. Worst of all is the condition of the youngest child, a girl of about two; her feet and calves are covered in ulcerated burns and the poor little mite never stops screaming. Yet when I told her mother that she should be taken to Gondar hospital *at once* I got the impression that no one considered her cure worth such a long journey.

The walls of this tiny *tukul* are flimsy and already the night air is cold; so despite my exhaustion I foresee getting very little sleep.


### 4 February. Kunzela

By now I feel like a shipwrecked nonagenarian. I was being optimistic when I foresaw 'getting very little sleep'. For the second successive night I got *no* sleep—a personal record which I would prefer not to have achieved. Possibly because of my exhaustion I felt the cold even more last night, and in that over-crowded hovel I had no room to move a finger. Fleas tickled and pricked relentlessly and bugs swarmed over me, inducing that peculiar, feverish irritation which cannot be imagined by those who have never experienced it. The unfortunate burnt child never stopped whimpering, my host never stopped coughing, the injured young man never stopped moaning and the local dogs never stopped barking. Rats raced all over everyone and two donkeys who 'live in' kicked me three times. At midnight I crawled out to the starlight, broken in spirit and shivering in body. I found a little pile of straw and burrowed under it, but it was too little to warm me—and anyway I'd brought the bugs with me in my clothes.

As I sat chain-smoking the moon rose over Lake Tana and lost itself in a drift of thin cloud that glowed above the water like a length of torn satin. Being deprived of any sleep for such an unnatural period strangely distorts one's sense of time. It would seem logical to feel that one has lived *longer*; instead, towards dawn, I found that having twice failed to cross the normal frontier between consciousness and unconsciousness I was aware of the past forty-eight hours as only one long day.

Not surprisingly we covered less than sixteen miles today. During the morning our path wound through sweeps of jungle grass that shone like bright copper, and on either side low ridges were covered in vivid green shrubs, and sometimes Lake Tana's blueness glinted between the hills.

At midday we came to a village where the marketplace was crowded—though all morning we had been walking through uninhabited country—and when I told my robber story in a *talla-beit* this ill-treatment of a *faranj* roused everyone's indignation, sympathy and generosity. The Medical Officer invited me to lunch and, though he is the poorly-paid father of nine children, he wanted to present me with five dollars and a blanket. His fair-skinned wife has a sweet, oval face and large, brilliant eyes; she is the same age as myself but looks ten years younger. At first she was very shy of me, but soon she relaxed, went to the iron bed and carefully opened an enormous bundle of clean blankets—to show off Number Nine, aged three weeks.

I would have liked to accept my host's invitation to stay, but now I'm in a hurry to get to the telephone at Bahar Dar, since it is just possible that the Gondar Police may be able to recover my irreplacable high-altitude sleeping-bag, which I bought from a Japanese Himalayan expedition in Nepal.

When I left this kind family I discovered that extreme tiredness leaves one abnormally vulnerable to *talla*. Beyond the village I found myself swaying and stumbling across rough ploughland and the landscape went unnoticed. I felt sick and drunk and horrible as I hung on to Jock's halter with one hand and leant heavily on my *dula* with the other. Inevitably we got lost, but that has proved a blessing. This little town is one of Lake Tana's chief ports, from where grain and coffee are shipped on small steamers and huge, unwieldy reed rafts to Gorgora and Bahar Dar; therefore it has some uncommon amenities, including one tin of insecticide which almost reduced me to tears of relief when I saw it beside my bed.

The Port Manager noticed our arrival and at once offered hospitality; then an agreeable young teacher appeared and the three of us walked beyond the town to this tiny, corrugated-iron shed beside a warehouse at the top of a stone jetty. Here my host put down a camp-bed for me, and produced a 'Visitors Book' to be signed. There was only one other name in the thin exercise-book—Chris Barry, Churchtown, Dublin, Ireland.

My compatriot had spent the night of 7 February, 1966, in this shed, on his way from Gorgora to Bahar Dar by steamer. It cannot be denied that we Irish get around.

### 5 February. *Zeghie*

After eleven hours' deep sleep I woke to find that my host and the teacher had decided that we must have an escort to get us safely across the Little Nile. Few people walk from Kunzela to Zeghie, because the short boat-trip is so much quicker, but there is a track of sorts, used by the locals, and a tribe of pagan boatmen runs a ferry-service. The teacher said that these boatmen are notoriously difficult to deal with and would be as likely to steal my load as to ferry it; so I greeted my escort enthusiastically, having had my fill of difficult lakeside dwellers.

We set off at 8.15, Jock being led by Fikre Selassie, a wiry little man of about forty who wore a permanently puzzled expression and was very polite but unbelievably dim-witted. As he wanted to get back to Kunzela before dark we walked non-stop for five and a half hours.

The track ran inland, at first across an uninhabited flatness where eight-foot thistles had flowers like foxgloves, and then through hilly, heavily-wooded country, inhabited by many small monkeys. Today the noon heat affected me more because of our forced march, and six of my swamp scratches have become throbbing streaks of pus—three on each leg—so I was not sorry when we passed a large settlement and came to the end of our marathon.

Here Lake Tana is very close, though invisible, and the Little Nile is some eighty yards wide, flowing deep and slow between low banks overhung by freshly-green shrubs. Wide, level pastures stretch away from both banks to the blue horizons and directly above the ferry-point the stream divides around a tree-covered islet. At times there is a disconcerting un-Africaness about these highlands. When I looked at this dark current, gently moving below its fringe of dense greenery, I could fancy for a moment that I was standing by the Blackwater River near my home. Yet some eccentrics still believe this stream to be the true source of the Blue Nile.

However, there was nothing homely about the human element here. At the ferry-point gravelly shores replace the banks and, as we approached, I could hear violent shouting. Then we saw one of three tall, bony, black-skinned boatmen viciously striking a passenger across the face, while abusing him for not paying the fee demanded. (I afterwards found that ten cents had already been paid for the ferrying of a small load of salt-blocks, but the boatman wanted another ten cents because the donkey had been towed by the same raft.) The passenger was a frail young man, hardly up to his opponent's shoulder, and now his wife courageously intervened by throwing a stone —which unfortunately struck her husband instead of the boatman. Then a second boatman joined in—the third was on the far bank—and at that point the young man gave up and produced the extra ten cents. These ferrymen certainly take full advantage of the highlanders' inability to cope with water-transport. By local standards eightpence is a most unscrupulous charge for a single crossing.

When one sees these rafts close to it no longer seems surprising that their management is an esoteric tribal skill. They are simple bundles of reeds, shaped like giant rugger-balls and no more than eight feet long and two feet above water amidships. One man punts them with a thin pole, some twenty feet long, and passengers ride astride with legs dangling in the water. If I were a non-swimmer I wouldn't cross a deep river on one of those contraptions for all the salt in the Danakil.

As I unsaddled Jock three interested men and two loaded donkeys formed a queue behind us. Someone asked where Jock came from and when I replied 'Makalle' there was an outburst of discussion and everyone assured me that a Tigre mule would not swim a river. Highlanders delight in arguing about a situation for as long as possible before taking any action and if they can build up an atmosphere of doom and drama so much the better; but at this stage I only wanted to immerse my sweaty, bug-bitten body in the river, so I postponed the Jock problem, pulled off my shirt and plunged in. (It is convenient to be among people who are not shocked by women stripped to the waist.)

The ferrying of our load and saddlery required two trips,

during which I swam watchfully back and forth beside the ridiculous raft, half-expecting my precious possessions to slide off at any moment. The water was cool, opaque, probably unhealthy and wonderfully restoring. I tried to dive to the bottom, but failed, so it must be about twelve feet deep.

Then the Jock problem had to be faced—and it is indeed true that Tigre mules don't like deep rivers. Clearly Jock had never met one before, and he so loathed the Little Nile that for the first time since our partnership began he turned mulish. When all my efforts to lead him in had failed I looked away, for I couldn't endure to see him being brutally thrashed by Fikre Selassie, the boatmen and the donkey-men. This was a poor return for his patient, life-saving loyalty.

Local donkeys are ferried by one man half-lifting them into the water towards another man, who is sitting waiting on a raft and who immediately grabs their ears and tows them across. So now the donkeymen suggested ferrying their animals first, to reassure and lure Jock. But this stratagem also failed. Then at last the poor devil was so tormented that he plunged despairingly in—and, following the men's advice, I rushed after him, seized the halter and swam beside him. When he broke away my efforts to head him off from the shore merely revealed the interesting fact that a mule swims faster than I do. Twice this happened, but the third time I quickly wound the halter round my shoulder and kept so close to him that I was in no danger of being kicked. Now another return to shore meant towing me, so he decided that crossing the river was the lesser of two evils and followed meekly—at which point even the sullen boatmen raised a cheer. Half-way across I noticed that the panic had gone from his eyes and when we scrambled on to the opposite shore he was looking faintly surprised. Probably he had just realised that swimming a cool river on a hot day can be quite pleasant.

By 3.30 we were following a clear path across close-cropped pastureland, where a few herds were visible in the distance. Some half-a-mile away, on our left, lay the lake, hidden by a fringe of tall, feathery reeds, and soon after five o'clock the path vanished at the edge of a swamp. This was a much swampier swamp than our last one, but it was also more predictable;

the reeds were only two or three feet high and beyond I could see trees along the horizon and black dots that meant grazing cattle. Yet the next fifty minutes were unpleasant enough, for I was wading through waist-high water, slushy with rotted vegetation. As always in hours of peril I held trustfully on to Jock's halter, but the slippery ground remained solid underfoot. The stink of decay was nauseating, and at every step we disturbed clouds of mosquitoes and other sharp-stinging flies. Later, when we arrived here, I looked at my legs and saw that they were covered with immense, swollen leeches. After burning them off I bled so profusely that my hostess came over all queer and had to sit down in the middle of preparing supper.

Beyond the swamp a continuation of our path soon brought us to roughly-broken scrubland, and as darkness fell we entered a thick forest, where the filtered starlight didn't help much. Yet by night a thin forest would be even more difficult; here one knew that the path went where the growth was least dense.

By 7.30 we were clear of the trees and about a mile away I could see a black, serrated mass against the stars—the blue-gums of Zeghie. Then I lost the path, amidst a chaos of boulders. Before long our way was blocked by an inlet from the lake, and having retreated from that we wandered into a stony gully which seemed to be a *cul-de-sac*, and on climbing out of this we became painfully enmeshed in a thorny thicket. I was about to give up and unload when suddenly the path reappeared, and twenty minutes later we were beneath the shadows of the blue-gums.

I stopped at the first *talla-beit*—identifiable because lamplight was reflected in rows of glasses upturned on a wooden bench inside the door. As I drank half-a-dozen men stared at me in unfriendly silence, and I felt relieved when a breathless teacher came to offer me hospitality. (There is a hint of magic about the speed with which teachers materialise when a *faranj* appears in a small town. We had entered Zeghie in total darkness and seen no one on our way to the *talla-beit*.)

Abraha is a tall, broad-shouldered, handsome young man from Debra Marcos—the capital of Gojjam province, which we entered yesterday. Like most rural teachers he longs for further education and has just been asking me wistfully if the

Irish Government offers scholarships to Ethiopians, and if so could I please arrange for him to have one—a pathetically common request. He detests life in Zeghie, where the school has about four hundred pupils (some from far-away villages) and five teachers. Many of the locals are so opposed to modern education that they boycott the teachers cruelly—which does not surprise me, for since leaving Gondar everyone with whom I have discussed my route has frowned and muttered '*Metfo!*' ('Bad!') at the mention of Zeghie. It would be interesting to discover why these people are so renowned for unpleasantness.

When he came here last year Abraha took a wife on a temporary basis. She is the twenty-two-year-old daughter of a rich local coffee-farmer and was divorced by her first husband after five years of childless marriage. Abraha said that if she bears him a child he may keep her, otherwise he will leave her behind when he gets a transfer. Meanwhile, he treats her considerately, though I noticed a marked difference in her demeanour compared with that of the average wife and mother. She shows a rather servile manner towards Abraha, and though her expression is cheerful enough there is a resigned sadness behind her eyes.

This is going to be another hellishly buggy night; within minutes of my sitting down the ghoulish brutes were attacking me and, having discovered that my flea-bag had been stolen, Abraha insists that I must sleep on his hair-mattress. I would much prefer to lie outside under the blue-gums, coldly bugless, but to do so would dreadfully offend my host.

*6 February. Bahar Dar*

This morning I saw that Zeghie stands on a high cliff overlooking a bay sheltered to north and south by wooded promontories. Many of its square, sophisticated houses seem quite new; they have high tin roofs, smooth, solid mud walls, little unglazed windows, and doors made of chopped-up packing cases. These dwellings are so well spaced out, amidst tall, dignified blue-gums, that the town parodies a European 'select residential area'.

Last night was as expected: I got no more than two hours' sleep, in uneasy ten-minute snatches. Apart from the battalions of bugs, rats were rattling continuously amongst the cooking utensils and quarrelling with high-pitched squeals.

We left Zeghie at 8 a.m. and arrived here six hours later, having struggled through three rivers, each more difficult to cope with than the last. None was wide, or above four feet deep—but all were fast-flowing, and it was never clear where one should or could cross, and Jock didn't want to cross any of them anywhere. If it wasn't treacherous oozy mud underfoot it was treacherous slimy stones and between Jock's nerves and the strength of the current I was submerged as often as not. This was a region of dense, green forest—the nearest I've ever been to a true jungle—and our path frequently disappeared. The three rivers were overhung by dark tangles of trees and creepers so that one could never go straight across—always it was necessary to wade up and down searching for the point of exit on the opposite bank. Twice, between rivers, Jock got wedged and had to be partially unloaded, while scores of little monkeys paused in their swingings to peer down at us and make impertinent remarks. Then at last we escaped on to a path thronged with people going to market and an hour later were back on the motor-road, which comes to Bahar Dar along the east shore of the lake.

At once I made for the newly-opened luxury Ras Hotel (the measure of my demoralisation!) and its dapper Ethiopian manager could hardly conceal his agitation when a room was booked by a repulsive object covered in mud and blood and wearing a shirt and shorts so torn that they had become mere tokens of the will to be decent. However, he relaxed somewhat when I changed a damp but valid traveller's cheque from the roll in my money-belt. Then he noticed Jock standing patiently by the veranda—and all was well. Jumping from his chair he exclaimed 'The Irish lady with the mule!' and held out his hand. Even before he said it I knew that Leilt Aida had been on the telephone.

When a platoon of wide-eyed servants had conducted me to my room I sent one of them to buy barley for Jock and another to buy insecticide for me. This enormous hotel consists of rows and rows of rooms on the edge of the lake, laid out in chalet style. Tonight two rooms are occupied. My spacious, elegant suite has a private (pale pink) bathroom, limitless boiling water, a bed with primrose-yellow sheets and an ankle-deep, wall-to-wall olive-green carpet. The whole thing seems Hiltonian and I'm loving every inch and minute of it: I haven't asked what the tariff is—and just now I couldn't care less.

After a bath and before a late lunch I telephoned Colonel Aziz, who suggested that tomorrow I should leave Jock here and return to Gondar by bus to guide a Punitive Expedition to the Scene of the Crime. This seemed to me an excellent idea, and I said so with un-Christian enthusiasm.

Then I ate a huge meal, slept for four hours, ate another huge meal, wrote this—and am now going to sleep again.

# 8

# *Vengeance is Mine*

Words fail me when it comes to describing the dreariness of Bahar Dar—so I quote from my guide-book. 'Bahar Dar is a small town on the bus route from Addis Ababa to Asmara. The only passable hotel in town is the Ras Hotel. The bus station is across the street from the hotel, near the Total petrol station. Ethiopian Airlines connects Bahar Dar with Addis Ababa. The airport is across the street from the hotel just beyond the Total station. Of interest to some is the Polytechnic Institute, a modern secondary school staffed by Russian and Ethiopian teachers and attracting an enrolment from all over the Empire. The school is just past the Shell petrol station and is distinguished by a number of large, modern buildings.' To complete the picture add hundreds of tin-roofed hovels and a textile factory. Yet Abraha, in Zeghie, had described Bahar Dar as 'a fine city'.

I overslept this morning, missed the early bus to Gondar and decided to hitch-hike instead of waiting for the afternoon bus. There was very little traffic, but I was soon picked up by an interesting American girl archaeologist named Joanne. She was driving a Land-Rover, with a mongrel pup on her lap, and beside her sat an elderly, fat, chain-smoking interpreter-guide, who had been appointed to help her by some cultural institute in Addis. Unluckily this man seemed to be convinced that digging in Ethiopia was a futile occupation.

After a twenty-five-mile drive over an arid, brownish plain we said good-bye and Joanne turned off the gravel road and went bumping away through the scrub towards a site. Four miles further on I was picked up again, by three young men in a W.H.O. jeep. They were officials of Gondar's Public

Health College and, despite Jock's absence, they had at once recognised 'the Irish lady with the mule'. The remaining eighty-five miles took us across a continuation of the featureless plain, and then over a splendid range of barren mountains; Lake Tana was rarely visible, as this road is far inland, and we passed only a few tin-roofed villages.

At half-past one I presented myself at Gondar Police Headquarters, where for ninety minutes I sat in a tiny office beside a rusty filing-cabinet reading *Talleyrand* while I waited for Colonel Aziz to return from his lunch.

Colonel Aziz is a stocky man of forty-five, with a round, brown face, keen eyes, a neat, slightly self-conscious moustache and a tinge of that pomposity common to most highlanders in responsible positions. His English is easily understood, though far from fluent, and I had much enjoyed our previous meetings; but obviously this official reunion was going to be embarrassing.

Already I had realised that the robbing of a *faranj* causes genuine shame and distress to the average highlander. This crime is 'not cricket' and had I wished to profit by my misfortune I could easily have done so, since every peasant was eager to compensate me to the limit of his resources. For those who know that I am writing about my travels in Ethiopia the situation is even worse, so when Colonel Aziz appeared— looking as guilty as though he had robbed me himself—my first task, as we walked to his office, was to cheer him up. I stressed that the robbery was an isolated reef in an ocean of kindness; I pointed out that Ethiopia is the sixth foreign country in which I have met robbers and—when he continued to look miserable—I abandoned patriotism and admitted that I had also been robbed in Ireland, where the police had made no perceptible effort to recover my property. At this the poor fellow brightened up. Pulling his chair closer to his desk, he rang a bell and said that of course things were quite different in Ethiopia, where stolen goods were normally restored to their owners within twenty-four hours.

A tall, slim young lieutenant appeared in response to the bell; he spoke excellent English, and after we had been introduced he sat down to take my statement. When I began to describe the priest the atmosphere suddenly became electric

and simultaneously the officers exclaimed 'Kas Makonnen!'
Then, as Colonel Aziz grabbed the telephone and demanded
Gorgora, Lieutenant Woldie looked at me and said 'You're
lucky!'

It hadn't occurred to me that my quartet were *shifta*: they
had seemed merely the extra-degenerate inhabitants of a region
where most people looked somewhat degenerate. I had imagined *shifta* to be colourful types on fast horses who came galloping down hillsides brandishing rifles; but apparently every
detail of my description of the priest fitted one Kas Makonnen,
a *shifta*-leader wanted for countless robberies and two murders.

Soon Colonel Aziz had arranged that at six-thirty tomorrow
morning he, the lieutenant, the Governor of Gorgora (who is
at present in Gondar), eight armed policemen and myself will
leave for Gorgora, where the Colonel and Governor will
wait, while the rest of us go man-hunting. When I explained
that it might take me more than a day to locate the settlement,
since I'd been thoroughly lost on my way there, it was decided
that we would take a motor-launch along the shore of the lake
and land where I recognised the *shifta* bay.

Colonel Aziz asked me not to discuss our plan or the identity
of my 'robber baron'. Only the Colonel, the lieutenant, the
Gorgora sergeant, the Governor and myself are in the secret:
neither the Gorgora nor the Gondar constables are to be given
any information about our objective until we are aboard the
motor-launch. This reversal of a familiar procedure interested
me. At home the help of the public would be enlisted for a
man-hunt; here not only the public but the ordinary police are
regarded as potential allies of the criminals—either through
fear or friendship. Tomorrow the aim will be to capture men
in terrain so difficult that if they once get a start pursuit would
be futile. Therefore the surprise element is of first importance;
and in Ethiopia the concept of a police-force is new and not
very popular.

This evening I am a little confused about Kas Makonnen's
status. One person has told me that he is not a priest but dis-
guises himself as one ('Kas' means priest); yet I have also been
assured that the Bishop of Begemdir will unfrock him when he
is brought in chains to Gondar. This assurance naturally

makes me suspect that the first statement was a face-saving manœuvre on behalf of the Ethiopian Church—though if he is a priest one feels the Bishop might justifiably have unfrocked him by remote control quite some time ago.

*8 February. Gorgora*

Today has been suffused with improbability. For an ordinary citizen of Ireland there is something not quite believable about the business of guiding seventeen armed men through a remote corner of Ethiopia in search of a murderer.

By this morning it had been decided that sixteen policemen might serve our purpose better than eight and when we left Gondar at nine o'clock the new police Land-Rover, driven by Colonel Aziz, was so overloaded that its driver would have been arrested in any other country. Two hours later we reached Gorgora and went straight to the launch, which was moored at a little Italian-built jetty—where sacks of *teff*, sorghum, millet and coffee were being unloaded off a great papyrus-raft just in from Kunzela. The next hour was spent waiting for the Governor to provide us with four baskets of *dabo*, *injara* and *wat*, two flasks of *tej* and several fat earthen pots of *talla*. Then, at twelve o'clock precisely, we pushed off, leaving the Colonel and the Governor waving on the jetty and calling final instructions and good-luck messages.

There were twenty-four of us aboard—a crew of three, sixteen policemen in civvies, two police officers, two undefined local officials and the *faranj*. Everyone except the crew and the *faranj* was so heavily armed—with a rifle and revolver each and a sub-machine gun between them—that I wondered the elderly launch didn't sink. The lieutenant and the Gorgora sergeant had been in uniform, but now both changed lest someone ashore should notice their dress and warn the *shifta*. I was impressed by the sergeant—a small, wiry man of about fifty, who greatly distinguished himself as a Patriot fighter against the Italians. He has a strong, shrewd, kindly face and a reassuring air of calm authority; only a lack of English has hindered his promotion.

For two hours we travelled at top speed, about a mile and a

half offshore, with the forested cliffs of the coast on our right. Frequently we passed between rocky, wooded islets of various shapes and sizes—each with its monastery or church half-hidden by trees—and all the time the sun shone and Lake Tana sparkled and the wind blew strong and cool. Standing at the prow I reflected that there are many less pleasant occupations than chasing *shifta*.

At about two o'clock I decided that we should move inshore. As we cruised along slowly I attempted to work out our position in relation to my route last week—but this was surprisingly difficult, for a landscape seen from half-a-mile offshore looks strangely unlike the same landscape seen from the middle, as it were. However, that ghastly semi-swamp put me right and at 2.30 we slid quietly into the wide bay. The crew refused to go close to the unfamiliar coastline, so a tiny life-boat was put down and we were rowed ashore in four groups.

We landed at the foot of the northern ridge and I suggested that, since surprise was vital, we should go along the water's edge to the south ridge (*see sketch, p. 155*) and follow it to the compound. Lieutenant Woldie then ordered everyone to bend double and we hastened along the lakeside with the fig-trees between us and the *tukuls*. By this time I was thoroughly enjoying myself. Skulking through jungle-grass, followed by my little army with its weapons at the ready, I felt like a cross between Napier on the way to Magdala and a child at play.

Suddenly a figure moved behind the trees. It was a scared-looking youth and instantly two policemen ran towards him, waving their rifles and gesturing that he must be quiet. He reacted by fleeing at top speed and then, since his flight could have been observed from the compound, we changed our tactics. The sergeant and six policemen went north-east, using the cover of a maize-field, while the rest of us sprinted west and followed the base of the ridge towards the settlement.

When we were thirty yards away, still hidden by an outcrop of rock, we paused to collect ourselves. Then we rushed into view, raced through the compound and saw our quarry sitting outside a *tukul*. He was seized as he rose to his feet. Whereupon I got the giggles, in reaction to this anti-climax at the end of our perilous man-hunt.

The compound was now surrounded by police and within moments I had identified the other three robbers and all four had been securely roped and manacled. Lieutenant Woldie told me that both the older man and the slim youth had recently been released from gaol—which may explain their disinclination to murder *faranjs*. At this stage I became convinced that Kas Makonnen is an ordained priest. His companions-in-manacles were being handled brutally, yet he was not ill-treated but was allowed to sit in the shade of a *tukul*—with a guard on either side.

At first all four vehemently denied ever having seen me before —though the horrified recognition in the priest's eyes when he found me standing beside him was a sufficiently eloquent admission of guilt. During our unsuccessful search of the eight *tukuls* police tempers became frayed, and then the older man was taken out of my sight. But he was not out of earshot, so it didn't surprise me to see him reappearing ten minutes later looking ill. He was now most anxious to guide the police on an hour's walk to a settlement where he said all my property would be found intact. The sergeant and eight policemen accompanied him, the rest staying to guard the prisoners and prevent anyone from leaving the compound, which had been put under 'martial law' pending the recovery of the stolen goods.

I then went to investigate a strange cave that I had noticed in the north ridge last week—when too distraught to pursue cultural interests. As I had suspected, it was a series of chambers and passages hewn out of the rock. My only light was from brands fired with matches, which was not very satisfactory— though it enabled me to see that the rock had been hewn smoothly and skilfully. I could find no traces of wall-paintings, but they may well exist, for my exploration was sketchy. When the system of corridors became too complex for my nerves I retreated: this is not my luckiest area. Later I was told that the place is called Selassie Washa and is believed to have been hewn out of the mountain six centuries ago—about a century after the creation of Lalibela's rock churches. But one can never rely on Ethiopian dates. The tradition is that Selassie Washa was used by kings (unspecified) as a refuge from their enemies and a place of religious retreat.

When I got back to the compound my 'army' was eating and drinking merrily and I was given a large meal of inferior *injara* and fresh milk. On such expeditions the police follow the ancient custom of highland armies and demand sustenance as their right. Indeed it may be said that they looted this compound, because on our return to the launch each man was laden with foodstuffs—none of which had been paid for.

At 5.30 the sergeant's party reappeared in the distance and we cheered loudly on seeing a canary-yellow dot—my precious flea-bag—being carried by the prisoner. Everyone had known of my obsessional desire to recover this particular item, so the sergeant and his men were grinning all over their faces as I ran to thank and congratulate them.

My torch and Jock's bridle had also been recovered, but nothing else—which didn't worry me in the least, as I sat gloating over my flea-bag. The police, however, were very worried, especially about my camera, which I only mildly regretted since I am incapable of using it effectively. As the 'fence' at the other compound was away at a wedding his mother had been arrested instead, and I was told that she would be kept in gaol until he gave himself up and handed over the rest of my property. She was a frail, bewildered, terrified woman of about fifty and this procedure appalled me. Yet it would have been absurd for the *faranj* to deliver a lecture on Justice in such a situation, so I simply begged to have her released. This silliness was ignored; but now the poor woman, perhaps realising that she had my support, knelt weeping before three policemen and resumed her protestations of innocence and her pleas for freedom. In response all three kicked her hard on the shoulders, back and breasts. Whereupon I intervened very angrily. During the afternoon several acts of needless brutality had enraged me and at this point all my pent-up indignation was released. I gave the nearest kicker a box on the ear and called Lieutenant Woldie, who immediately reprimanded the constables—not, I fear, for kicking the woman, but for allowing me to see them kicking her.

Then we left, with our 'bag' of seven prisoners—my quartet, the fence's mother and two other 'wanted' men who had been captured incidentally at this *shifta* headquarters. On our way

to the shore I asked Lieutenant Woldie a question that had
been puzzling me for hours—why these *shifta* neither carried
rifles nor had them in their *tukuls*. He replied that the men of
this region are professional cattle-thieves, who operate over a
wide area of Begemdir and Gojjam provinces, and when most
of them are 'away on business'—as at present—they take all
the available arms with them, having no reason to fear police
raids in their absence. Several other questions were also bothering me—why the *shifta* risked robbing me when I was then
let loose to inform the police, why certain things were stolen
and others not, and why the quartet remained in their settlement when there was danger of a police raid. However,
Lieutenant Woldie was vague about all these points, so I can
only assume that the naïve *shifta* thought it unlikely that I
would survive the shores of Lake Tana, or didn't realise that
an English-speaking *faranj* could communicate effectively with
Ethiopian police officers, or miscalculated the impetus that
the robbery of a *faranj* would give to police activity. Tonight
I feel flickers of ridiculous sympathy for the quartet—their
capture was so obviously a victory of sophistication over simplicity.

We reached the lakeside at sunset—when the water was a
rippling expanse of copper, lemon and blue-green. As I was
being rowed out the sky flared briefly to blood-red and the
masts of the launch formed a black cross against it. Pulling
myself aboard I sat in the stern, with the fence's mother sobbing
on my shoulder, and watched the light being swiftly absorbed
behind the ridge beyond the swamp.

By 7.45 everyone was aboard and, as the engine quickened,
our celebration party began. With their valuable cargo of
prisoners securely roped together on deck, all the police were
in good humour—and before long they were in high good
humour. A mysterious flask of *araki* soon appeared, to supple-
ment the Governor's generous supply of *talla* and *tej*, and as we
swished through the starlit water we mixed our drinks recklessly. Towards the end of the voyage a group of policemen
began to quarrel among themselves about rifles and in the
cramped cabin I found it a sobering experience to have four
drunken highlanders disputing possession of as many loaded

weapons. Lieutenant Woldie was sitting beside me, asking progressively less intelligent questions about European history, and now he blinked benevolently and remarked that really these peasant lads were like children—which was precisely what was worrying me. But luckily we slackened speed then, and were soon beside the jetty.

By torchlight, we climbed a rough path to the local gaol— a solid mud building, with clean straw on its floors. Here the six men were locked into one room—manacled in pairs—and the wretched woman was left alone; but at least they all have more comfortable accommodation than they are accustomed to at home.

When the lieutenant, the sergeant and myself came to this doss-house—where I spent my last night in Gorgora—we heard that Colonel Aziz had had to return to Gondar during the afternoon, but already he has been told of our victory and tomorrow he will come to collect us.


*9 February. Gondar*

It is now 11 p.m. and I have just returned from a party at the Police Officers' Club. Indeed the whole of today has felt like one long party, starting from the moment when a beaming Colonel Aziz arrived at Gorgora this morning and we had *tej* for breakfast. When we got to Gondar I was somewhat disconcerted to find myself the Local Heroine. Apparently yesterday's excursion was reported on the Addis news bulletin this morning, and the citizens of Gondar are behaving as though I had captured the *shifta* single-handed. This afternoon I was invited to have tea at the Palace with the Governor-General's wife (a cousin of Leilt Aida) who has just returned from Addis. She speaks fluent English and once the initial *shifta* embarrassment had been overcome we enjoyed a long talk about the more cheerful aspects of highland life.

Today my books, insecticide and medicines were recovered, but the camera and money are still missing and I must remain in Gondar until they have been found. Then I will be required to give evidence in court when the quartet are being tried for this particular robbery.

*10 February*

There were no police developments today and I'm getting restive. I long to be with Jock again, on the track to Labibela —though Jock himself doubtless prefers inactivity and barley in Bahar Dar. I telephoned the Ras Hotel just now and the manager assured me that my *buccolo* is receiving full V.I.P. treatment. And so he should.

This morning the Governor-General returned from Addis and this afternoon I was summoned to the Presence. Though he has only been here eighteen months he gives the impression of taking an exceptionally intelligent interest in the province and he was eager to discuss with me the little-known area between the Takazze and Buahit. In his general approach to regional problems he seems wise, kindly and considerably more than just a figurehead representing the Emperor.

*11 February*

My patience-test continues. Luckily for me Joanne is stranded here too, awaiting a permit to dig in Begemdir province. She is the only *faranj* I have met in Ethiopia who sleeps in *tukuls*, drinks *tukul talla* and eats *tukul* food. She also speaks Amharinya, swims in Lake Tana, rides unbroken horses through the Semiens and is oblivious to the multitude of infected insect bites at present covering her legs. We like each other.

To-day's diversion was a visit to a barber who gave me a *barbaric* hair-cut. The operation took thirty-five minutes and I had the sensation of being scalped rather than barbered. My Gondar boy-friends are shocked and saddened—they say that now my virtue will certainly be safe on the way to Addis.

Morale is low this evening. Two of the six septic cuts on my legs have turned into inflamed, suppurating messes from which arrows of pain are shooting up my thigh and making me feel queasy. This is the logical consequence of having neglected them completely, amidst all the other alarms and excursions, and on Nancy O'Brien's advice I've started a course of antibiotics.

*12 February*

I had a grim night with my throbbing leg, which was accompanied by the throbbing of wedding drums in a compound just behind the hotel and by incessant chanting, hand-clapping and dog-barking. Today was spent lying on my bed, dozing and reading. Colonel Aziz says that the Court won't sit tomorrow, but perhaps on Tuesday. . . . Or perhaps not.

*13 February*

Today the robbers were told that if my camera had not been found by noon they would be given fifty-five lashes in the market-place tomorrow morning. The police expected me to rejoice at the prospect of my enemies receiving a public whipping—which I was cordially invited to attend—and Colonel Aziz announced the decision to inflict it in self-satisfied tones, as though he were displaying some extraordinary virtue of the Ethiopian police. His astonishment was considerable when I turned pale green and begged him not to do any such thing on my behalf. Then, recovering himself, he looked at me scornfully and exclaimed, '*This* is why you have so much crime in European countries!' Mercifully the threat of a whipping was sufficient. My camera is now at Police Headquarters and the Court will sit at ten o'clock tomorrow morning.

*14 February*

At 11.30 a.m. I was summoned to the Court-house and led along filthy corridors between rows of men who were squatting on their haunches with their backs to the walls, arguing quietly. The high-ceilinged courtroom was about sixty feet long and twenty feet wide. On a dais at one end three judges, robed in rusty black silk, sat behind a table covered with a green plastic cloth. The 'witness-box' was a small wooden table in the centre of the floor, behind which I sat with my 'recovered goods' and an Amharic Bible before me and a teacher as interpreter beside me. The 'dock' was a waist-high corrugated-iron pen on a dais to the right of the door as one entered. There was no jury, but the public—about fifty men—occupied benches behind the witness-box. Some of these men were waiting for their own cases to come up, others were indulging in one of the favourite pastimes of these litigation-loving highlanders.

The proceedings were orderly and subdued. When I had sat down the Public Prosecutor—also robed in black silk—took the chair on my right and read to the Court an Amharic translation of my statement. (No one present spoke English, except the teacher and Lieutenant Woldie.) Then the teacher read my original statement, and I stood up, laid a hand on the Bible, swore that it was a true statement and identified both my property and the prisoners. Next Lieutenant Woldie described the arrests and the finding of the stolen articles, and finally three of the four spoke in their own defence, only Kas Makonnen remaining silent. No one interrupted or hurried the accused. But they didn't speak for long, being obviously without hope, and the cross questioning was brief.

While the judges were deciding on the sentence the prisoners were taken to the corridor and I went to an adjacent room with my interpreter and Lieutenant Woldie. Twenty minutes later we were recalled, and the Chief Justice stood up and made a long speech about the loathsome iniquity of robbing *faranjs*. He then sentenced the four to two years imprisonment each and thirty lashes of the whip in the market-place at nine o'clock on next Saturday morning—this being the hour at which the greatest crowd is assembled for the biggest market of the week. Immediately I stood up and pleaded for the whipping to be reprieved—whereupon the whole Court, including the judges, rocked with mirth at this exhibition of quaint *faranj* squeamishness. The Chief Justice told me to sit down and stop being silly, or words to that effect; but later I learned that had an Ethiopian made a similar plea he would have been promptly sentenced to three months' imprisonment for contempt of Court.

At two o'clock I was back in my room, sombrely swigging *tej* and plunged in remorseful gloom. The judges had implied that the sentences were so severe because by robbing a *faranj* the prisoners had sullied Ethiopia's fair name, and it is shattering to feel responsible for three men being punished out of all proportion to their crime. (My compassion does not extend to

Kas Makonnen, who presumably will soon be receiving a far more severe sentence at the Central Criminal Court.)

These broodings were interrupted by a telephone call from the Palace, announcing that the Provincial Government had decided to replace my missing E. $120. I protested strongly, for all my expenses during this Gondar delay are being paid by the Government—most unnecessarily, since no Ethiopian asked me to go wandering alone amongst nests of *shifta*. However, my protests were ignored: and putting down the receiver I reflected that anyway the making of this generous gesture would lessen the locals' shame.

Just then Lieutenant Woldie walked into the bar, so I told him of the Governor's kindness and grovelled slightly about being an expensive nuisance to Ethiopia. But he only laughed—and by way of cheering me up explained that the E. $120 would be taken from the prisoners' families.

Now I was flung into the uttermost depths of guilty depression. Almost certainly these families got none of the money, so this system involves penalising a number of innocent people to whom E. $120 mean as much as E. $1200 would mean to me. Leaving the bar, I went to cosset my depression in the Royal Compound—where I've spent a lot of time during this past week.

Sitting outside the shell of Iyasu the Great's castle I eventually got things in perspective by dwelling on the deeds done within this very compound, and reasoning that my contribution to the history of cruelty in Ethiopia is not significant. I also began to see that it is impertinent for a *faranj* to criticise Ethiopian police methods in general, though obviously one should criticise particular excesses. In a country where the rural population cannot be communicated with through newspapers, or by radio, public floggings are the only effective method of publicising the fact that criminals have been caught, and of instilling respect for law and order. Nor does it do to forget that a century ago public executions were among the more popular entertainments of our own civilisation.

On my way back to the hotel I concentrated on silver linings. The sergeant at Gorgora is at last being promoted, as a reward for the efficiency and secrecy with which he organised things at his end, and the Ethiopians are now unique in my experience for no other police force has ever found what I have lost. When I was robbed at home the Irish police showed not one-tenth of the intelligence, efficiency and energy of Colonel Aziz and his men: but perhaps they would have exerted themselves a little more had I been an Ethiopian.

My plans to leave for Bahar Dar tomorrow morning were abruptly changed this evening. At the Itegue Menen Hotel I found John Bromley sitting in the lounge—newly arrived from Asmara—and half-an-hour later Peter rang, heard of my tribulations and commanded me to come to Asmara for a rest, before rejoining Jock. The idea of relaxing for two days in 'a little bit of England' seemed not unattractive, so I have booked seats on tomorrow's early bus to Asmara and on Sunday's flight from Asmara to Bahar Dar.


*15 February. Enda Selassie*

The large, comfortable Addis–Asmara bus left Gondar at 7.10 a.m. and arrived here at 5 p.m. It was only slightly over-crowded and had a cautious Eritrean driver whose caution was fully extended as we zig-zagged through the western extremity of the Semiens. I detest bus-travel, yet I am glad to have seen this road: even in the Himalayan foothills there is nothing comparable, for the terrain there makes no such outrageous demands. To cross the Takazze Gorge we descended steeply for eight miles in a series of tight hair-pin bends and then climbed north in a twin series. Those passengers from Addis who had never before seen the Gorge thought this wildly exciting; yet to me it was an anti-climax, since the road naturally crosses the Takazze at its tamest point.

Enda Selassie is a regular over-night stopping-place for bus-travellers and we are staying in the most pretentious of its few small hotels. The chief snag about a pretentious hotel in a drought area is the loo. Here it is unspeakable—and my room is next door. It would be far healthier to scrap this impractical Italian innovation and revert to the wide open spaces, where everyone is responsible for digging their own hole or finding their own flat stone.

*16 February. Asmara*

We left Enda Selassie at 7.30 a.m. and two hours later came to the Tigre–Eritrean boundary. Here a tall stone monument commemorates the re-unification of Ethiopia and the rough, gravel-topped road changes to smooth, well-kept tarmac.

We stopped for lunch at the Italianate town of Addi Ugri, where the sky quickly clouded over. Then, to my delighted astonishment, it began to *rain*, and as we approached Asmara a strong wind was sending low, grey clouds racing raggedly above the parched landscape. This was the first rain I had seen since leaving London, and while everyone else shivered and closed their windows I opened mine wider, the better to enjoy cold drops on my bare arms. However, the rain-storm didn't last long and in Asmara a hideous dust-storm was blowing instead.

When the bus pulled up at the terminus Peter was waiting for me. It was a joy to be with her again—and to be greeted by the big, silent grins of Christopher and Nicola.

*17 February*

Amidst a neolithic trek this interlude of English domesticity feels extraordinary—bacon and eggs for breakfast, afternoon tea, log fires, dogs on chairs, books everywhere, *The Times* only two days old and news from the B.B.C.

Tomorrow John arrives from Gondar with Sir Thomas and Lady Bromley (the British Ambassador and his wife), who are doing the Addis–Asmara trip by Land-Rover. So today preparations were being made for two official parties and I spent much of my time in the kitchen shelling walnuts, stoning prunes, grating nutmeg and beating eggs. Normally this would not be my idea of relaxation, yet here I enjoyed it enormously.

This afternoon thunder rumbled loudly around Asmara, followed by heavy rain that was being driven before a strong, cold wind—even the climate is making me feel at home.

*18 February*

The Land-Rover arrived at midday, and though John has a streaming cold and Sir Thomas has lumbago we achieved

such a gay lunch party that I slept away the afternoon. At six
o'clock the cocktail schemozzle started and I slunk back to my
room, being allergic to such entertainments. But as I lay reading Wodehouse the children rallied round so loyally that the
final accumulation of empty glasses looked positively de-
bauched. Now early to bed, for I must be at the airport by
7 a.m. tomorrow.

*19 February. Bahar Dar*

On arrival here I was enraged to find Jock in wretched condition, though I had left an ample 'feeding-fund' for him.
Obviously no one has bothered to supervise the servant in
charge, who seems to have pocketed most of the money and
given Jock some vile fodder that has blown him up dreadfully
and made his coat more starey than I have ever seen it. When
I called to him as I approached he pricked his ears and then
came towards me—which was indeed touching, for by now he
must associate his *faranj* owner with a variety of strenuous
horrors and unnerving predicaments. Evidently he knows that
he is appreciated.

Our tiny Ethiopian Airlines plane left Asmara at 7.30 a.m.
and arrived here three hours later, having stopped at Aksum,
Gondar and Debre Tabor. Asmara has an International Jet
Airport: elsewhere we came down on crude landing strips.
The crew were all Ethiopians and the pilot was extremely skilful, but inevitably there were lots of bumps. As we flew low over
the Semiens I heard my fellow-passengers exclaiming in awe
and the Englishman on my left remarked that this was such a
bloody impossible country one could only get around by air.
I agreed politely.

Then I found myself looking into the future instead of the
past. Debre Tabor lies on our route from Bahar Dar to Lalibela
and it was strange to think that the fifteen-minute flight will
probably be a four-day walk. From what I could see of the
terrain our next lap will not be an easy one.

Bahar Dar is 2,000 feet lower than Asmara and feels almost
tropical by comparison. I spent most of the afternoon swimming in Lake Tana—and now I must pack my sacks.

# 9

# *The Natives were Hostile*

Four years ago the Israelis, by way of 'aiding' Ethiopia, built a horrid bridge over the Blue Nile where it flows out of Lake Tana, and the desecration of this spot—once among the most romantic in Africa—has been completed by rows of shacks, a petrol station and a textile factory.

Beyond the bridge we left the motor-road, went north-east for a few miles through rough scrubland, climbed a forested hill and slithered down to wide, hot grasslands, where the issue was confused by many rivers. One flowed broad and deep through a patch of thick, dark jungle, and beside it Jock looked at me reproachfully; so after a quick swim I led him back to the grasslands, where for two hours we wandered up and down the high banks of several narrow, shallow rivers, whose fording points were always elusive. A few settlements lay on distant hillsides but we only met one local, a youth who asked all the usual questions in Amharinya: 'Where are you coming from? Where going to? Why alone? Why on foot?' Trying to answer, I walked on through the knee-high grass, leading Jock —who dawdled today, if not led. (The girths had to be tightened three times during the morning, as he got rid of his wind.) Then I felt a nervous jerk on the halter and looked round to see our companion racing away, clutching my sun-hat and an *injara*-basket which had been tied to the top of the load. I was furiously angry—the more so as I had been about to stop to put on my hat—but pursuit would have been futile. This theft is serious, for the basket (recently purchased in Gondar) contained compass, map, altimeter, torch, tin-opener, spoon, today's lunch-tin of tuna fish, water-pills and malaria pills. The pills and tin-opener I should be able to replace in Dessie, but the map and compass are irreplaceable between here and Addis —and without them it may be rather difficult to find Addis. At this latitude the mid-day sun doesn't help much and my sense of direction is not reliable on wriggly tracks.

When we got clear of the rivers a path of sorts led us across wooded hills and level grasslands until two o'clock. Then I saw a few compounds on a ploughed slope and a group of men beckoned me to join them for *talla*. This settlement seemed poor, yet all were eager to give me food as well as drink. I reported the theft here, and my host named a village from which the youth was likely to have come, declaring that its inhabitants are '*metfo*'.

Another series of hills, plains and rivers brought us to this settlement on a slope overlooking a broad valley. By chance I sought hospitality at the priest's compound, with a result that has been more diverting than edifying. My tall, thin, elderly host—who for some reason wears only his turban and a *shamma* —has friendly though cunning eyes and a stately manner. Like everyone else he was deceived by my Gondar hair-cut, and I hadn't been sitting long in the compound when he led his grand-daughter towards me and offered her love at two dollars for an hour or five dollars for the night. She was a very beautiful girl, who looked most willing to earn an honest dollar, and I pretended to consider the offer carefully. Then I settled for an hour, explaining solemnly that having walked from Bahar Dar I mightn't be up to an all-night session. By now the whole family had gathered round, and everyone saw this point and nodded understandingly as the girl sat close beside me, intending to give good value by not limiting her co-operation to one hour after dark. A moment later Grandad's little error had been discovered.

The poor girl exclaimed '*Set nat!*'—and there was an astonished silence, during which I grinned broadly at the company. Then everyone, including Grandad, roared with laughter. Immediately one man stood on a high rock to relay the joke to the next compound, illustrating his words with some not very decent gestures.

Here the cattle are sheltered at night in one enormous, communal stockade, elaborately reinforced with thorn bushes and guarded against thieves and wild animals by a group of youths and a pack of dogs. When we arrived the herds were still grazing on the valley floor and from all directions shepherds came running up the slope to inspect the *faranj* before darkness fell. It is strange to think of the responsibility borne by these little boys. As soon as they can walk they learn how to herd, and by the age of eight or nine many of them are in charge of almost the entire wealth of a family.

As I write two-thirds of a moon is brilliant overhead and lightning frequently spurts up the sky from behind the southern mountain. Neighbours by the dozen have been coming to view me and we are all sitting outside the *tukuls*—where it is so much brighter than inside—drinking *talla* and *araki* and eating *atar* from the pod. The loquacious womenfolk have become so engrossed in this impromptu party that there are no signs of supper, but I was given two raw eggs an hour ago and I'm now going to unroll my flea-bag on deep *teff* straw.

### 21 February. A Compound on a Mountainside

This morning I was shown the faint path to Debre Tabor by my host—still casually clad in a *shamma*, though canonically equipped with cross and fly-whisk. There is little traffic on this route and we were soon climbing into the first real mountains we've met since leaving the Semiens. This range is precipitous, heavily forested and almost entirely uncultivated; between 8 a.m. and 4 p.m. we passed only two distant settlements.

Soon after midday I saw a leopard—and my heart bounded with a mixture of delighted excitement and ancestral fear. The handsome creature had been lying along the branch of a tree, apparently asleep, and when our footsteps disturbed him he sprang to another tree and thence to the undergrowth in one swift, sinuous movement. I had tightened my grip on the halter, expecting some nervous reaction from Jock, but evidently his ancestral fears were not operating and he just plodded on, unflappable as ever.

From the top of this mountain I could see our path winding for miles along a grassy ridge that was narrow in relation to its length and had a deep valley on either side. Beyond these valleys two other long, high, unbroken ridges induced a peaceful sense of seclusion and here I sat on a boulder to eat raisins while sniffing at the sweet pungency of sun-beaten herbs, listening to a gentle orchestra of bird-song, and looking at a glory of flowering shrubs—pink, white, blue, yellow, purple, red. A few white clouds were making the intensely blue sky look even bluer and I hoped that soon they would cover the sun. With my head shaven and my hat stolen I'm already suffering from a burnt nape and burnt ears. (My ears being at right angles to my head makes them extra vulnerable.) As we continued a high, cool wind rose suddenly, driving masses of grey cloud before it—and once it even tried to rain. (For two months, from about mid-February, the highlands enjoy what are known as 'the Little Rains'—heavy showers that usually fall in the evenings.)

On the next mountainside I lost the path, and by 4.30 the sun had told me that we were going due south instead of north-east. However, we soon came to a village where I found a wide track that took us east for five miles over high, ploughed hills. The few people we met seemed rather surly—though not sufficiently so to prepare me for my reception here.

This settlement consists of five or six impoverished compounds near the top of a mountain. The first two families I approached not only refused me permission to sleep in their compound but shouted 'Hid!' and made threatening gestures with dulas. I hidded, endeavouring to combine alacrity with dignity, and cautiously continued towards two tukuls that stand in a stubble-field a little apart from the rest of the settlement. Here the gaunt young man of the house was far from welcoming, but he did grumpily agree to my sleeping in his compound, where there are two ferocious curs to repel hyenas and leopards.

While unloading, I heard loud moans coming from one tukul —where I found my host's young wife lying on a mud bed with a high fever. As she was complaining of severe pain in her lungs I decided to administer antibiotics and the first capsule seems to be working well. Her husband demanded murfee as soon as he realised that the faranj was carrying medicines and he turned quite sulky on hearing that I have none. These highlanders— like the Tibetans—much prefer injections to oral medicines. However, despite his churlishness towards the guest, my host is being endlessly patient and gentle with his wife. For the past three hours he has been sitting beside her, massaging her back, stroking her forehead and persuading her to drink tea and coffee. He also attempted the traditional 'horn treatment,' which seems to have affinities with Tibetan medical magic. Taking a long cow's horn he wrapped a large green leaf around the hole in the tip and tried to attach it to the body, on the site of the pain, by suction. To my disappointment his repeated efforts failed, so I don't know what the next step would have been.

This is an extremely poor household; the whole family looks undernourished and neither *injara* nor *talla* were served at supper-time, though there are three women sitting around the fire. Everyone had two fistfuls of boiled haricot beans and as much coffee as they wanted, for coffee is now commonly grown at this altitude.

Half-an-hour ago a worn-looking man of about fifty—who had earlier chased us from his compound—came to give me five tiny new-laid eggs. He is the father of my patient and this valuable gift has been presented, I gather, as 'compensation'. On learning that I am a woman he promptly volunteered to sleep beside me, as a bodyguard, and he seems quite overcome by remorse and gratitude—which confirms my opinion that these people's hostility was based on fear rather than ill-will.

Now I must give my patient another capsule and go to bed, hoping that I'll wake during the small hours to administer the next dose. As I write the poor woman is trying to suckle her frantically screaming two-year-old son—which seems unwise, but is at least a sign that she feels better.


*22 February. Camping in a Valley*

Last night I slept brokenly, but this morning had the reward of leaving my patient smiling and feverless.

We set off at seven o'clock and for two hours were walking east on a much-used track across undulating country. Many slopes were being ploughed and from every direction came the sharp cries and curious whistles of youths driving yokes of oxen, and the gun-shot cracks of long whips echoed and re-echoed over the wide, serene landscape. Then the terrain became rougher and the track vaguer, but I never quite lost it and at eleven o'clock we reached a big village shaded by tall blue-gums.

Already thirst was torturing me, for without water-purifying pills I am dependent on *talla*. So I toured the compounds, and at the fifth *tukul* was offered a feeble brew and a meal of stale, slimy *injara* and fiery *berberie* paste. Several young men came to sit around me, stopping on their way to examine Jock's load, and the atmosphere was unpleasant. They lacked the normal highland courtesy and made no attempt to talk with me, but were all the time discussing me and my *buccolo*.

When I stood up to leave my elderly hostess blocked the doorway and aggressively demanded two dollars for less than fifty cents worth of food and drink. This sort of thing angers me. I had intended giving one dollar, but now I handed over fifty cents and firmly pushed past her, to find myself followed by three youths, who attempted to take my purse from my pocket. I was about to be discreet instead of valorous when a gunman appeared around the side of the *tukul*, wearing a bush shirt, clean jodhpurs and an air of authority. He must have been a local official, for at once the youths slipped away around the other side of the circular hut. I then picked up Jock's halter, exchanged greetings with the gunman and departed.

The people of this area seem so unpredictable that I'm glad we didn't begin our trek here. By now familiarity with highland ways has given me a lot more self-confidence, in relation to the highlanders, than I had when I landed at Massawah.

Beyond the village I detected a faint path running east through tall jungle grass. Here we met another gunman who stopped to warn me, dramatically and emphatically, about the number of *shifta* said to be at present infesting the forests on the way to Debre Tabor. His was the first of six similar warnings I received today; but even if it is true that *shifta* abound locally I can do nothing about it—except pray that they won't notice us.

The noon sun felt brutally hot as we climbed a stony, shrub-dotted mountain. On the plateau summit, where much *teff*-threshing was in progress, we passed two locked churches and a few settlements before descending a precipitous, thickly-forested slope on a crumbling path. At the foot of this mountain, beyond a group of three dejected compounds, the path vanished and for the next four hours I saw no vestige of a track going in any direction.

At 2.30 I enjoyed a long swim in a deep, narrow river. All day I had been sweating hard, so my self-control collapsed here and I drank avidly. I wonder if those experts who tell us that our sexual appetite is the strongest know what real thirst feels like; I can imagine the desire for water driving someone to commit a crime to which sexual desire could never drive them.

Crossing the river we climbed another high hill, populated by grey baboons, and here a surprisingly unalarmed leopard went strolling through the grass thirty yards ahead of us—to the great annoyance of the baboons. For the next half-hour thick forest forced us to go in whichever direction was possible, rather than in the approximately right direction; and when the trees thinned we crossed two more hills, where flowering shrubs were bright between massive outcrops of rock. Here I heard several new bird-calls and saw some spectacular butterflies and many busily buzzing bees—one of whom got over-busy and gave me an agonising sting on the back of my neck.

By 4.30 we were on top of a third hill which, like the other two, might be more accurately described as a mountain—if the climbing of three mountains in rapid succession didn't sound a little improbable. I spent twenty minutes finding a way down from this broad summit. On one side the forest was impenetrable, on another there was a sheer 500-foot precipice overlooking a wooded ravine, and ahead there were minor precipices, fearsome tangles of thorny scrub, high grass and low trees. This scrub was excruciating. Its thorns proved easily detachable from its branches, but not easily detachable from one's skin; just now I have been painfully picking them out of my arms and legs. Also the dry, slippery waist-high grass concealed treacherously broken ground, and on one steep slope I skidded, tumbled sideways into a gully and wrenched my right knee. This was slightly alarming, but having recovered from the first shock of pain I realised that the injury was not severe. Soon after I saw how we could descend, by zig-zagging to avoid cliffs, gullies and scrub-tangles, and half-an-hour later we were on level grassland, where hundreds of grey baboons swarmed between gigantic trees.

Another mile brought us to inhabited country. Here three small boys, collecting wood beside a stream, fled into the undergrowth at our approach and a pathlet led us to a slope where a young man was ploughing, chanting as he followed his oxen. Like many of the people of this region he was very dark-skinned (evidently Agow blood is unusually thick here) and when he noticed us he paused to stare in silent astonishment, before shouting a *shifta* warning. Then—his duty done—he showed no further interest, but turned back to his oxen, cracked his whip and resumed his chanting.

One of the most obvious highland characteristics is a lack of interest in the passing *faranj*. Even the few people who spontaneously offer hospitality remain essentially aloof from their guest, which can be disconcerting. Yet this aloofness is no longer creating the barrier it once did. My return to the true highlanders, after that 'urban' interlude, has made me realise what an unexpectedly deep affection I am developing for them—though the people around here are not conspicuously lovable.

By now my knee had become troublesome and as we approached a large settlement of scattered compounds I was in real pain. Our appearance roused a hostility that seemed more deep-seated than last evening's, and for some reason my antennae warned me not to trust these people. I was immediately chased out of the first two compounds I entered and, when the women stoned me vigorously in the third, while the men stood by applauding their wives' initiative, I decided to get away from it all.

As I retreated—rubbing an elbow, where one sharp missile had found its target—dusk was thick in the valley below the settlement; and by the time I had hobbled down to this level stretch of grassland at the foot of the mountain it was dark, but with a promise of moonlight. While I was unloading Jock we had the first rain of the trek—a downpour that continued for twenty minutes, leaving the air deliciously fresh.

Travelling in this country fosters an abnormal degree of fatalism, doubtless produced by one's subconscious as a protection against nervous breakdowns. Tonight I'm past caring about untrustworthy locals, *shifta*, leopards or hyenas. The probability is that Jock and I will survive, and the possibility that either or both might be attacked has ceased to worry me.

*23 February. Debre Tabor*

At some time last night I woke suddenly, to see a sky wonderfully patterned with slowly-sailing, silvered clouds—and among them was the full moon, radiant against a royal blue background. I turned, and lay gazing up for some moments in a curiously disembodied state of enchantment; it seemed that I had ceased to exist as a person and had become only an apprehension of the beauty overhead. Perhaps such a sky may be seen quite often but, unaccountably, there was for me some supreme loveliness, some magical glory in this silent, drifting movement of silver against blue. And the memory of it has strengthened me throughout a painful day.

My knee was stiff and swollen this morning, and it didn't improve during our ten-hour walk. Yet not even constant pain can dull one's enjoyment of these endlessly varied highlands, where our trek has never taken us through the same sort of country for more than half a day.

I hadn't hoped to be at Debre Tabor by nightfall, and it is a sheer fluke that we have got here so soon without benefit of map, compass, intelligent peasants or clear tracks. Today I lost count of the mountains we crossed. Until 3 p.m. we passed no settlements, yet occasionally I heard shepherds calling in the distance, so there must have been compounds somewhere. Often the path disappeared, but always I found it again, though at the time I never knew whether it was the right track or not. We forded several rivers and I had three swims—noticing evidence of local inhabitants, who had left their marks along the banks or on flat stones in midstream. It seems odd that the imprudence of using one's water supply as a latrine is not obvious even to the most backward people. During the morning I almost trod on the tail of a leopard who was asleep under a bush by the path. Momentarily I mistook the tail for a snake; then its owner woke up and streaked into the undergrowth with a snarl of fear—which did slightly upset Jock.

Soon after 3 we reached a mountain-top where a large church, surrounded by ancient oleasters, indicated that we had left the forested wilds. From here I could see many blue-gums on another, higher mountain-top, beyond a wide valley, and I guessed correctly that these marked Debre Tabor.

This last lap took three hours and the final tough climb, to 8,500 feet, left me weak with pain.

In the valley were several settlements and a few flocks of mangy sheep. Below Debre Tabor the mountainside was crudely irrigated, which is unusual, though the early Semitic settlers introduced irrigation to the highlands and in Tigre there are many traces of canals. But this skill, like Semitic architecture, never spread south and has long since been lost in the north.

From the edge of Debre Tabor delighted children escorted us up a long, rough 'street', between stalls displaying the usual limited array of goods, to the main 'square' where two Peace Corps boys promptly appeared and invited me to be their guest. Debre Tabor is the most isolated Peace Corps post in Ethiopia, so I didn't hesitate to accept this invitation—though in general I am against sponging on volunteer workers.

However, I soon discovered that my acceptance had created an International Situation. Days ago the Governor-General had telephoned from Gondar and arranged for my entertainment here, and the local Governor was all set to receive me. This really was awkward. I would have preferred to stay with the Governor, and it seemed ungracious not to; but the Americans looked crestfallen at the prospect of losing their *faranj* guest and to treat their invitation as a 'second-best' would seem worse than ungracious. Therefore I compromised, and when my knee had been tightly bandaged I hobbled off to the Governor's house, split a bottle of *tej* with him and had supper there. He is a kindly man, who understood my predicament and settled for entertaining Jock instead of me.

*24 February*

Today my knee needed so much rest that I have seen little of Debre Tabor. I lunched with the Governor and his inter-preter, whose English is not much more fluent than my Am-harinya. Having listened to this language during so many long evenings, and been forced sometimes to struggle seriously with it, I find that even my linguistic blockage is now giving way a little.

Debre Tabor was an Italian outpost, so the Governor's quarters, the police barracks and the school are ugly, one-storey concrete buildings at the edge of the town. The Italians also built a motor-road from Gondar through Debre Tabor to Dessie, but many of the twenty bridges between Gondar and here were blown up by the Italian army as it retreated before the British liberators, and the rest have been allowed to collapse —as has the road itself. It seems that the Government is as casual about roads as the local chieftains are about tracks. In Nepal, where in most areas communication is also confined to mountain tracks, the village headmen co-operate to organise track maintenance; but here such a communal effort would be unthinkable. If a highland track becomes impassable it is usually repaired by the merchants who are most dependent on it, otherwise maintenance is carried out only if the Emperor or a Governor-General is to visit a particular area, and then the work is so inefficiently done that the track soon relapses into its natural 'state of chassis'.

On my way back from the Governor's house I called at the Seventh-Day Adventist Mission, which was established here in the 1930's and runs a large school and a hospital. It is illegal for missionaries to proselytise Ethiopian Christians and the few Falasha or Muslim converts to Catholicism or Protestantism are not regarded as true Christians by the highlanders. How-ever, to qualify for all the advantages offered by this school a number of locals do become temporary Seventh-Day Adventists.

I don't expect to find twin souls in missionary compounds, but the ideals of this contingent completely unnerved me. After listening for some fifteen minutes to an earnest young woman I took out my cigarettes and said automatically 'Do you mind if I smoke?' The air froze. My hostess looked at me as though I had uttered an obscenity. Then she said, 'We never permit habit-forming drugs here'—and went on to explain that tea is a sinful stimulant. Whereupon I looked at my watch, muttered wildly about an improbable urgent appointment and retreated in disorder.

My Peace Corps hosts have now been here long enough to realise that at present the education of young highlanders is 95 per cent farce and 5 per cent achievement. Most of Debre Tabor's twenty-five Ethiopian teachers are themselves poorly educated and have had little or no training for their job. Many of the 1,050 pupils come from settlements or villages two to six days' walk away, as is usual, and they live with relatives or in rented *tukuls* or rooms shared by six or eight children. About one-fifth are girls—a surprisingly large proportion—and everyone's ambition is to qualify for Gondar Secondary School. Yet the few who do qualify rarely achieve much in competition with city-born pupils—unless they are Muslims, whose average intelligence is higher than that of the Christian majority. However, this superiority increases their unpopularity with the local authorities, so the winning of scholarships can be even more difficult for them than for the others.

## 25 *February*

This morning I did a test walk to the local 'famous church'. It stands on a high mountain, overlooking the (comparative) lowlands that we crossed on our way from Bahar Dar, and to the north-east I could see the towering barrier of rough ranges which lies between here and Lalibela.

The church was locked and in the nearby settlement no one would volunteer to open it. Situations like this repeatedly reveal an ingrained unhelpfulness in the highland character. Beside the enclosure, on the highest point of the broad summit, stand the overgrown ruins of one of those Italian stone forts which were constructed on many hilltops to repel Patriot raids. Climbing up, I sat there for more than an hour, gazing over the vastness and thinking of the nineteenth-century Englishmen who made their way to Debre Tabor.

Early in the nineteenth century, when Gondar was still the nominal capital, Ras Gugsa, the most powerful noble of the day, chose this town as his headquarters; and he was succeeded by Ras Ali, to whose court Lord Palmerston sent Walter Plowden as consul in 1848. Plowden was accompanied by John Bell, who had been with him on his first visit to Abyssinia in 1843 and who was to become a close friend of the Emperor Theodore. On arrival Plowden wrote, 'Debre Tabor ... is cold and healthy, but there is no stone house in it but that of the Ras.' Three years of negotiation led to a trade treaty, which was signed in Ras Ali's inner tent where the nobleman and the consul sat on carpets laid over the bare earth. Plowden wrote, 'After the Abyssinian manner he (Ras Ali) kept talking . . . about a horse that was tied in the tent, and that was nearly treading me under-foot a dozen times.' A few months later Ras Ali was conquered by Kassa (Theodore to be) and after his coronation Kassa also made Debre Tabor his headquarters because he despised Gondar as a 'city of merchants'. Then, before moving to Magdala, he burned Debre Tabor to the ground—not a difficult feat, if there was only one stone house among hundreds of *tukuls*.

In 1879 General Gordon arrived at Debre Tabor from Egypt, to make peace on the Khedive's behalf. The rebuilt town had become Yohannes IV's capital and Gordon was not impressed by the highland nobles. He wrote, 'I have seen many peoples, but I never met with a more fierce, savage set than these. The peasantry are good enough.' At that time there were several foreigners at the court. Gordon mentions meeting the Greek consul from Suez and three Italians—and this after-noon, in a *tej-beit*, I met an English-speaking local merchant who told me that his great-grandfather was 'an Egyptian Greek'. Yohannes IV and General Gordon did not get on well. The only thing they had in common was their destiny, for both were soon to be killed by followers of the Mahdi.

Returning to the town, I spent a few hours drinking in *tej-beits* and walking along rough laneways beneath tall blue-gums between solid houses of stone and mud. The population is now about 7,000 and the people are polite and friendly; as this is one of the province's most important market-centres 3,000 out-siders sometimes attend the Saturday market. Debre Tabor is also renowned for the number of its hyenas, the largeness of its donkeys and the potency of its *araki*—which is sold in Gondar, and sometimes even in Addis.

At 5.30 I returned to the Governor's house to eat strips of fried dried beef and drink more high-class *talla* and *tej*. The highlanders must be among the world's heaviest drinkers; several teachers have told me that children often roll in to school in a semi-inebriated condition, or give total inebriation as their reason for non-attendance. Yet I have never seen a drunken adult Ethiopian; and *talla* and *tej* are such healthy drinks that they cannot produce a hangover.

My knee doesn't feel quite as painless tonight as it did this morning; but tomorrow we leave for Lalibela.

# 10

## *Mapless in Lasta*

*26 February. Kummerdingai*

Today's landscape was a complete contrast to last week's hot, silent world of golden-brown hills and valleys. Here we are on wide, cool uplands, where cattle and horses graze off sweeping yellow-green pastures, and the new-ploughed fields are grey-flecked with stones, and each hilltop has its tree-shaded settlement and streams sparkle every few miles.

Soon after midday we came to a compound where the men-folk were sitting drinking. One of them asked our destination, told me that we had gone astray and invited me to stop for *talla* before being guided back to the right track. Then, as I sat on a goatskin brought from a *tukul* in my honour, and felt kindliness lapping round me, I had to admit to myself that the locals' attitude is important—though one may pretend at the time that it doesn't much matter if most people glare and some people throw stones. Loneliness never touches me in uninhabited country, where my solitude is complete: but I do feel twinges of it where people are particularly unresponsive.

By four o'clock I was limping so badly that I received much incomprehensible medical advice from a group of men driving five spavined horses, piled high with hides, to Debre Tabor. Soon after we were overtaken by a tall, thin, elderly man with bright, deep-set eyes. He looked at my knee—now swelling again—muttered '*Metfo!*' firmly took Jock's halter, led us to this big village, installed me in his square, bug-infested hut and ordered his wife to scramble eggs for the *faranj*. He, too, had walked from Debre Tabor, and soon his young daughter appeared with a tin of warm water and a wooden bowl, to give us both a foot-wash and thorough massage from toes to knees.

She paid special and rather painful attention to my right knee, and ended the ceremony by respectfully kissing my left big toe.

Kummerdingai is on a flat, windswept plateau, overlooked from the north by a range of rounded mountains. All day we had been climbing gradually and now the night air is so cold that I reckon we must be at about 9,000 feet. This seems a prosperous area, but my host's family is very poor. They have no *talla*, and for Sunday supper they ate only *injara* and *berberie* paste; yet fifteen minutes ago the guest was given a second meal of *injara* and scrambled eggs.

*27 February. Sali*

Beyond Kummerdingai our track switchbacked for three hours over a series of steep, arid, smooth-topped ridges. Then we climbed to a wide, green plateau, where scores of horses were grazing, and from a large settlement two teachers came running towards us, shouting invitations to drink coffee. Settlements don't normally have schools, but I soon discovered that the local headman is an unusually civic-spirited individual, who went to Gondar and persuaded the authorities to open a school, guaranteeing to organise the building of a school-house by volunteer workers, and to provide for the teachers at his own expense. Happily, he has got the teachers he deserves—two refreshingly idealistic Gondares, who don't at all resent living in discomfort and isolation.

Both the headman and his wife are charming, and he is one of the handsomest men I have ever seen—aged about fifty, well over six feet, broad-shouldered, with the head of a lion and the bearing of a king.

For two hours we sat in a large, clean, high-roofed *tukul*, drinking *talla* from glass carafes and coffee from tiny cups. Our conversation flowed with unusual ease, partly because the teachers spoke reasonably good English and partly because my host and hostess asked such intelligent questions. The coffee was being roasted, ground and brewed by a good-looking woman of twenty-eight, who had come from Gondar with the twenty-three-year-old boys as their joint temporary wife;

recently her husband divorced her on grounds of infertility, but already she seems happy in her new rôle.

My *dula* split this morning, and when I was leaving my hostess noticed this and immediately fetched me a replacement which is much stronger than the original. It was now 11.30 and the sun felt uncomfortably strong, despite a cool, steady breeze. Yesterday the sky had become half-clouded over by eleven o'clock, but today there was no such relief and at this altitude the ultra-violet rays are quite fierce.

Before long I had again lost the right track, so we descended to a river, failed to receive directions from youths who were watering cattle, climbed a steep, forested mountain, crossed a few barley fields and went wandering over wide, windy slopes of short, golden grass. Here there were no paths and Jock found the slippery turf difficult; but soon I saw a clear stretch of main track, on the flank of the opposite ridge, and for the next two hours we were crossing undulating ploughland—mile after mile of it, sweeping brownly up to the deep blue sky.

From the edge of this plateau I was suddenly looking down into an enchanting little valley, set deep amidst rough grey peaks. On a floor of red-gold grass tawny-thatched *tukuls* were surrounded by slim green trees and each colour glowed pure and soft in the mellow afternoon brilliance.

These scattered compounds make up the village of Sali, and this morning's teachers had given me a letter to their two *confrères* here. When we arrived my hosts were still at school, but their servant—a squat adolescent girl, plain by highland standards—welcomed me warmly, though timidly, and provided a foot-wash and massage, followed by a meal of fried dried meat and cold *injara*. Then the headman brought gifts of *talla* for me and fodder for Jock. The locals are more likeable than my singularly unintelligent Debarak-born hosts, who long to give up teaching and get 'better jobs', preferably as bank clerks in Asmara or Addis.

Tomorrow I'm going to the village of Bethlehem, where Thomas Pakenham discovered a well-preserved medieval church in 1955. To get from there to Lalibela I must return to Sali, so Jock will have a day off.

This two-roomed mud hovel was built three years ago, when

the school opened, and it seems to be bugless though it vibrates with fleas. (Compared with what I feel for bugs my feeling for fleas is a tender affection.) The boys want to sacrifice one of their beds in the inner room but, as I have not enough faith in the establishment's buglessness to risk this, I will share the living-room floor with the servant.

*28 February*

What misery! Last night I woke with a searing pain in my chest, a savage headache and what felt like congestion of the lungs. Groping through my sacks in the dark I found aspirin and antibiotics and then sat with my back to the wall, painfully struggling to breathe—if I lay down I at once experienced a terrifying suffocating sensation. Yet I had gone to sleep at 9.30 feeling perfectly well, so this was no ordinary influenza or bronchitis germ. Presumably it was sun-stroke and, as I wheezed agonizingly through four long, dark hours, I tried to forget that sunstroke can cause pneumonia. Dawn was breaking before the suffocating sensation lessened—but an hour after taking the second acromycin I felt so much better that I decided to act on the 'Fresh Air and Exercise' principle and stick to my plans for today.

At nine o'clock I set off, with two schoolboys as guides, and four hours' walking took us to Bethlehem. All the ascents were steep and at every breath my lungs felt as though they were being simultaneously compressed by some instrument of torture and scraped with sandpaper. I had brought my spare shirt to drape over my head and neck—a precaution I should have taken yesterday—but by 10.30 kind clouds had half covered the sky.

Part of this walk was through 'conventional' mountain scenery that might have been in the Himalayan foothills, but most of it was across roughly beautiful ridges—some thickly forested, some ploughed, some grassy—and from each crest wild ranges of dusky-blue mountains were visible against the horizon.

Bethlehem is a big settlement on a high spur. When we arrived a service was being held, to celebrate one of the innumerable Coptic feasts in honour of Mariam, and from without the enclosure we could hear splendid chanting and the beating of many drums and the clicking of many *sistra*. I felt reluctant to distract the faithful by appearing during the service, but my guides hurried me in, and at once I was surrounded by the entire congregation and welcomed by several polite, unpredatory priests.

At first sight Bethlehem's church looks like any other circular highland church. To quote from Thomas Pakenham: 'The *tukul* church was simply a rude veneer overlying an older church. Preserved inside the circular mud walls and under the conical roof was a rectangular mediaeval church of the most exciting design: the vast stumpy timbers of the doorways, and the pink stone walls polished like porphyry were finer of their sort than any yet known . . . I had . . . discovered an entirely unknown mediaeval church of the most dramatically exciting style.'

At that time (eleven years ago) 'there were many eighteenth-century frescoes painted on linen hangings superimposed on the pink stones of the west facade'. Now there are only marks on the walls, indicating where these frescoes once hung. The priests—assuming that I had come specially to look at the paintings—released a cataract of apologetic explanations, which conveyed nothing whatever to me. In fact I was not particularly disappointed, for the church itself had made my painful detour seem well worth while.

At the end of the service my guides and I were invited to accompany the priests, the village elders and the boy deacons to a broad ledge below the enclosure, where we sat under giant wild fig-trees that looked as old as the world, and ate blessed hot *dabo* and drank thick grey-green *talla* from huge, yellow-brown gourds.

Beneath us a profound semicircular gorge separated our mountain from the blue-green-ochre slopes of its neighbours—and to all this wild glory cloud shadows ceaselessly brought subtle changes.

Soon a deacon came down the path carrying on his head a goat-skin full of roast *atar*, and when the peas had been poured on to wicker platters these were laid within reach of every little group. Meanwhile other deacons were refilling gourds, fetching fresh pots of *talla* and distributing second rounds of *dabo*; and the priests and elders were discussing their own affairs, having lost interest in me as a *faranj* with characteristic rapidity. As a guest, however, I was not neglected: the chief priest repeatedly used his fly-whisk for my benefit and never allowed my gourd to be empty of *talla* or my fist of *dabo*. And here I felt such a deep contentment that this became—all unexpectedly—one of my happiest hours in these highlands.

There are two phases of enjoyment in journeying through an unknown country—the eager phase of wondering interest in every detail, and the relaxed phase when one feels no longer an observer of the exotic, but a participator in the rhythm of daily life. Now I am at ease among the highlanders, for wherever I go, in this static, stylised society, everything seems familiar. Not only the graceful formalities—significant though minute—but the long, lean faces and the clear brown eyes, the way men flick *atar* from palm to mouth, the movement of settling *shammas* about their bodies when they sit, their stance as they stand and talk, leaning their hands on the ends of a *dula* that rests across their shoulders, the harsh, staccato language, the expressive gesticulations, the sudden bursts of apparent anger that can quickly change to laughter. All this makes up a world which only two months ago seemed puzzling, amusing and sometimes a little frightening, yet which now seems as normal as my own far world away to the north.

Soon after we left Bethlehem it rained heavily for about twenty minutes. At sunset we were crossing the wide plain that lies below Sali and here the scene was so autumnal that it reminded me of Ireland in late September: above a gold-brown ridge lay sombre, torn clouds, against a blue-green horizon, and the cold wind was gusty.

This evening the headman and his wife called to see me, bringing another kettle of *talla*. All the usual questions were asked and my answers provoked the usual reactions. It really distresses the highlanders to hear that I have no parents, brothers, sisters, husband or children. Some of the women almost weep in sympathy and an Amharic proverb is often quoted: 'It is better to be unborn than to be alone.'

*1 March. A Village on an Amba*

I felt better this morning, despite a restless night of wheezing. When we left Sali at 7.30 the sky was grey and for four hours we were climbing gradually across still, sunless widths of ploughland and moorland. From the edge of this plateau I saw a little town which seemed hardly twenty minutes walk away; but below the plateau there were so many deep chasms to be negotiated that it was one o'clock before we reached Nefas Moja.

At a *tej-beit* a kind woman filled me with *talla, tej* and tea, but would accept no payment. When we continued the sun was out, so I tied my spare shirt round my head. We were now back in 'precipitous' country, and during one nightmare descent poor Jock almost lost his footing on a narrow path overhanging a sheer drop of at least seven hundred feet. Then the track levelled out and for six miles wound round the flanks of forested mountains, with deep, golden valleys on our left, an upheaval of blue ranges beyond them and no settlements visible.

Soon we were overtaken by two men driving a donkey. The elder, aged about fifty, was small, slim and one-eyed—and I disliked the look in that one eye. The other, aged about twenty, was burly and thick-lipped, and at once he took Jock's halter and urged me to walk on ahead. This is a common highland courtesy, but it was clear that my present companions were not being inspired by good manners. However, I feigned friendliness and walked beside the older man, behind Jock, watching my load. I felt so uneasy that had we met travellers going towards Nefas Moja I would have returned to the town with them.

Then my one-eyed companion began to beg whiningly for clothes and medicines. When I denied having either his whining changed to truculence and he ran ahead, prodded the sacks and demanded to be told what was in them. As I replied 'Faranj injara' the young man turned suddenly and asked where my money was. I said that I had no money, whereupon both laughed unpleasantly and remarked that every *faranj* has much money. For a few moments they stood discussing the situation *sotto voce*, and then they invited me, with artificial cordiality, to spend the night at their settlement. Obviously they feared to unload Jock on a main track and to gain time I accepted their invitation.

The next fifty minutes felt like as many hours. Often I glanced back to see if anyone was overtaking us; at every turn of the path I looked hopefully for someone ahead or for signs of a settlement, and all the time I was listening for the calls of shepherds or ploughmen—but these mountains were too thickly forested to be grazed or cultivated. As I was considering asserting myself before we reached the settlement, where everyone would be likely to support their relatives against me, the path turned another corner and I saw a man and woman ahead, walking very slowly. Grabbing the halter I ran as fast as Jock would trot and we overtook them just where a faint path branched off towards my companions' settlement.

The couple had been walking slowly because the woman was ill; her eyes were glazed with pain and she scarcely noticed me. Both husband and wife were, I should think in their forties, and the man, too, looked unwell. He stared at me blankly when I offered him Jock's halter, pointed ahead and emphatically repeated, 'Debre Zeit! Debre Zeit!'. Then the two toughs caught us up and his expression became uneasy as they began to talk angrily, pointing first to Jock and then towards their settlement, high above the track. They were claiming to have been put in charge of me by the local Governor, and my friend seemed a person of minimal intelligence who only wanted to keep clear of the situation. Making a gesture of indifference he turned away, beckoning his wife to follow. I despairingly pulled out my purse, thrust a dollar into his right hand and the halter into his left, and repeated pleadingly 'Debre Zeit!' He gazed for a moment at the money, frowned and returned it—but to my astonished relief he retained the halter, suddenly shook his dula at the toughs with unexpected vigour, and quickly led Jock down the main track. Strolling nonchalantly after him, I looked back and saw the toughs climbing towards their settlement, still glancing covetously in our direction. It is most unlikely that they would have harmed me, but in this country one never quite knows what might be regarded as a sufficient motive for murder.

At a small village I said grateful good-byes to the pathetic couple. Here we were back in a region of overwhelming heights and depths, of symmetrical *ambas*, sheer escarpments and grotesquely eroded peaks. As the afternoon advanced the valleys were filled with a wonderful light, like pale blue smoke, through which I could see expanses of rose-coloured earth glowing on steep slopes above green-gold forests.

Near the base of the gruelling escarpment below this plateau we met a handsome young gunman who claimed to be 'the Police'. I knew that he was lying, and I disliked his plausible manner and mistrusted his speculative glances towards Jock's load, but as my knee was now throbbing again it helped to have someone to show us the easiest way up the escarpment and when we reached this settlement everyone looked so surly that I choose the devil I knew slightly and accepted the youth's invitation to sleep within his compound.

My host's family consists of his mother, a child-wife and two other women, and the atmosphere in this *tukul* is unique. All the time I am being laughed at unkindly—a discourtesy I wouldn't have thought possible among Ethiopian highlanders —and payment in advance has been demanded for every glass of *talla* I've drunk, for my *injara* and *berberie* paste and for Jock's fodder.

As I write, *injara* is being cooked beside me. The batter is poured on to a flat iron skillet from an earthen jar (in which it has been fermenting for three or four days) and is then covered with a conical pottery lid. A round takes hardly five minutes to cook, over a hot wood fire, and when the housewife has skilfully slid it on to the *injara*-stand she wipes the skillet thoroughly with a filthy rag soaked in vegetable oil, and starts again. *Injara* jars are never washed so scraps of stale dough speed the fermentation of each fresh mixture.

To-day I noticed some *tukuls* solidly built of stone and a few men wearing brown, or brown and black check blankets instead of *shammas*. These reminded me of the shepherds' blankets in the Kangra Valley in northern India, though here the workmanship is much inferior to anything one sees in Asia.

Now I'm going to take my flea-bag out to the smooth turf of

the compound and sleep beneath cool, brilliant stars; but because of the ferocity of the local hyenas Jock is being stabled in the *tukul*.

## 2 March. A Settlement on a Hillside

This morning my host woke me before it was light and seemed most anxious to see our backs, though highland hosts usually try to delay a guest's departure. He had already brought out my kit from the *tukul* and was attempting to load Jock but could make no sense of the Italian saddle. He had tied the sacks, which I left open last night, and when he saw me untying one of them, to insert my flea-bag and Huskies, he became abusive. Investigating, I saw that he had stolen my tin-box of coins and everything else had been examined, though nothing else was missing. Now he was standing over me, scowling, and when I stood up he poked me roughly with his rifle and told me to load quickly and go. His fear suggested that by reporting to the headman I could recover my money, but remembering the unfriendly glares when we arrived last evening I decided to ignore the theft. This incident was another illustration of the average highlanders' lack of intelligence. Had my host behaved normally this morning I would never have thought of checking my possessions before leaving.

As we were walking across the table-flat plateau, towards a lemon-streaked, red-flecked east, I heard someone yelling '*Faranj! Faranj!*' and looked round to see a young couple with three small children running to overtake us. They were going to visit relatives at Debre Zeit—twelve miles away, at the end of the plateau—and the father asked if their sickly five-year-old boy might ride on top of my load. Already the child was whimpering, so I could hardly say 'no', and he beamed delightedly when lifted on to the sacks. His eight-year-old sister walked sturdily with the adults, but his three-year-old brother rode all the way on Father's shoulders.

For six miles our path ran level over parched grassland. Then it switchbacked through scrub—where baboons barked at us, and two hyenas went slinking into the bushes at our approach —and at 9.45 we saw the blue-gums of Debre Zeit against the horizon. I stopped briefly for *talla* at my companions' destination, and then several boys guided me to the edge of the plateau and pointed out the downward path—a narrow, rocky stairway of blood-chilling instability.

I paused here, and looking north saw one massive square mountain, towering above scores of other blue giants. Undoubtedly this was Abuna Josef (13,747 feet), which overlooks Lalibela—and when without map or compass it is reassuring to have such a conspicuous landmark. Then I gazed down at the intervening chaos of mountains and gorges, and remembered that somewhere among them, hidden deep, the tortuous Takazze Gorge was waiting to renew our acquaintance. There are two special moments in a trek like this—the moment of challenge, when you first sight such a stretch of country, and the moment of triumph, when you look back over the same stretch as its conqueror. In the present case that moment of triumph still feels very far away.

From the base of the escarpment we slithered down a precipitous ploughed slope and were suddenly confronted with the most difficult descent yet. This was not a straightforward progress from high to low, but an involved scramble up, down and across a confusing complex of cliffs, ridges, and crags on which the path sometimes overhung drops of up to 1,000 feet. I enjoy rugged mountains, deep valleys and precarious situations—but one can have too much of anything.

We were three-quarters down when Jock lost his footing and went over the edge. I could hardly grasp the horror of it as I watched him fall. My mind refused to register that this really was happening. He landed on his back, on a narrow ledge some thirty feet below the track—and then rolled off on to the next ledge, twenty feet lower. Mercifully this second ledge was about fifteen feet wide. Had he again rolled off he would have crashed onto rocks three hundred feet below.

Knowing nothing of the durability of mules I was astounded to see him scrambling to his feet, apparently intact. Impatience to examine him sent me down that cliff like a baboon—forgetful of my knee, which was severely re-wrenched on the way. The poor fellow was trembling all over—and so was I—but he seemed quite unharmed, and when I realised this I flung my

arms around his neck and burst into tears. One could easily
buy another mule, but one could never buy another Jock.

When we had pulled ourselves together I set about collecting
my kit, which was strewn all over the two ledges. Yet the
saddle was still in place: probably it had been both the cause
of Jock's fall and the shield which preserved him from injury.
(Very likely Italian loading techniques were not adopted here
because in these mountains it is safer to avoid protuberances on
either side.) Little damage had been done, apart from a box of
carbon paper being ruined by a burst tin of insecticide. Even
my precious bottle of ink and my still more precious fountain-
pen were unbroken. However, I soon discovered that it is not
easy to load a mule on a ledge fifteen feet by ten, above a sheer
drop of three hundred feet—particularly when the nerves of all
concerned are in bits. It took me twenty minutes to get organised, and then we began timorously to pick our way across the
cliff to rejoin what here passes for a path.

Twenty minutes later we were on the floor of a long, hot
valley, where the arid earth was a dirty white and even the
scrub looked unhealthy. Now I knew that my knee had been
badly injured. Each step was such agony that I decided to
spend the night in the nearest compound. But the second of the
month is not our luckiest date. During the next four and a half
torturing hours I saw not even one *tukul* in the distance—and I
was afraid to camp out, lest a stiffening knee should leave me
incapable of defending Jock from the possible attacks of hyenas
or leopards.

The rough track led us out of the valley, up, across and down
an *amba*, and then again down, down, down through dense
forest to a broad river-bed where a shrunken stream flowed
filthily between green-slimed stones. By then I was past caring
about filth or slime. I drank pints to match Jock's gallons,
bathed and massaged my knee and in a daze of pain tackled
the last lap—a ninety-minute climb to a wide plateau scattered
with patches of stubble. A settlement lay half-way up a mountain at the plateau's western edge, and though our arrival
caused some alarm my agonised exhaustion quickly reassured
everyone.

Seven *tukuls* make up this compound (four for humans and

three for animals) and the poverty and disease are heart-rending. I'm sitting now on a huge, smooth boulder, being demented
by clouds of flies as I write on my usual food-box desk. Already
the injured knee feels better, having twice been massaged expertly and lengthily by my hostess.

A few moments ago two shepherds drove the family's wealth
into the compound—one sheep, two lambs, a billy-goat, three
nannies, two kids and five cows. All look dreadfully emaciated.
This is the edge of the Lasta famine-area, which has been
afflicted by drought during the past several years, and tonight
Jock has had only half an armful of straw and I am on emergency rations. One of the shepherds, aged about fourteen, has
limbs so frail and a head so disproportionately big and eyes so
sunken that he seems to epitomise all the starvation in the
world. Nor is his younger brother much better. There is a
harrowing difference between sitting beside human beings in
this condition and seeing Oxfam pictures of famine victims.
Both boys, and the three younger girls, are clad in scraps of
worn cow-hide. As I write two older girls are coming into the
compound, bent double under huge water-jars; they must
have had to carry these from some distant well or river, for
they look near collapse. One of them has a gruesome leg,
covered from knee to ankle with suppurating sores. Yet she
seems quite cheerful, so now I feel ashamed of the fuss I have
been making about my knee. Here medicine is not in demand—
a sign that these people have had little or no contact with
*faranjs*.


*3 March. A Camp in a Gully*

What a day! If any path to Lalibela exists in this region I've
yet to find it, and at present Abuna Josef is my only hope of
salvation.

This morning my knee felt less painful than I had expected
and we were on our way by 6.30, but during the next three
hours we can't have gained more than three miles. Repeatedly
our attempts to descend to river-level were thwarted by sheer,
jungle-covered cliffs, which forced us back to the plateau to
try another route; and when we did get into the gorge I

couldn't find a way out, for this was not one simple gorge, but a very beautiful labyrinth of deep ravines. We spent over an hour ploughing through soft, scorching, silver sand in search of a path on any of the forested cliffs that walled the various river-beds. Then, as we were following the most northerly stream, I saw people ahead—a surprise, amidst this motionless, soundless wilderness. They were a laundering-party—eight children with their father and mother—and everyone was trampling patched clothes in stagnant pools.

When Father had recovered from the shock he pointed to a boulder and told me to wait for guidance out of the gorge. It was now 9.30 and I was glad to rest, while the younger children left their work to study me with awe and Jock grazed enthusiastically off the few green plants that grew by the water. This family was unusual in having some affection for their dog, who was smaller than the average highland cur.

After half-an-hour the wet clothes were ready to be carried home in bundles on their owners' backs. As mother was shouldering an immense load of firewood, Father tied her bundle and his to the top of Jock's load before leading him up a path so faint that *faranj* eyes would never have detected it. On the cliff-top we joined a clearer path which climbed through arid scrubland to another high plateau.

Our progress was funereal. Mother walked very slowly and Father kept pace with her, making encouraging noises and calling the children back whenever they scampered disrespect-fully far ahead. It would have been unspeakably *infra dig* for him to carry the firewood, yet he was certainly not indifferent to his wife's struggle as she toiled, panting, up one long slope after another. Many *faranjs* condemn the treatment which high-land women receive from their husbands, but my own im-pression is that most couples show a normal degree of mutual affection and consideration. Highland tradition undoubtedly gives women a lowly status in some respects, as is symbolised by their carrying of loads in a country where I have never yet seen a man carrying anything but his *dula* or rifle—and perhaps an *injara*-basket, if he is not accompanied by his wife. However, it is unfair to deduce from this that most men always treat their wives callously or that there is no such thing as a hen-pecked highland husband. In at least two *tukuls* on my route I have noticed that the unfortunate head of the household lived in constant dread of his overbearing wife and became almost as subdued as a highland child when she was present.

My rescuers' large settlement seemed wretchedly poor. No *talla* was available because of the crop failure, so I was given a gourd of curds. As I sat on a boulder, eating, the whole population—friendly though timid—came to stare wonderingly. At first there was much speculation about my sex, but already the cotton shorts I bought in Gondar have reached a stage which renders lengthy speculation unnecessary—and this caused great and charmingly unshocked amusement.

At 11.30 Father led me to the edge of the settlement, with scores of people following, and pointed out the path to the Takazze Gorge. He and several other men had argued strenuously against our continuing towards Lalibela, for they said that beyond the Takazze I would find no tracks, no *tukuls* and many wild animals. So after much hand-shaking and bowing everyone stood in gloomy silence watching us leave.

For the next hour we were descending steeply through a harsh, drought-stricken world of sharp rocks, grey-brown, crumbling earth and dying scrub. I had been able to get no information about this stretch of the Takazze Gorge and my heart lurched with fear when suddenly we were overlooking a ravine that was deeper than any other ravine I have ever encountered. The descent looked tolerably safe for a cautiously-moving human being with a reasonable immunity to heights, but for a loaded mule it looked murderous. I hesitated, then decided to reconnoitre on my own and tethered Jock to a stunted tree lest his superlative loyalty should prompt him to follow me, even here. About one-third of the way down the vertical, ill-defined stone stairway I saw donkey-droppings. These reassured me—though it is certain that no animal burdened with an Italian pack-saddle has ever before used this route—so I returned to Jock, said my prayers and directed him over the edge.

The next twenty minutes were the most nerve-wracking of my life. Even Jock's unflappability came undone and in his pardonable panic he tended to leap towards level ledges of rock from which he could never have escaped had he once reached them. And my repeated efforts to check his fool-hardiness were perilous, for this was no precipice on which to frisk baboonishly.

At one point the load got jammed between shelves of rock and Jock was wedged head down, his hind legs feebly scrab-bling. By then I had been reduced to such a state of numb desperation that I no longer feared the sheer drop on to the boulders of the river-bed, hundreds of feet below. Recklessly I pulled myself on to the inner shelf, said a few would-be-steady-ing words in an unsteady voice and bent down to untie one sack. As Jock unwedged himself I seized the halter. Had he continued with an ill-balanced load he would have been in more acute danger than ever and for a hideous instant I thought that he was going to plunge ahead; but by one of those telepathic miracles which distinguish our relationship he stood still below the rock-pincers while I—braced against the cliff-face and sweating with tension—roped the sack back into position.

When at last we reached the river-bed Jock's sides were heaving and his coat shone ebony with sweat. He was so far gone that he didn't even want to drink; and I was so far gone that I vomited before drinking. I considered filling my water-bottle here, but as one could think of no more lethal liquid than the Takazze in March a last flicker of what seemed to be common sense inspired me to keep bacteria to the minimum by leaving my bottle empty.

To my relief Jock now moved towards the water and while he was drinking I lit a cigarette. Here the river-bed curved, limiting my view to about eighty yards in both directions, and the dark rock walls of the gorge had been eroded to soaring, fluted pillars of an eerie symmetry. Only opposite our point of descent was the cliff not quite sheer and the rock mixed with soil. There, presumably, lay our ascent route.

As the gorge felt oven-like beneath the midday sun I soon led poor Jock onwards, over a jumble of burning boulders. While we climbed sweat streamed off me, clouds of powdery dust irritated my lungs and often it was one step up, two steps back. However, neither of us was in mortal danger, so what would normally have seemed an ordeal now seemed a Sunday afternoon stroll.

At the top I realised what a mistake I had made by not filling my water-bottle; already thirst was tormenting me and my dusty throat felt raw. A faint path led us over a desolation of burnt-up grassland, but an hour later Abuna Josef reappeared through a gap in the nearer mountains and showed me that we were straying wildly. Turning towards him, we descended a long, pathless slope between bare ridges that converged at the foot of the slope. Since leaving the settlement I had seen no trace of humanity, but near the meeting of the ridges four girls were gathered round a water-hole, their pots on the ground beside them. Thirstily, I hurried forward—and then they saw me, shrieked piercingly, abandoned their pots and fled up the northern slope. As I reached the edge of the hole a fifth girl pulled herself out of it, glanced at me like a hunted animal, shrieked too and followed the rest. It amuses me to remember all that I have heard about *faranjs* being afraid to travel among highlanders—when so many highlanders are afraid to be travelled among!

At this water-hole I drew the line. Probably it was less contaminated than the Takazze but my thirst was not extreme enough for me to drink the liquid brown mud that lay in a pool two inches deep, eight feet below ground level. It must take half a day to fill one pot here.

From the crest of the northern ridge we descended to a wide, dusty stubble-field. The girls' settlement, where I hoped to find some drinkable liquid, lay a hundred yards ahead—isolated on its parched plateau, surrounded by silent ravines and rough blue mountains. The scene was a beautiful one, and tranquil in golden sunshine. Yet death hovered over it.

The settlement was unusually well fortified; its thick, six-foot thorn stockade seemed to have only one 'gateway' and each compound had a high, strong fence. Obviously the girls had warned everyone that something very peculiar was in the vicinity and the place looked deserted. Nor did anyone appear, or make the slightest sound, as we walked along the narrow paths between the compound stockades: but all the time I was aware of being watched from every side.

Eventually I entered one of the compounds. As we approached a *tukul* two men came to the door, tense with suspicion, and behind them women were exclaiming in alarm as they peered out. When I asked for water the men turned and muttered with their womenfolk, then tentatively beckoned me inside.

As usual, a thaw followed rapidly. I was given two small gourds of foul water, faintly flavoured with honey (a diluted form of the non-alcoholic drink called *birz*) and, as I gulped it most of the population—now reassured—came to stare silently, packing the *tukul* and crowding outside the door. The general atmosphere seemed neither friendly nor hostile and it was depressingly evident that the lethargy of malnutrition explained this neutrality.

At first I had been bewildered by the number of men wearing turbans, especially as there appeared to be no church anywhere near. Then I realised that this was a Jabarti* settlement, hence the strong stockades and *birz* instead of *talla*.

The woman of the house offered me half a round of *injara* —something that has never happened before since scraps are considered fit only for servants or children. As I declined it I wondered why these people remain in this accursed region, where some 5,000 people have recently tied of typhoid, malaria and starvation, while most of the few survivors have migrated. Perhaps Jabartis would find it difficult to obtain land elsewhere.

When we left this sad settlement it was impossible to continue towards Abuna Josef. Turning west, we crossed a slope of impoverished ploughland on a thread-like path that soon

---

* These Muslim highlanders are racially similar to their Christian neighbours and religiously dissimilar to Muslims anywhere else. Few of them observe Ramadan, go to Mecca, or pray regularly, and they know as little about orthodox Islam as the Copts do about orthodox Christianity or the Falashas about orthodox Judaism. The majority are descended from Copts converted by the Galla invaders or the armies of Mohammed Gragn. Deprived of hereditary land-ownership by several Imperial Decrees, many Jabartis weave and trade, thereby earning the contempt of the Copts. In their dress and buildings they are almost indistinguishable from other highlanders, though their compounds are often enclosed extra-securely as a defence against *shifta*, who are implicitly encouraged to attack Jabartis rather than Copts. Thousands of Jarbartis were forcibly converted by Theodore, in 1864, yet they now form about one-tenth of the highland population.

vanished, and for three hours were in a hot wasteland of thinly-forested hills. I saw two hyenas, a leopard lying under a bush happily playing with his tail and one abandoned settlement, roofless and overgrown. There were no traces of cultivation or paths, for already the bush had reclaimed every slope.

By six o'clock the terrain had become rougher and the forest thicker. Hundreds of baboons delighted me as they hurried along the crest of a low ridge, silhouetted against the sky and pausing often to swear discordantly at the intruders. I was no longer hoping to find water, so when we came to this dry river-bed it seemed as good a camping site as one could expect. It is about thirty yards wide and the ground rises on both sides, giving the place a cosy feeling. Many flat slabs of rock lie amidst the fine silver sand and on one of these I've built my fire, thus avoiding the possibility of sending the whole mountainside up in flames.

While collecting wood I moved some way down the gully—and suddenly the sweet music of running water rippled through the stillness. My thirst was now an ache dominating both body and mind and when I saw a shallow river, some 400 feet below this ledge, I rushed back for my bottle and made three attempts to reach the ravine. Thirst is so compulsive that sufferers within sight of water tend to disregard safety; but it was no use—everywhere the last hundred and fifty feet were sheer, smooth rock. The baboons now reappeared, far below me at the water's edge, and I realised that when last seen they had been on their way to the local, as it were. For a few moments I stared at them gloomily, contemplating the disadvantages of having evolved. Then I precariously climbed back to camp and ate a tin of tuna fish, which considerably increased my thirst.

Earlier a sprinkling of rain had fallen and as I ate ghostly, starlit cloudlets went drifting by overhead. Jock was munching above me, on the jungle-grassed eastern slope, and while unpacking my writing things I glanced up at his comforting black bulk, moving slowly between the bushes. Then my heart jerked. Close to him was a brilliant, malevolent yellow eye, glinting near ground level. It looked no more than a leopard's spring away and seizing a heavy length of firewood I charged the slope, marvelling at his placid stupidity. It took me some moments to discover that my One-Eyed Savage Beast was in fact the planet Venus, just risen above a mountain crest and glittering through the scrub.

During these past few hours my self-esteem has been restored by two large pairs of genuine eyes reflecting the firelight from various points on the upper slopes. Neither pair was near Jock, who gave no sign of being alarmed, so I took my cue from him and remained seated in a dignified way. I'm glad that I have an open space on which to sleep; it would not be relaxing to spend a night entangled in this forest.

Soon after sunset a strong wind rose and the fire has been burning quickly. Its leaping, twisting, crimson-orange flames are lighting up an extraordinarily wide area, which in an odd way seems to belong to me, as I sit at its centre—while beyond are the black walls of the night, shutting out a country that belongs now to no man. At this comparatively low altitude (about 6,000 feet) being beside such heat makes one sweat continuously, so my thirst is steadily increasing.

Already it is eleven o'clock. I have been writing for four hours, by the light of candles sheltered from the wind between boxes in the lee of a boulder—but with many pauses to enjoy a flawless tranquillity which here seems to have absorbed me into itself. Despite thirst and glinting eyes I know that this evening will forever remain among my finest memories. Here the solitude has a quality such as I have not experienced since crossing that plateau between the Ataba and Buahit. Almost certainly there is no other human being within a radius of ten miles; and the spirits of the local plague-victims must feel friendly towards me, for my peace is complete.

Now the sky is cloudless again, and alive with the golden vigour of its stars. A moment ago a jet passed on its way from Asmara to Addis, and I thought of the passengers—briefly my nearest neighbours—sitting back after their five-course dinner, reading magazines and sipping iced drinks. But

> When I survey the bright
> Coelestiall spheare
> So rich with jewels hung, that night
> Doth like an Æthiop bride appear

I can't wish, even for the sake of an iced drink, to be up there hurtling towards Addis.

> Thus those coelestiall fires,
> Though seeming mute,
> The fallacie of our desires
> And all the pride of life confute.
>
> For they have watcht since first
> The World had birth:
> And found sinne in it selfe accurst
> And nothing permanent on earth.*

### 4 March. Lalibela

It is impossible to mule-sit efficiently after climbing mountains all day. Last night my sense of duty roused me only once, for long enough to heave two huge branches on to the fire. I then slept deeply until six o'clock, yet when I woke our hillock of embers still glowed rosy in the silver dawn-light—and Jock was safe, though not, as I soon discovered, sound. There was a great joy in that solitary awakening to the cool stillness of a mountain morning.

While I was eating a tin of sardines the baboons came quite close and sat round scratching and making insulting gestures and abusive remarks; but when I stood up they retreated, protesting raucously.

By 6.45 we had begun a two-hour struggle with a series of broken, thickly-forested hills which sometimes threatened to defeat us utterly. Abuna Josef was disobligingly invisible, but that didn't matter much, for my immediate concern was to escape in any direction from this formidable complex of gullies and spurs. Then suddenly we were free—overlooking a broad, gradual slope of sun-powdered grey soil. And at the foot of the slope gleamed water.

This tributary of last evening's river was laced with minute strips of green slime, but I reasoned that these must be composed of some health-giving vegetable matter. Beyond the high riverside dunes of fine grey sand I again looked for Abuna Josef, but on every side towering ranges restricted my vision to

* William Habington (1605–1654).

a few miles and warped my sense of direction. So I went vaguely towards the least stern-looking mountain, hoping that from its summit Abuna Josef might be more co-operative.

It was during this climb that Jock began to fold up. He moved only very slowly, his breathing was heavy and his expression was the ultimate in dejection. I felt seriously alarmed, but not at all surprised. He has had little corn since we left Debre Tabor and we have been averaging twenty miles a day through demanding country. At the thought of his collapsing in this godforsaken spot I almost panicked. I myself was now safely within reach of Lalibela, but the desertion of Jock, to save my own miserable skin, would be an experience from which I could never hope to recover; and I doubted if my common-sense would prove robust enough for me to abandon a sick animal and a good friend to beasts of prey.

My own empty stomach was sick with anxiety as Jock battled on, game as ever, to the top. Now I looked desperately for Abuna Josef but the giant was still hidden behind a new array of nearer mountains.

While Jock rested I studied the terrain ahead. Lalibela, I knew, was at about the same height as this summit, so I decided to try to avoid further steep climbs by keeping, where possible, to the upper flanks of the intervening ranges—even if this meant doubling our mileage. However, we were soon forced down by scree slopes so steep—and above such a deep chasm—that I dared not risk them with a weakly stumbling Jock. We then followed a level, winding, silver-sanded gully; it seemed to be going in quite the wrong direction, but the only alternatives were other possibly futile ascents.

It was 10.40 when a faint path appeared on the left-hand slope. Relief exalted me—and perhaps infected Jock, who here quickened his pace in response to my eager tugs at the halter. Twenty minutes later we had reached another wretched Jabarti settlement, on a grey, desiccated hilltop. The compounds were fortified with ill-kept 'Connemara' stone walls, and the people—who must see tourists if they trade in Lalibela—observed our arrival apathetically. They had neither fodder for Jock nor food for me; but from this hilltop a man pointed out the route to Lalibela.

The miles that followed were the most trying of the whole trek. Had Jock behaved mulishly his suffering might have been a little less heart-rending, but he struggled on—becoming hourly more enfeebled—with a faithful courage that I shall never forget.

My earlier ambition to avoid climbing now looked absurd. Below the settlement the path expired in a broad, barren valley and for a few miles we followed a deep, dry river-bed, overhung by dense forest, between mountains which eventually merged so that we had to climb one of them. (My reward for this was the reappearance of Abuna Josef; he still looked dishearteningly far away, yet his presence had a steadying influence.) Then came another descent, another valley, another river-bed—this one retaining stagnant pools of malarial water —and yet another mountain on which we again went astray amidst gullies and thorn thickets. All that brought us to the most harrowing stage—a continual two-hour climb up a massive mountain wall which stretched unbroken for miles between us and Lalibela. At this point I faced the possibility that we might have to camp out, though one more night without adequate fodder would be likely to leave Jock too weak to continue in the morning. Here he had to pause about every ten yards to recover his breath; when he had stopped panting I would tug hard on the halter and he would meekly make the painful effort necessary to cover the next ten yards. Each time he stopped I stroked his nose consolingly and he gazed at me with dull, sad eyes. I hope never again to live through two such hours.

Below the crest the inevitable rock escarpment was not very high, but the absence of any established route to the top made it exceptionally difficult. Now poor Jock was near complete collapse. At the foot of the cliff he hung his head and refused to budge. This was the moment that I had been dreading; I had no alternative but to go behind him and use my *dula*. Reluctantly he responded, and I would like to think that he understood the spirit in which I was thrashing him. As he scrambled on to the crest ahead of me I was sick with suspense, knowing that if just one more climb lay between us and Lalibela he couldn't possibly make it. I almost sprang on to the top in my anxiety, looked over the wide, new panorama—and thanked God to see tin roofs and blue-gums in the distance, on a level with ourselves. A deep valley intervened, its floor littered with hills, but our path swept semicircularly around the upper flanks of the high mountains to the north.

It took us two and a half hours to cover the last four miles and the several severe inclines were agony for Jock. Near Lalibela the track falls abruptly, to cross the river Jordan; then it climbs steeply. When we reached Lalibela Jock stopped in the middle of the 'Main Street' in a determined way and gave me a look signifying that as far as he was concerned we had arrived. Seeing his point, I unloaded him on the spot—surrounded by unhelpfully staring locals—and hired three youths to carry our saddlery and sacks to the Tourist hotel, which is on a high ledge above the town. Elsewhere one wouldn't have to pay people to help a traveller in obvious distress—but Lalibela is one of Ethiopia's main tourist centres.

As I led Jock up this last steep hill, through the dusk, I suddenly became aware of my own miserable state and the pain of my knee and the soreness of my lungs swept over me like a wave. Not having eaten anything like a square meal for days I again got the knocks, as I did outside Gondar. Yet here I couldn't eat when I dragged myself into the restaurant; and tonight, for the first time in this country, I have that stabbing, fiery bellyache which is the prelude to dysentery. Perhaps those strips of green slime were not, after all, health-giving.

# 11

# *Wading through Wollo*

Here everyone says briskly that of course Jock must now be sold and another mule bought; but such insensitive talk of buying and selling outrages me. As events have proved, Jock is no ordinary pack-animal, and to part from him would blight the rest of my journey. The experts admit that his only complaint is malnutrition, so I have decided simply to give him a week's well-fed rest and to reduce his future load by abandoning the Italian saddle and sending my books to Addis.

Today I left the hotel compound only briefly, to lunch with the Governor at his nearby home. Much of my time was spent fidgeting around Jock, supervising his feeding, and between fidgets I lay reading on my bed, cosseting my divers diseases. The dysentery attack seems to have been successfully repelled by sulphaguanidine: but Jock isn't the only one who needs a week's rest.

*6 March*

Once upon a time Lalibela—then known as Roha—was the capital of the Zagwe dynasty, whose Hamitic Agow Kings replaced the Solomonic line for some three hundred years, from about 920. These kings are now officially if illogically regarded as usurpers, by way of upholding that Solomonic legend which gives such moral support to the present dynasty. However, they were Christian Agow, and one of them—Lalibela—is a saint of the Ethiopian Church. According to a manuscript now in the British Museum he was the last but one of his line, and between 1182 and 1220 (Ethiopian calendar) he sponsored the construction of ten of Lalibela's famed rock churches.

The eleventh is said to have been built by his widow, as his memorial.

These churches have been sculpted out of living rock and they are among the few renowned 'wonders of the world' which, when seen at last, gave me a shock of joy. Tradition says that for their construction King Lalibela employed four or five hundred skilled workers from Jerusalem and Alexandria, as well as innumerable locals; and in the sixteenth century Francisco Alvarez, the Portugese traveller, was told by monks at Lalibela that the eleven churches had been completed within twenty-four years. Soon after their completion an Ethiopian scribe wrote: 'What tongue is capable of giving a description of them? He who beholds them will never be able to gaze his fill; his marvelling is so great that his heart is never tired of admiring them.' I quite agree, and am glad that we are taking our rest-cure here.

## 7 March

Much as I am enjoying Lalibela's churches, the atmosphere of the town depresses me. Until three years ago this was a remote mountain village, visited only by a few *faranjs* and by highlanders on pilgrimages to King Lalibela's tomb. Now Ethiopian Airlines provide a link with Addis six days a week, the Seven Olives Hotel provides a reasonable imitation of Home Comforts, the local children form a corps of professional beggars and the taint of greed lies heavy on the air.

The hotel is owned by Princess Ruth, a younger sister of Leilt Aida and reputedly the Emperor's favourite grandchild. Since it was opened two and a half years ago it has been managed by an American ex-missionary who sports pious texts on the rear windows of his Land-Rover and took twenty-four hours to realise that I am not Mr Murphy. (He still wriggles all over with apologetic embarrassment every time we meet, though I have repeatedly assured him that his error is in the best highland tradition.) The charge for a single room in the main building is 42/–, and I'm paying 18/– for a cell (in the annexe) which is furnished only with twin beds and has a low tin roof, mud walls, a stone floor and a tiny unglazed window—anywhere else in this country a similar room would cost 3/–. However, the profits are spent on the drought victims of Lasta and during recent years the regional ills would have been even worse but for the Seven Olives Hotel.

Yesterday the kindly District Governor was flying to Addis at noon, and he took an S.O.S. from me to Lady Bromley. I am against the transferring of travellers' worries to Embassy shoulders, but the present crisis seemed to excuse my appealing for a sun-hat, water-pills and Biros, to be put on a plane to Lalibela one day this week. Then, at 11.30 a.m. today, I received a large canvas Britannic Majesty bag, solemnly sealed, and containing not only the essentials I had requested but two tin-openers, a compass, a pair of sunglasses and a fat wad of mail. This generous efficiency filled me with awed gratitude. The Governor had gone straight from the airport to the Embassy and delivered my letter into the very hands of Lady Bromley, who had gone straight to the shops, filled the bag and sent it post haste to the airport. May St Lalibela bless them both!

*8 March*

Lalibela's houses look unusually attractive; many are circular, two-storied, stone buildings, with thatched roofs—I have seen nothing similar elsewhere. Priests and their families form the greater part of the population and, like most highlanders, these people are much less dour than they seem on first acquaintance. During my rambles today I was twice invited into *tej-beits* for drinks on the house (Lalibela *tej* is exceptionally good), and one group of old Agow women asked me to stop and eat roast corn with them, as they sat in the sun outside their *tukul*. After our conspicuous arrival here everyone has made enquiries about us, so I am basking now in Special Treatment. Even the hotel waiters give me double rations at each meal, on the grounds that walkers need more food than fliers.

This evening Jock is noticeably plumper and the small girth sore on his belly has healed completely. My own state is also satisfactory. The knee injury has responded well to lack of ill-treatment and the chest pain has gone; but I am being persecuted by a peculiar cough which keeps me awake and seems immune to antibiotics.

### 9 March

Today my medical state was far from satisfactory; the sulpha-guanidine has given up fighting whatever exotic bacteria I now contain and I have been almost annihilated by a blitz of dysentery. This evening I feel kittenishly weak, and can no more imagine myself walking to Addis on my feet than on my hands; but with luck I'll revive as suddenly as I collapsed. Meanwhile I lie on a comfortable bed, counting my blessings between excursions to the loo. It was exceedingly benevolent of my Guardian Angel to preserve me from this onslaught until I had arrived here.

### 10 March

I woke this morning feeling much better belly-wise, but as my cough was worse I walked slowly down to the new Health Centre after a prudent breakfast of anaemic tea. The Medical Officer impressed me by his intelligence and dedication; prob-ably Princess Ruth hand-picked him for this post. He is not a doctor, but simply a sincerely concerned young man with a stethoscope around his neck and lots of common sense in his head—the ideal type to achieve maximum results with the minimum of fuss.

When he had written out a prescription for me I took it to another room—stepping over dozens of groaning patients—where an equally impressive Addis-trained nurse poured thick chalky liquid out of a 'Grant's Whisky' bottle into a smaller bottle, and wrapped a fistful of tablets in a scrap of Amharic-printed newspaper. She told me to take the medicine four times a day and eight tablets a day for a week. No one would commit themselves to naming either remedy, but I paid my 4/- and bore them away, hoping for the best. The tablets were obviously of the sulpha group, the medicine could have been anything. I was astonished when my cough dwindled after the first dose and almost stopped after the second.

I had planned to trek tomorrow to Imrahanna Kristos—a church built in a cave on the western slopes of Abuna Josef— where I intended spending a night. Before my visit to the medicine man it had seemed that this expedition would have to be forgotten, but by noon I felt so restored that I set out to climb to a church near the summit of the mountain directly above Lalibela, and I got there—so now the trek to Imrahanna Kristos is *on* again. Granted I turned back at the church without reaching the summit, which signifies a weakened condition; but if I proceed tomorrow at a sedate, convalescent pace all should be well.

## *11 March. Imrahanna Kristos*

All is well, to the extent that I have got here, though today's walk was a singularly unsuitable excursion for convalescents. Otherwise all is far from well, and this evening I am in a very bad temper.

As a concession to my semi-invalidism I decided to bring a porter-boy with me and last evening Giorgis, a charming four-teen-year-old, came to my room and said that he had been sent by Mrs Dettenberg, a German artist who is Lalibela's only foreign resident—apart from the hotel-manager—and who has been a good friend to me during this past week. Giorgis is the son of a priest and is himself a deacon. He looks pitiably under-sized and being a pupil of the Church school he speaks no English, but he is an unspoiled child with a sudden smile that wonderfully lights up his small brown face.

We set off at eight o'clock, collecting on the way a letter from the Governor's office requesting the priests here to 'grant me every assistance'. After a spectacular plunge into a wide, dusty valley we climbed on to one of Abuna Josef's powerful 9,000-foot shoulders, from where I was again overlooking the land of our travail between Lalibela and Debre Zeit, whose plateau was now a long, clean-cut, cobalt chunk on the far horizon. I well remembered first seeing this landscape—and Abuna Josef —from the edge of that chunk.

It felt good to be back on the uplands, breathing keen air and seeing the world through that pure light of the heights

which adds splendour to every colour. This well-watered plateau is strewn with colossal granite boulders and herds of horses
and mules keep the fresh pastures so close-cropped that they
look like well-tended lawns. Around them lie acres of brown
ploughland and golden stubble-fields, all dotted with tiny
settlements; and directly above, to the east, rises a further
craggy 4,000 feet of Abuna Josef.

At midday the path again climbed steeply, taking us about
a thousand feet higher across the face of a rock escarpment.
Then another easy walk—over still greener pastures, where the
wind was cold—ended dramatically on the edge of the plateau
and at my feet lay a vast, fierce turmoil of mountains and
valleys.

A difficult path led us down from ledge to ledge along Abuna
Josef's mighty flanks. Eventually we came to the remains of an
ancient forest and walked to the foot of the mountain through
a cool gloom beneath huge, deformed conifers.

Imrahanna Kristos appears unexpectedly when the path
plunges into the narrow, shadowed head of a valley, from
which high mountains rise steeply on three sides. Under the
centre mountain is a deep cave, and within this cave stands
the church. I first glimpsed it from above, while scrambling
down the last rocky thirty yards, but a six-foot wall guards the
cave's wide mouth and only the roof is visible from the level
space outside the enclosure.

Here I sat down heavily on a boulder. Nearby stood the
priests' residence—a two-storied, circular stone hut—and within
moments we were surrounded by three priests and sundry
deacons. Respectfully I dragged myself to my feet, bowed and
handed the Governor's chit to the senior priest, but without
even glancing at this official introduction the ordained trio
aggressively demanded a down payment of five dollars. They
sounded more like *shifta* than clergy and I promptly lost my
temper and snapped, 'Cents *yellum*!'—though I had brought
five dollars as a parting donation. In such an impoverished area
insistent begging from 'rich' *faranjs* is understandable, but there
was no excuse for this truculence.

Then I decided to compromise by offering one dollar—and immediately all three closed around me, gesturing towards the

path and yelling '*Hid!* Lalibela! *Hid!* Lalibela!' Possibly this was an attempt to cow me; they may have assumed that I would be afraid to spend a night on the mountain. I was about to leave, in a fury, when a tall youth stepped forward from among the *debtaras*. He spoke a few words of English—with which he tried to soothe me, before turning to the priests and suggesting that they read the Governor's chit. Apparently none of them was sufficiently literate for this, so he himself laboriously read it aloud; but the voice of officialdom made no impression.

Meanwhile I had been retrieving my temper. I explained that if the clergy would show a minimum of civility, and unlock the church, I would make a suitable donation on departure; but they obstinately repeated that they wouldn't open even the enclosure door for less than five dollars. Whereupon I beckoned to poor Giorgis—who had been cowering behind a boulder— and started back up the path. Forgetting my tiredness in my rage, I moved fast—but was checked by shouts from below, offering to open the enclosure for E. $1.50. I was tempted to ignore this haggling, yet I did want to see Imrahanna Kristos. So I returned, handed over the 'reduced fee' and was admitted to the cave, with a promise that I would be shown the interior of the building tomorrow morning.

This 800-year old church has horizontal bands of whitish plaster and black wood which, seen through muted cave-light, surprisingly recall medieval England. The building is only forty-two feet long and its sanctuary is roofed by a low dome, not unlike a Buddhist *stupa*. It was built by a priest-king, Imra-hann Kristos, who reigned from about 1110–1150 and of whom it was written in an ancient manuscript (seen here in the 1520's by Francisco Alvarez) that 'during the whole life of this King he had not taken dues from his vassals, and that if anyone brought them to him he ordered them to be distributed among the poor'. It seems that these royal ideals have ceased to inspire the local clergy. Walking around the church, past the tombs of the king and his saintly daughter, I noticed another link with Buddhism in the swastika design which decorates some of the very beautiful carved wood and pierced stone windows. And suddenly, in this remote shrine of fossilized sanctity, the mori-bund religion of modern Ethiopia seemed intensely tragic.

At the back of the cave, which is roughly half-moon shaped, lies a mysterious mound of scores of disintegrating mummies. Clambering over them through the gloom I found myself breaking a child's ribs—and its left arm and hand were a few feet away. This embalming effort was so unsuccessful that there are many more skeletons than mummies—though most of them are still partly enclosed in 'shrouds' of wicker-work, tied with string, which seems to indicate that they are not very old. No one has any definite information about their origin. The most plausible theory is that they are the remains of a pilgrim group who died here during some epidemic, but it is not clear why they should have been embalmed and deposited in such a sacred spot, instead of being buried like anyone else—unless perhaps they were particularly distinguished pilgrims, whose corpses deserved this special honour.

When I left the cave one of the younger priests informed me that I could eat and sleep in his *tukul* on payment of E. $2. I replied acidly that I was in no need of hospitality, gave him E. $1 for Giorgis' board and lodging and retired to this ledge below the settlement—where I'm overlooking a long, wild valley, now softly filling with dusk.

It is unfortunate that so many tourists get their only impression of the highland peasantry from meeting priests at such places as Aksum, Gondar and Lalibela. Donald Levine has remarked with restraint that 'though there are devout and kindly men among them, the Ethiopian priests have never been particularly noted for their moral qualities'. Exercising less restraint, I would add that the highland priesthood seems to attract the worst type of highlander—or rather to breed him, since the priesthood is mainly hereditary.

It is interesting that the clergy here treated the Governor's chit with such contempt. During the past thirty years Haile Selassie has been gradually reducing clerical power in the interests of progress, but evidently his reforms have not yet penetrated to Imrahanna Kristos. On this issue the Italian occupation helped the Emperor, for many traitorous priests lost the respect of their flocks and two bishops publicly supported the enemy—one so forcefully that he forbade Christian burial for Patriot fighters. But Haile Selassie's greatest victory, in his subtle anti-clerical campaign, has been the cutting of the umbilical cord between the Ethiopian Church and the Alexandrian Patriarchate. This victory has flatteringly raised the status of Ethiopia's own church dignitaries; but it has also given the Emperor complete power over the clergy, who previously —under their Egyptian Abuna—wielded an authority independent of the state.

*12 March. Lalibela*

It was dark when I woke this morning, yet the priests were already celebrating the Eucharist. I lay warmly in my flea-bag, gazing up at a starry highway running between black mountain massifs and listening to that antique, solemnly beautiful chanting, which has been so strangely preserved amidst the decay of church buildings, doctrines and morals. Ten minutes later day came—at first faintly, to the crests high above, then with a quick flood of light that poured gold into the valley.

At 6.30 we entered the cave but to my indignant surprise I was again refused admission to the church, by a group of sullen *debtaras* who were obviously acting on orders from the priests. I waited until the service was over but the priests didn't leave the church immediately, as is usual. Then the *debtaras* rudely pushed Giorgis and me towards the enclosure gate, pointing up the Lalibela path and *looking 'Hid!'* without actually saying it. Poor Giorgis had been in a state of mingled fear and embarrassment ever since we arrived yesterday, and now he indicated that it would be best for us to go. So we went, with my main objective unachieved.

I suspect these priests of having recently illegally sold some church treasures to a *faranj*. This trade has become fairly common and in an effort to curb it the Government is aided by reputable foreign experts who, on visiting a church, take an inventory of all its treasures. It is a pity that I am not recognisable as probably the greatest non-expert on church treasures ever to visit Imrahanna Kristos.

I felt so much fitter today that I was only half-tired when we arrived here at three o'clock; and Jock looks quite rejuvenated, so off we go in the morning.

*13 March. Kulmask*

Today we were following the jeep-track (my guide book elegantly terms it a 'provisory road') that links Lalibela with the Asmara–Dessie–Addis motor road. About once a month a vehicle uses this track (the 130-mile journey takes ten or eleven hours) and it seems miraculous that even a jeep can cope. Last week a W.H.O. Malaria Eradication team left Lalibela and today the tyre marks were still discernible—luckily, since I was often dependent on them to guide me over stretches where nothing else indicated that here lay a track.

From Lalibela we descended to a wide, hot, arid valley and during the next two hours I found myself becoming depressed by my surroundings, for the first time in these highlands. This valley is still inhabited and we passed several settlements, two small herds of emaciated cattle, and a few neglected, un-ploughed fields from which the last thin *teff* crop has long since been harvested. Yet I saw not even one shepherd-boy, and as we walked between endless low, grey-brown hills, disfigured with dead scrub, the whole sun-plagued scene reeked of misery. The junipers, which somehow contrive to look freshly green everywhere else, were withered here and even the cacti hung limply. One felt that the remaining population had accepted the nearness of death and were sitting dully in their *tukuls*, not trying any more. Deserted, uninhabited landscapes delight me but the memory of that still, suffering valley will haunt me for a long time to come.

A gradual two-hour climb took us to a higher valley—long, broad, well-cultivated and walled by tremendous chunky ranges. I paused at the rectangular rock church of Geneta Mariam, which has an unexpected, magnificent colonnade under a sloping roof; but no keeper-of-the-keys was to be found in the nearby settlement.

During the afternoon the steady breeze became a strong wind, which by six o'clock had risen to gale force and blackly clouded the sky. We arrived at this little town half-an-hour after sunset and when I saw a young man in a Western suit standing at the lamp-lit doorway of a shack I guessed, correctly, that he was a teacher. I am now installed in his room and Jock is audibly munching corn at the other side of the wall.

For the past two hours my host and I have been conversing in shouts above the welcome drumming of heavy rain on the tin roof. Hailu is Addis-born and full of grumbles about having been forced by the Government to come to this godforsaken town for two years. There are five other teachers here, two of whom are women, which is unusual.

Now the servant is unrolling my flea-bag on a cowhide on the earthen floor—to Hailu's distress, for he wants the guest to have his bed. It is very agreeable to be in a country where one needn't hesitate about sharing a bedroom with a young man whose face one hasn't even seen clearly. Whatever the other hazards of highland travel, a woman knows that as a woman she can trust every man in every circumstance. This remarkable chivalry is so integral a part of the highland atmosphere that I had come to take it for granted—until it was underlined recently by the behaviour of an ostensibly civilised *faranj*, who was also staying at Lalibela and who never suffered from the hotel-manager's initial delusion. His attempts to make me drunk, and then to invade my room, provided much food for thought on the subject of Comparative Civilisations.

Cynics like to explain away the highlanders' code of chivalry by referring to their habitually varied sex-lives. However, even in Ethiopia variety is not easily obtainable in settlements or villages and an explanation which appeals to me much more was given by Colonel Aziz. He said that traditionally the highlanders regard unknown women as representatives of the Virgin Mary, and he added—with a realism which acted as a splendid foil to this romanticism—that if any unknown woman indicated that she would appreciate some relaxation on her way then the local men would be happy to oblige; but the initiative must be hers. Here the cynics may scoff, yet my own experience of the highlanders' behaviour convinces me that Colonel Aziz's explanation is essentially true.

*14 March. A Compound in a Valley*

When we left Kulmask this morning the air was sharply fresh, running water sang on every slope, the track was deep in sticky mud and it seemed that the valley below Lalibela must surely be a thousand miles away.

From Kulmask to Waldia the 'provisory road' goes a long way round, so we followed the old track through high ranges that were utterly different from anything else I've seen in Ethiopia. This fertile region is thickly populated and we were crossing irrigated fields and richly moist ploughland, or walking between bright slopes that swept greenly down in unbroken lines from the grey jaggedness of high escarpments. On these generous pastures grazed many herds of cattle, horses and goats; and at midday we reached sheep-level, where there were few settlements or fields.

Here a piercingly cold gale opposed us from the east and by 1.30 surly purple clouds were hanging low above us, and thunder was incessantly crackling and roaring around the near-by summits and with its echoes producing a strange, wildly beautiful rhythm. Then hail briefly scourged this high plateau with such violence that I took refuge beneath Jock's belly.

Ten minutes later we stepped on to the edge of the tableland and below us, to north and south, lay stairways of lower mountains, their giant steps gleaming white. For a moment I imagined that it had been snowing; then I realised that this was where the hail-storm had spent itself. Here the sun shone again and the lighting was almost intolerably beautiful. Beyond these sparkling ledges were motionless layers of dove-grey or navy-blue clouds, half concealing rough summits, and far, far beneath, in a golden valley, ripe grain glistened like a silken carpet.

While Jock grazed I sat on a rock and looked with joy at all this loveliness; but soon after we had begun the descent I was regretting not having looked more intelligently at the precipice and less ecstatically at the loveliness.

This 500-foot escarpment provided a new kind of wrack for my nerves. It was almost sheer and it jutted out over the valley —which lay another 1,500 feet below, with nothing but good

fresh air in between. Even Jock took a pessimistic view and had
to be led. Then, a third of the way down, I lost my nerve and
we got stuck. Looking about in wild surmise I saw that we had
taken the wrong route, for directly below the top there had
been no definite path. Now, however, the correct route was
visible—two hundred yards away, separated from us by a wide,
perpendicular crack in the cliff-face.

When I decided to return to the crest to make a fresh start
I discovered that Jock couldn't turn. Never before have I been
so near to panic. This was completely irrational, as a drop of
2,000 feet is no more dangerous than one of 500, but I shud-
dered at the sight of the ground so very far below and at the
extreme insecurity of this friable precipice; and Jock's trembling
appeared to justify my own jitters. Yet we couldn't spend the
rest of our days like carvings on a cliff-face so I set about
regaining my nerve by gazing steadily down at the valley floor,
in the hope that familiarity would breed sufficient contempt
for me to be able to continue calmly. Then I moved forward,
and Jock reluctantly followed. For the next forty slow minutes
we were descending—with occasional ascents, necessitated by
deep gullies or insurmountable outcrops of rock. Half the stones
I trod on went hurtling into space: the loose clay crumbled
at every step: a minor landslide started if I lent on my *dula*:
the thorny scrub 'came away in me 'and' if I despairingly
grabbed it. And all the time I was waiting for the worst to
happen to Jock.

When at last we rejoined the path our route was clear, though
awkward. We continued along the base of the escarpment,
away from the golden valley, before again descending into a
deep gorge where a river flowed strongly through dense, dark
green forest.

Sometimes the kaleidoscopic quality of these highlands seems
dreamlike. Beyond this swirling brown river we walked beneath
a twilit tangle of trees, creepers and ferns—then we were in a
hot, wet valley where young wheat and lush pastures glittered
emerald, the air was gay with the rushing of flood waters and
around the many compounds grew tall cacti, their brilliant
clumps of coral-pink berries like brooches pinned on the breast
of the earth. Yet only this morning we had been on a cold,

austere plateau of close-cropped turf and rough granite, and less than thirty-six hours ago we crossed that shrivelled, colourless, waterless 'Valley of Death'.

This luxuriant landscape made walking difficult. For a few miles our track was the bed of a two-foot deep stream that raced downhill over round, slippery stones. Next came gradually sloping pastures, where I sank to my ankles at every step while poor Jock slithered miserably on the black mud—and here the load slipped, though it is now so light and compact. Luckily we were by then meeting many mule and donkey caravans, on their way home from Waldia market, and two kind men paused to help.

For the last hour we followed the river through a wide ravine between wooded cliffs. Repeatedly we had to cross the swift, cold, dark-brown flood, but it was never deep. As we approached this five-*tukul* compound, on the outskirts of a village, dusk was thickening to darkness and the sky had again clouded over. I'm now installed in the main *tukul*, which is bigger than average —and it would need to be, for at night it shelters seven adults, four children, three donkeys, a mule and sundry poultry.

This evening I'm anxious about Jock. Despite his improved working conditions he seems in poor shape after today's twenty-six miles, even though they were easy, apart from that precipice.


*15 March. Waldia*

Last night must go among the Top Ten of hellish vigils. Within moments of entering that *tukul* I had realised that it was uncommonly well-stocked with fleas, bugs and body-lice—a new plague. These lice tend to induce an unpleasant fever so it was disconcerting to find that my last tin of insecticide had all leaked away. Then a violent thunderstorm broke and the force of the rain on the thatched roof loosened showers of large and very peculiar insects, who stampeded over me vigorously but elusively. This double downpour continued until 2.30 a.m., by which time the stench of animal urine was so strong that it might reasonably have been expected to asphyxiate any number of insects. But unhappily it did not.

Soon after 10 p.m. the fire was covered, everyone curled up

beneath cow-hides and I began my eight-hour ordeal. However, there were diversions. A mirthfully inebriated all-night party was being held in the next-door *tukul* and we were treated to one donkey-fight and one cock-fight. The kicking, biting, squealing donkeys wakened everyone; and an hour after they had been separated, and tied to opposite walls, the populace again rose as one man to intervene between a pair of apoplectic cocks, one of whom was imprisoned, with difficulty, in a sack. The other then returned sulkily to his roost, some two feet above my head, and at about 3 a.m. he caused me to leap like a shot rabbit when he made a machine-gun-like noise with his wings before beginning to crow stridently. During the rest of the night he crowed every ten or fifteen minutes. If I had been capable of feeling anything at 6 a.m. I would have felt glad that the sun had risen.

My host was also coming to Waldia, bringing three donkeys loaded with hides, and at 6.45 we joined a caravan of nineteen other donkeys and seven men. The sky was clear, but I have never anywhere encountered so much or such slippery mud. For an hour we were slithering into and out of a series of flooded ravines; then suddenly we were beyond the area of last night's storm and the track went winding over bare, grey hills that looked as though they hadn't had rain for a decade. A tough climb up a forested mountain brought Waldia's blue-gums within sight and by eleven o'clock we had arrived at this dreary little town.

I felt exhausted as we approached the tin roofs and truck noises. By 1 p.m. I had bought a big feed of dried peas for Jock (oddly, no corn was available), and had renewed my supply of insecticide. Then I retired to my cleanish room, in this Italian-built, Ethiopian-run truck-drivers' 'hotel', and slept until 5 p.m.

When I woke rain was crashing on the tin roof and one of the local teachers was awaiting me in the bar. He invited me to have dinner in his room and an hour ago I waded back here through an ankle-deep torrent of thin mud. If these are the 'Little Rains' one can easily believe that travelling is impossible in the highlands during the 'Big Rains' of June to September.

*16 March. A Shack by the Roadside*

Today we were following the motor-road for all of our twenty-three miles, yet Jock seemed alarmingly tired towards evening.

This morning Waldia stank like a neglected public lavatory but beyond the town the rain-clear air was delicately scented by a flowering tree, with blossoms like balls of pale-yellow fluff, that grows here on many of the steep slopes. A long climb took us over the first of several passes, the road coiling around sheer, bare, brown mountains, from which streamed frequent miniature landslides of rain-loosened soil. Then we descended to a broad valley of many settlements and stubble-fields, where maize seemed to be the main crop. The landscape was bright with fifteen-foot-high pointed stooks of maize straw, looking like so many golden wigwams, and each stook had a thorn fence around its base as a protection against hungry cattle. These tall, thick maize stalks are a common local building material, being used to reinforce *tukul* walls and to form ceilings under the usual grass thatch. Most of the cattle here grow enormous, spreading horns—something I haven't seen since leaving Tigre. This breed is lightly built and if the animals are underfed they walk as though their horns were too heavy for them to carry.

Soon a strong wind arose and by one o'clock the sky was two-thirds clouded over. Colossal mountains towered ruggedly around us and here the road became another example of Italian engineering genius. Today Jock was slightly temperamental about traffic but luckily we had to contend with no more than eight buses and nine trucks.

This big Jabarti compound is beside the road and high above it a Coptic settlement clings to the mountainside, half hidden by tangled bush and giant cacti. Despite its size the compound contains only one small *tukul*—the home of a young couple—and a long, Italian bungalow which may have been an army post during the Occupation. Five of the six rooms are no longer habitable and in the other lives a trio of ancient crones—one without a right eye, another without a left hand and the third pitifully burn-disfigured. These are my hostesses, and soon after

I had entered their unfurnished, high-ceilinged home—illuminated only by the flicker of a tiny oil-lamp—the three abruptly
rose, faced Mecca and began their evening prayers. They used
a cow-hide prayer-mat and made a weird picture as they stood
close together near the door, performing their rituals in unison,
silhouetted against the cloudy dusk.

A meagre supper of *injara* and bean-*wat* was brought from
the *tukul* and though the poverty of this family is extreme
everyone insisted that I should have some. Now two donkeys,
a cow, a calf and Jock are being driven into another room,
which I have decided to share with the livestock in preference
to being a meal for bugs.

*17 March. A Camp under a Bridge*

St Patrick's Day—appropriately, my first all-cloudy day in
Ethiopia. When we set out at 6.30 it felt like a wet summer's
morning in Ireland, for soft rain was falling steadily and clouds
hung low over a warm, dripping world. From the first pass I
could see three new ranges with rags of silver mist trailing across
and between their blueness. As we reached the valley floor the
rain became a deluge and soon I was suffering from humidity
—a strange sensation, after three months of exhilarating dry-
ness. Here we slogged through mile after mile of thick, sticky
mud and it was impossible to keep swarms of tickling flies off
my face and neck. However, these incidental discomforts
seemed well worthwhile when I looked around at the gloriously
green countryside. Twice during the morning I stopped to graze
Jock, who tore ravenously at the sweet, fresh grass. I hope his
bowels survive this drastic change of diet.

Then came another long, sweaty climb to a high pass where
a sleety wind flayed us. From here sections of the road were
visible for many miles ahead, descending around mountain
after mountain, and it was three o'clock before we reached the
valley floor. The rough terrain ahead seemed likely to be uninhabited so I called at a settlement, bought a bundle of straw
for Jock's supper and tied it to the top of the load, ignoring
Jock's hint that it was already supper-time. He is indeed an
astute animal. Normally he never stops to shake himself more

than once a day, but today he chanced to shake after I had bought the straw and a little of it fell off, so I foolishly paused to give him time to eat it. Cause and effect were not lost on our Jock. Soon he stopped to shake again, turned expectantly towards the few dislodged mouthfuls and looked cheated when I cruelly picked them up and stuffed them back with the rest.

At the end of the next climb the road levelled out to wind around forested slopes where there were no sounds of voices or signs of cultivation. At sunset a barren valley appeared below us and on the far side I could see our road climbing another high, *tukul*-less range. I could also see a wide bridge, spanning a half-full river-bed, so as the sky promised more heavy rain I decided to camp beneath one of its arches. By the time we reached the bridge it was dark, and because Jock was stumbling wearily after our twenty-eight miles we had some difficulty getting down to river-level and finding a site. I cursed myself for having neglected to buy a torch in Waldia, where it hadn't occurred to me that it might be necessary to camp out on the main road.

In the morning I'll have to wait for a passing truck-driver to load Jock. However, this shouldn't cause much delay, as south-bound trucks often stop overnight at Waldia.


## 18 March. Dessie

It rained heavily last night, but the Italians built solid bridges and I woke dry, though stiff. My bed was a pile of small boulders, yet having once arranged my body in the most comfortable position even this unpromising couch didn't seem to matter. Wakening at 5.30, I saw that my tethering of Jock in the dark had been so inefficient that he had broken loose and had joined me under the arch, no doubt to shelter from the downpour.

As I was packing up, the distant roar of a giant petrol-truck reverberated through the valley. The driver and his mate made a clumsy job of the loading—possibly because they were so astonished by the whole situation—but in a village on the crest of the next ridge, where I stopped at a rudimentary 'bar-restaurant,' the servants reloaded carefully.

I was relishing my third big glass of tea when a tall, elderly man entered the shack, wearing scanty rags and carrying a bundle tied to his *dula*. Sitting near me, he ordered a small glass of tea, which costs only five cents in many areas. Then he quickly asked 'How much?' and, on being told 'Ten cents', cancelled his order and stood up to leave without argument or complaint. Obviously he was starting a long day's walk so I ordered tea and *dabo* for him, and after a moment's surprised hesitation he accepted his change of fortune with dignified gratitude. This tiny incident affected me more than any number of statistics on poverty.

All morning the road climbed gradually, the light breeze was cool and puffy white cloudlets drifted across a deep blue sky. We passed many settlements and on glistening pastures herds grazed contentedly, while from the smooth greenness rose long, brown mountains, with pine-woods darkening their lower slopes and round clouds resting on their summits—seeming to reflect faintly the cinnamon tinges of the earth beneath.

At 10.30 we stopped in a small town and Jock applied him-self to the fresh grass that grew around the *talla-beit*. On the way from Waldia I have rested in several towns and villages and I find the people of this (Wallo) province exceptionally friendly and hospitable. They seem less susceptible to the 'main-road infection' than the people of Begemdir—or perhaps they have been less exposed to it—and in the village homes one sees few foreign innovations.

On the long climb to the pass above Dessie the road wound around mountains so colossal that I felt like a midge on a cathedral wall; here every slope blazed with the waxy, orange-red flowers of a small cactus plant which grew amidst a scatter-ing of shimmering blue-green eucalyptus saplings. Because of the contortions of these mountains one first sees Dessie—hardly two miles away, but far, far below—about three hours before one arrives. After a long westward detour over the pass the road swings south-east, crosses a minor mountain and drops abruptly to the provincial capital.

On the pass we were joined by a friendly couple, also bound for Dessie, who offered to show me a short cut. Together we left the road and descended steeply to boggy, level pastures, which soon became water-logged ploughland, divided into sections by channels some three feet wide and four feet deep. Here it was almost impossible to keep upright for this newly-turned, flood-sodden clay was like a mixture of butter and treacle. Then, as we were crossing one of the channels, Jock misjudged his jump and slipped backward into the water. At first only his hind legs were stuck, but in his struggles to free himself he turned, slipped again, and became wedged between the walls of the channel.

For the next horrible half-hour the three of us, assisted by two small local boys, floundered through mud and water encouraging poor Jock to help himself. There was little else to be done, apart from removing his load and saddle—in the course of which operation I twice fell into the foul liquid at the bottom of the ditch. I could hardly bear to watch the unhappy creature again and again heaving up towards relatively solid ground, but always being defeated by slipperiness and lack of manœuvring space. Then at last he freed himself sufficiently for me to force him to turn in the other direction and I persuaded him to work his way along, slowly, to a point where the channel widened enough for him to jump clear. He looked shaken and miserable as we reloaded and liquid mud had increased the weight of both load and saddle. So I decided to give him a day off tomorrow.

On the outskirts of Dessie the friendly couple said good-bye and, as we continued towards the Touring Hotel, scores of delighted children were attracted to us by my mud-blackened person.

According to the official guide-book this Italian-built hotel 'offers fair service at moderate prices, but it is usually empty and has a gloomy atmosphere'. I have noticed before that the author of *Welcome to Ethiopia* makes it a point of honour never to mislead *faranjs* on the subject of Ethiopian hotels, and in his anxiety to be objective he sometimes goes too far. This enormous, clean building is furnished with elaborate tastelessness and, to the extent that only two of its one hundred and four bedrooms are occupied tonight, it does perhaps justify the adjective gloomy. Yet the staff welcomed us so cheerfully that it seems to me quite a jolly place. Two maid-servants conducted me to my room, down an interminable carpeted corridor on which I deposited ounces of mud at every step; and when I apologised for the havoc in my wake they laughed loudly, patted me forgivingly on the shoulder and told me that I was like a *buccolo* in the *tukul*. Perhaps they were glad to have something to do.

My 12/– room has a large window that opens, a knee-hole writing-desk, a comfortable bed, a bedside lamp, a wash-basin into which water will flow (I am assured) tomorrow morning, and a palatial wardrobe whose door-handles fall off at a touch. (This last point is of merely academic interest, since I have no robes to ward.) But the most valuable feature of the whole extraordinary establishment is its garden—some three acres of uncut grass, on which Jock is now gorging in the company of four bullocks, two sheep and five turkeys. This opulent grazing more than compensates for the fact that none of the taps in the innumerable bathrooms produces water, so I had to de-mud myself under a hesitantly-dripping cold shower. The Manageress is a blonde Italian woman, who was born sixty years ago in Eritrea. Universally known as 'Mamma', she is by far the fattest and one of the kindest people I have ever met.


*19 March*

There is a tragi-comic incongruity about some Ethiopian place-names. Dessie means 'My Joy', yet never have I seen such a depressingly ugly collection of human habitations. This is the third city of Ethiopia, with a population of about 80,000; but, as my guide-book explains, 'It is actually hard to call Dessie a city or a town; rather it fits the description of "overgrown village". Though the "town" is cramped in a small valley, its important position between the lowlands and the plateau and between Addis Ababa and Asmara, has contributed to its growth as an important commercial centre.'

However, by switching off the current between eyes and brain it is possible eventually to derive some joy from Dessie. The friendly people seem much more outgoing than most highlanders and, despite its monstrous ugliness, I greatly prefer this city to alien Asmara. At least Dessie is genuinely Ethiopian, with donkeys browsing in front gardens throughout the 'residential district', and women washing clothes in the gutters of the main streets.

Today I got into conversation with my fellow-guest—a withdrawn young government official from Addis, whose strained expression worried me until I discovered that dysentery is the cause. The patient blamed Dessie's water and asserted that Ethiopia is a very dangerous country for travellers. This is the first time that he has left the capital, in all his twenty-six years, and he hopes never to be forced to leave it again.

Jock's condition is not reassuring tonight. I have misgivings about his ability to cope with our last lap across the high plateau of Manz.

# 12

## *Mournfully to Manz*

*20 March. A Compound on a Mountain Top*

Not since leaving Asmara have I seen anything like the crowds that were coming into Dessie this morning. As we descended a steep path through thick eucalyptus woods our pace was slowed by the opposing 'rush-hour' traffic of hundreds of pushing humans, scurrying flocks of goats and sheep, scores of laden donkeys, horses and mules and many men and a few women riders, each with an attendant gun-bearer. This province seems to have an unusually big population of pack-horses, pack-mules and riding-mules.

At the foot of the mountain we crossed a bright green, semi-waterlogged valley where we were joined by a caravan of six men, ten donkeys, five horses and three mules, on their way home from yesterday's market. As usual, Jock was keen to trot in the lead—but, alarmingly, he soon lagged behind with the slowest of the donkeys.

A long, tough climb took us to a high pass from which our track dipped and rose through a magnificent wilderness of broken mountains. But it never dipped very far and we were steadily gaining altitude.

Since noon the sky had been cloudy and at 3.30 one shattering clap of thunder was followed by a rainstorm that came sweeping across the slopes before an icy wind with the force of a waterfall. Immediately I was soaked and my companions, now wrapped in heavy blankets, were very concerned about my pathetic state—which was even more pathetic than they realised, for my flea-bag and Huskies on Jock's back were also being saturated. Here we were at about 10,000 feet and soon the rain turned to painful hail as we sloshed muddily through a premature twilight.

At five o'clock this cluster of compounds appeared on the mountainside above the track and as I slid with Jock up the precipitous path an amiable old man, carrying two new-born lambs, shouted an invitation above the roar of the wind and led us into this already overcrowded *tukul*. It is the biggest hut I have stayed in—some fifty feet in circumference—and it now contains nine humans, one mule, two horses, three donkeys and innumerable sheep, lambs, goats, kids, cocks and hens. They all make such a din—especially the kids and lambs—that one can hardly hear oneself think.

The design of this *tukul* is exceptionally complicated. Its outer circle accommodates the livestock—except for one 'kitchen' section, where a cooking fire burns—and the stabling for mules, horses and donkeys is lower than the rest, so that their heads are almost on a level with the floor of the (theoretically) human preserve, where their fodder is thrown in heaps.

When we arrived extra wood was piled on the 'sitting-room' fire and I have spent the past two hours attempting, rather unsuccessfully, to dry my sodden clothes and flea-bag.

### 21 March. A Compound in a High Valley

The saddest date—for here I am parting from Jock.

Last night my sleep was somewhat disturbed by dampness, coldness and the occasional sheep or goat strolling over me. During the small hours I woke, reached for my torch and felt a disconcerting substance under my hand; it proved to be the afterbirth of a ewe, who had just lambed by my ear.

When we set out at 6.30 it was a cool, bright and very lovely morning, with a pale blue sky faintly cloud-streaked above wide brown sweeps of mountain. A few round stone huts were visible in the distance and on some lower slopes grew a scattering of twisted trees that might have been evergreen oaks. There was an oddly Scottish feel here. Acres of a green-brown herb, growing densely in little bushes, gave the illusion of heather and outcrops of silver-grey rock gleamed on the peat-dark soil.

Our track continued to climb steadily and I was alarmed to see Jock making heavy weather of it at the start of the day. When we came to a stone shelter where two little boys were selling pint tumblers of tea I stopped and led Jock to a grassy patch—but he wouldn't eat.

There were two other travellers already in the hut, chewing hard *dabo* with their tea and, as I drank, a pathetic family group came slowly up the track. The wife was horribly blind —her eyes, face and neck were covered in open sores—and she was being guided by a daughter of about twelve who walked ahead holding over her shoulder a long *dula* to which her mother clung nervously, whimpering with misery every time she stumbled on the rough path. The father was an advanced tubercular case. After each bout of coughing he wiped his blood-stained mouth with the end of his threadbare *shamma* and his sunken eyes held an expression of hopelessness that was more harrowing than any physical symptom. He didn't even beg medicine from the *faranj*. Indeed, when I paid for the family's teas and gave them my own *dabo* he looked utterly bewildered, as though this minute shred of good luck was something entirely new in his life. Clearly, both he and his wife are dying on their feet. One can only pray that they die soon.

Jock and I continued with the two men and their donkeys and half-an-hour later we were overtaken by another caravan of five men, four horses, twelve donkeys and a mule. This party was returning home from Dessie market so most of the animals were unladen; only a few donkeys carried blocks of salt or sacks of raw cotton.

The track fell steeply into a narrow valley, before climbing to a windy pass strewn with drifts of unmelted hail. Here we must have been at about 11,500 feet and we got little heat from the bright sun. On this Semienesque plateau only giant lobelias grew on the level turf, yet there was no Semien atmosphere of desolation and we met several heavily-laden caravans coming towards Dessie. The view from the edge of the plateau was overwhelming; but my appreciation of Ethiopia's unique magnificence is now tinged with sadness for in less than two weeks I will have come to the end of the road.

As we descended a few compounds appeared, amidst broad strips of ploughland and green pastures. Then the track switch-backed over mountain after mountain and at each ascent Jock moved more and more slowly—until at last, near the provincial border of Wollo and Shoa, he stopped at the foot of a hill, hung his head and could go no further.

By now I had established the usual comradeship of the track with my companions and immediately an agreeable man named Haile Malakot, who seemed to be in a position of some authority, ordered a youth to transfer my sack to one of the free donkeys. Jock then continued wearily and I followed with a heavy heart. Obviously he is so out of condition that he needs a month's rest, with top-quality feeding.

We arrived here soon after five o'clock and, judging by the temperature and vegetation, I should think we must be at about 9,000 feet. This settlement stands in the middle of a circular, undulating, fertile plateau, bounded on three sides by high mountains, and Haile Malakot's compound is by far the biggest for it contains three dwellings, two stables and two well-filled granaries. My host is the local headman, yet even so his *tukul* is shared with horses, calves, sheep and a mule.

Every local detail interests me as I have decided to leave Jock here and to take a donkey instead. Haile Malakot will gain about £12 on the exchange but he is welcome to it, for I feel sure that he will treat Jock properly. I have carefully inspected his horses and donkeys, who are in good condition, with not a sore among them. Another encouraging sign was the welcome given him by his dog as we approached the compound. This big, black, woolly creature (an uncommon type) came bounding and tail-wagging to greet his master, though most highland dogs cower and tremble when their owners appear.

The return of the travellers occasioned much kissing and many elaborate greetings all round, especially between Haile Malakot and his five small children. Instead of those children's presents which would have been brought from the city in a more affluent society, the youngsters got hunks of stale *dabo*, left uneaten by their father on his way, which were received with delighted grins and low bows. Their mother was given a present of several cheap, gaudy glass bangles, imported from Czechoslovakia.

Haile Malakot's family is one of the nicest I have stayed with; depressed as I am tonight, I do realise how lucky we were to meet him on this crucial day. At supper-time it became apparent that he has a total of nine children, four of whom are large, and it's difficult now to imagine everyone finding sleeping space in this *tukul*. But no doubt we'll eventually get huddled down somehow.

*22 March. Worra Ilu*

We did eventually get huddled down somehow and I slept quite well, though children were packed so closely around me that I could hardly wriggle my toes. When nature called me to the compound during the small hours it was impossible not to waken everyone. The exit was blocked by a complicated web of hide thongs, devised to keep the horses from moving into our compartment, and as I hesitated Haile Malakot impatiently pointed to the animal compartment, where I had earlier heard several human urinations in progress. Obediently manœuvring under the thongs I added my mite.

At 5.30 my hostess and her eldest daughter rose to begin the day's grain-grinding in one corner of the dark *tukul*. Inevitably they walked on me en route, so I lay awake wondering how many hours a highland woman spends each day at this task. It is strenuous work, but this morning mother and daughter were singing softly and happily, as they settled down to it. The rubbing of stone on stone, with grain between, and the calls of shepherd boys in the mountains are the two sounds of Ethiopia that I shall never forget.

As soon as it was faintly light I started to pack, crawling over and around various recumbent bodies. Then Haile Malakot rose, to let the animals out and fetch my chosen donkey. I didn't say good-bye to Jock, who went cantering off with the rest to enjoy a peaceful day on rich pastures.

Yesterday I had been impressed by the sturdiness and docility of one particular donkey, who now stood meekly while being loaded, and then went trotting briskly before the little boy who led me on to the path for Worra Ilu. However, when the child had turned back disillusion set in. Sturdy this creature certainly is, but nothing less docile can ever have stood on four legs. Very soon I had named him Satan.

To begin with I tried to lead the devil; but highland donkeys are never led, so he reacted by laying back his ears, rolling his eyes malevolently and riveting himself to Mother Earth. For some moments we remained thus, personifying Immovable Object and Irresistible Force. Naturally, Immovable Object won that round, so Irresistible Force decided to take rear action. Administering a whack on the rump, I uttered a fierce appropriate sound in my best Amharic—whereupon Satan wheeled abruptly and headed for home at a gallop. When I had cut off his retreat another whack sent him trotting—momentarily—in the right direction. What I needed now was one of those mountain paths off which you cannot move; on a plateau Satan held all the trumps for there was nothing to prevent him from going wherever the fancy led him.

Over the next ten miles I had to pursue Satan repeatedly, as he fled to east, west or north. Oddly, south seemed the one point of the compass to which he could not reconcile himself. Nor did the weather help. It had been heavily overcast when we started out and soon a gale was sweeping sheets of sleety rain across the plateau and turning the ground to slippery, sticky black mud, which meant that every step demanded twice the normal expenditure of energy. Despite my exertions I quickly became so numb that my stiff fingers couldn't open the buttons of my shirt-pocket. Not even in the Semiens have I experienced such intense cold.

Instead of adjusting to his new situation Satan became increasingly xenophobic and when we arrived here I felt too demoralised to continue without a donkey-boy—though I guessed that it wouldn't be easy to find anyone willing to accompany me into Manz.

Worra Ilu, the birthplace of the Empress Zauditu, is the usual spread-out collection of tin-roofed mud hovels, set among blue-gums. The 'hotel' is a tiny doss-house, run by the Amharic wife of a Yemeni trader who settled in Ethiopia fifteen years ago. This man now speaks fluent Amharinya and has successfully adapted himself to the local way of life. These Yemeni small-town traders are more integrated with the highlanders than any other foreigners, yet the moment I met Hussein I was aware of a strong bond between us. He doesn't speak one word of English, but he and I have established the kind of intuitive understanding that could never exist between me and the local English-speakers. As I now feel so at ease with the highlanders this is a significant measure of the extraordinary degree of 'ingrown-ness' that marks their character.

I had just changed from my soaked shirt into my slightly less soaked jacket when Worra Ilu's four hundred schoolchildren, freed for their midday meal, 'discovered' me. Not since my arrival at Mai Cheneta have I been so enthusiastically mobbed. Despite this town being only two days' walk from Dessie few of these children had ever before seen a white person (though their parents must have seen many Italians) and, because education of a sort has made them aware of the *faranj* world, they were avid to meet a real live European. For seven hours I was submerged by them, often almost to the point of suffocation, as scores of bodies seethed around me. When it was time for afternoon classes the eleven teachers found it impossible to reclaim their pupils from my 'hotel', where the senior boys were packing the restaurant–kitchen–bedroom, while the juniors rioted outside the door, impatient for their glimpse of the *faranj*. As the teachers were scarcely less interested than the children I was invited to the new school—a handsome stone building—to make a lecture tour of the classrooms, so my afternoon was even more exhausting than it would have been had I continued towards Manz with Satan.

An hour ago the headmaster produced a twenty-year-old schoolboy, fittingly named Assefa, who will drive Satan to the bus terminus at Sali Dingai if I pay his bus fare north to Dessie. He doesn't mind walking alone from Dessie to Worra Ilu, but he says that it would be 'dangerous' for him to return alone through Manz, where the people are 'very wild'. The fact that he will miss a week's schooling seems not to worry anyone, and I gather that many of these pupils attend classes only irregularly.

*23 March. A Compound on a High Plateau*

On our way out of Worra Ilu I stopped at the school to say good-bye just as that familiar ceremony, which marks the start of each highland schoolday, was about to begin. Every morning all the pupils line up in military formation around a tall flag-staff to sing the National Anthem while Ethiopia's flag is being raised, and this attempt to foster nationalism in a tribal society is followed by a prayer for the Emperor. One boy faces the assembly, bent double, and gives out the prayer—to which everyone else, also bent double, vigorously responds. Today, however, the Worra Ilu assembly didn't bend very far, most eyes remaining on me.

Satan's mood was no less satanic this morning. He tried to bite my leg as he was being loaded, and for the first five miles Assefa and I were fully occupied keeping him on the right track. Crowds were coming to market, many carrying balls of wool measuring at least two feet in circumference, for we are now in Ethiopia's only wool-producing area. Elsewhere, highland sheep are rarely sheared and the idea of breeding sheep to sell their wool is unknown.

Here Satan allowed little leisure for admiring the landscape, but occasionally I paused to gaze over the rain-freshened miles of boulder-strewn turf that swept to the horizon on our right, or to peer into the chasm that separated this plateau from the next. Then our path temporarily left the edge of the chasm and wound across a few miles of pasture and ploughland, scattered with compounds enclosed by solid, shoulder-high walls. Some of the stone *tukuls* were two-storeyed and all seemed to have been built with unusual skill.

Soon we were again overlooking the gorge, from the point where our track began a four-hour descent. Visually, this was among the most dramatic moments of the whole trek. Standing on the edge of the escarpment I had an unimpeded view of the floor of the gorge 4,000 feet below, and the Uacit river was barely visible though it is now a considerable torrent. Beyond the gorge another long, level tableland rose sheer and to the south-east stretched a third, which was Manz.

The descent took us gradually south, on a giants' step-ladder formed by three flat, wide ledges. An almost vertical rock stair-way led down the escarpment but from its base the gradient was easier and sometimes we were walking on level ground, through thick forest above tremendous drops, as the path sought another point from which it could continue the descent.

On each ledge were a few impoverished compounds and once we stopped to ask for *talla*. Approaching the *tukuls*, I saw a sight that briefly curdled my blood. In a stubble-field, beside a pile of red embers, an old man was hacking the head of a hideously human-looking form. When I came nearer, and realised that the corpse was a roasted baboon, I felt quite weak with relief. In this area baboons do enormous damage to crops so they are sometimes pursued by men and dogs and clubbed to death when cornered. The victim is then roasted and fed to the dogs to increase their enthusiasm for the chase.

In this compound we were warmly welcomed by two old men and three old women. They gave us many pints of rough *talla*, many cups of weak coffee, an unfamiliar kind of chocolate-coloured *dabo* which was surprisingly palatable though it had a strange consistency (perhaps half-set cement would be similar), and cold stewed beans which both looked and tasted repulsive. The squalor of the *tukul* was extreme and the old people were grief-stricken because yesterday their only cow—due to calve soon—and their only ox died of some disease which has dysentery as its chief symptom. The magnitude of this disaster is hard for us to grasp. These animals were their most valuable possessions—worth at least two hundred dollars—and they have no hope of replacing them. The women wept as they told us, the men sat gazing dully at the floor. Now they are without an ox to pull the plough and the neighbours are too poor to lend them one. Yet when we left, full of their food and drink, they refused to accept any money.

During the rest of the descent it got hotter every moment and on the floor of the gorge the temperature must have been about 90°F. When I looked up at the plateau from which we had come it seemed utterly inaccessible: and when I looked up at the plateau to which we were going that seemed equally inaccessible. Here we stood at the confluence of two rivers, both about two hundred yards wide. A week ago they would have been almost dry and even today they were hardly one-third full, but several streams of new flood-water (the colour of strong milky tea) went racing over boulders from between which little shrubs were being uprooted and swept away towards the Blue Nile, the White Nile and the Mediterranean.

Having crossed the Uacit we turned west up the tributary gorge. At the foot of each colossal mountain-wall strips of rich arable land were being ploughed and irrigated by men from invisible settlements on the plateaux, and twelve times we had to cross branches of the river. As we ascended, the ravine narrowed and the streams became deeper and faster, until we found it difficult to keep our feet on the stony bed against the powerful, waist-deep current. Here a slip would have been unfortunate, for no one could possibly swim in this swirling, boulderous torrent. Satan tackled these fordings gamely—give the devil his due. Half-way up the gorge we had been joined by a young priest riding a white horse and by two men driving donkeys. Undoubtedly this asinine company heartened Satan, who has probably never before travelled alone.

Even between wadings the going was tiring—over deep, fine sand or across stretches of big, loose stones. The discomfort of these stones was compensated for by their variety of tints—pale pink, primrose yellow, dark and light green, mauve, silver flecked with white, dark red, and a few chunks of what looked like Connemara marble.

The gorge had narrowed to about fifty yards when we came to the start of a two-hour climb as severe as any Semien ascent. Before going up we paused to rest and I offered the wilting Assefa some *dabo*, which Hussein had given me as a farewell present. Knowing it to have been baked by Muslims he sniffed at it suspiciously and asked if it contained milk, which would break his Lenten fasting laws. I took a chance and said 'No milk—water', and at once he ate it ravenously.

At 5.45 we began to climb and by 6.45 daylight had become bright moonlight, without any perceptible dusk. The exhilaration of such an ascent is so tremendous that I enjoyed every sweating step, though we were at the end of a long day. There was only one brief, unpleasant stretch, where the moon was hidden by an immeasurably high cliff. My torch didn't help much and on one side of the rough rock stairs lay a deep ravine.

Then I heard a sound that took me back to the Semiens— the barking of hundreds of Gelada baboons. From every side they were abusing us and their shrieks, yells and screams, amplified and distorted by echoes, created an unearthly effect on this moonlit mountain, where previously the immense silence had been broken only by our footsteps.

I paused to wait for the others at the base of the escarpment and never shall I forget the beauty of that scene. Around me jagged escarpments rose sheer, and beyond the gorge lay the symmetrical, ebony line of the opposite plateau, and beneath a brilliant moon the strange splendour of this landscape seemed utterly unreal, with every abyss a well of blackness and every rocky pinnacle a monstrous tower of silver.

When we reached the top of the 10,000-foot Manz escarpment my shirt was sodden, for the normal highland evaporation had been unequal to the sweat produced by this climb. Here, to heighten the other-worldly feeling of my arrival at Manz, lightning such as I have never seen before went spurting in quivering flares of red and orange along the cloudy northeastern horizon. I had expected an easy walk at this stage but several steep hills lay ahead and when the priest had remounted he led us towards them. During that last half-hour I exulted in the simple romance of our little procession, as we climbed a high ploughed hill towards the tall black trees on its summit, following by moonlight the white horse with his white-robed, white-burbaned rider.

In this large compound the circular top storey of a stable is the guest-room. Within moments of our arrival a big fire had been lit so I took off my drenched shirt and sat close to the flames, eating new-baked *dabo* and curds. The local *talla* (*karakee*) is the best of all the highland beers—dark, slightly thick, bitter as unsweatened lemon-juice and miraculously restoring.

Our host and his sons are delightful, though very shy of the *faranj*. Oddly enough, no women have yet appeared. I asked if the locals often go to Addis—the capital is less than a week's walk away—but none of the company had ever been there.

During supper Assefa told me about his own family, who live beyond the gorge. A year ago his two brothers and an aunt were killed by lightning, while sitting chatting in the aunt's *tukul*, and he is the only surviving son. Because his parents are poor—'a little land, one donkey, one ox, two horses and three cows'—his schooling is being paid for by a rich uncle who works as a waiter in Addis. Assefa's intelligence is so limited that schooling is unlikely to be of the slightest benefit to him. But his parents imagine that once 'educated' he will be able to support them in their old age so, despite his brothers having been killed, they allow him to remain away from home and provide all his food—flour and spices.

## 24 March. Mehal Meda

This morning the clear dawn air felt icy. While Satan was being loaded I looked around my first Manze compound, which was built on a steep slope, with giant Semien-type thistles growing above it. There were three large dwellings, four two-storied stables-cum-granaries and three unusual igloo-type stone grain-bins. Everything had been solidly constructed with exceptional skill. Unlike the Semien people, these Manzes have been architecturally inspired by their climate. I noticed that cow-pats, with halved egg-shells embedded in them, had been stuck to the wall at eye-level beside each *tukul* door—presumably to ward off evil spirits.

By 6.30 a.m. the priest was leading us around the flank of the mountain on to a wide plain, dotted with round hills and flat-topped protuberances of bare volcanic rock which was riven by spectacular chasms.

On this vast expanse of yellow-green turf grazed thousands of tiny sheep. Their colouring was remarkably varied—black, red-brown, white, nigger-brown, grey and every combination of all these colours. Many cattle also grazed here, and mules, horses and donkeys: but I saw no goats.

At ten o'clock we stopped at the priest's wife's grandmother's compound and were entertained for two hours on roast barley, coffee, *injara*, bean-*wat* and, for the non-fasting *faranj*, three gourds of curds. This was a typical Manze compound with an attractive thatched archway over the entrance in the enclosure wall. Two cylindrical, straw-wrapped mud and wicker-work beehives were hanging below the eaves of the granary, each about four feet long and eighteen inches in circumference with a hole two inches in diameter at one end. Assefa told me that the highlanders consider bee-keeping 'men's work' and traditionally the hives are cleaned on New Year's Day, in September. Most of the honey is used for making *tej*, but sometimes it is eaten plain, as a delicacy. In Lalibela, at the Governor's home,

I was given a toffee-like confection made by spreading honey on a tray and leaving it beneath the sun for a few hours.

The priest was staying with his in-laws for the day so we continued on our own. All the morning Satan had been trotting contentedly behind the horse but now he lapsed into his evil ways and Assefa, who was complaining of leg-pains and general debility, left most of the work to me. However, on these glorious uplands—where the wind was cold, the sun warm and the sky patterned with high, white clouds—I felt so jubilant that the chasing of a demoniacal donkey seemed just another pleasure.

At three o'clock we reached this village, which is soon to be made the district administrative headquarters. Sheets of tin and piles of stones and building timber lie all over the place and I was startled to see a small tractor amidst the half-built houses. In the six years since Donald Levine wrote *Wax and Gold* there have been many changes here. He was the first *faranj* to explore Manz, but now a rough motor-track links it with Addis and during the dry season a slow bus rattles through twice a week to Mehal Meda, where one can buy Italian-made wine and beer. The rapid 'progress' of this area is perhaps owing to Haile Selassie's special affection for Manz—the homeland of the present dynasty.

I wanted to spend the night in a settlement, and after half-an-hour at a *talla-beit* we continued down the main street. Then someone shouted and looking round I saw two angry men pursuing us. Within a moment we had been overtaken; they gripped my arms and claimed to be policemen, saying that I must come with them for questioning. One man was obviously drunk, neither wore anything remotely resembling a uniform and both were behaving outrageously. I therefore 'resisted arrest' and during the brawl that followed—watched by half the village and by a cringing Assefa—the metal buckle of my bush-shirt was bent, my arms were bruised and the drunk gave me an agonising punch in the stomach. Then a third man intervened. He was wearing the remains of a uniform beneath a filthy *shamma*, and in poor English he confirmed that my attackers were policemen and explained that they wanted to see my passport. I replied furiously that though I have been in

Ethiopia for three months the police had never before demanded
my passport—which I don't have with me, since the Begemdir
Chief of Police had advised me to send it to Addis lest it should
be stolen on the way. At this the third man accused me of
lying, twisted my arms behind my back and marched me off to
the police station—with the other two in attendance and a
trembling Assefa driving Satan in our wake.

On the rare occasions when I lose my temper the loss is total
and I was shaking with rage as we entered the mud shack
'police station'. The police C.O. matched his subordinates. He
sat behind a wobbly desk in a dark little room, wearing a four-
day beard and a torn army great-coat under his *shamma*. Pushing my way through a group of arguing men I told him exactly
what I thought of the Mehal Meda police force. Then insult
was indeed added to injury, for the man who had arrested me
said sneeringly, 'Don't be so afraid!' Glaring, I snapped that
fear was the last emotion likely to be aroused in me by such a
dishevelled bunch of no-goods; and I observed spitefully that
he and his companions would have their own reasons to be
afraid when I reported this incident to the Addis authorities.
For good measure I threw in the names of Leilt Aida, Ras
Mangasha and Iskander Desta—whereupon everyone stopped
yelling at me.

After a moment's silence, the C.O. remarked that I had
better see the local Governor. I was then conducted to a
recently-built shack, where a neatly-dressed but unimposing
man sat rather self-consciously behind a brand-new, mock-
mahogany desk with a pile of virginal ledgers on either side of
the blotting pad. He was soon taken far out of his depth by the
situation, as four men were simultaneously giving him different
versions of the story of my arrest. He brusquely signed that I
was to sit on a bench by the wall and wait.

Ten minutes later an adequate interpreter appeared. Amsalu
is the local Medical Officer and a most agreeable young man.
He begged me not to be so angry, though my rage had already
gone off the boil, and he clearly explained the situation to the
Governor, Ato Balatchaw. Now the Big Man was awkwardly
placed. To release me would be to admit that I had been
'wrongfully detained'; to keep me in custody, after all this talk

about royalty, might prove calamitous. I suggested, as an honourable compromise, that Leilt Aida be telephoned by way of establishing my credentials. However, Mehal Meda has no telephone, so after much discussion and deliberation it was decided that a police officer would accompany me to Molale tomorrow morning and telephone Makalle from there. This satisfied everyone—though the Governor looked slightly apprehensive at the prospect of my discussing his police force with Leilt Aida.

I was then escorted back to a subdued C.O. who spent the next forty minutes 'taking my statement' for the records, with Amsalu's assistance. Obviously my account of the incident was being carefully edited and I would give a lot to know what sort of statement I signed at the end of this performance.

I am now relaxing in a minute 'hotel'. Its one earth-floored room contains two small iron-beds, with broken springs and revolting sheets. Bugs abound and the wall-paper consists of pictures from American, English, Italian and French magazines, many of which have been stuck on upside-down.

Mehal Meda is suffering from collective guilt this evening. Crowds of men and women have come to call, deploring my unlucky encounter, emphasising that none of the policemen involved was a Manze and consoling me with gifts of *talla*, *tej*, coffee, tea, roasted grain, stewed beans, curds and hard-boiled eggs. Nowhere in the highlands have I met with greater kindness.

Meanwhile Amsalu and the local teachers have been asking me the usual questions about my own country and my impressions of their country. When Dr Donald Levine was mentioned affectionate smiles lit up the grave faces of the non-English speakers who were sitting around us and one elderly man asked eagerly if I knew 'Dr Donald'. I replied that I hadn't the honour to know him personally but that I had read his book, and at once Amsalu seized my arm and begged me to send him a copy. He is prepared to spend almost a month's salary on it, but inevitably *Wax and Gold* has been banned in Ethiopia. This political censorship of books seems to me a serious mistake, for it arouses suspicions that things are more rotten in the state of Ethiopia than they actually are. Several

English-speakers have asked me what scandalous governmental secrets are revealed in *Wax and Gold,* and they look understandably bewildered when I explain that it is not an exposure of official iniquities but a scholarly study of their culture at its present stage of transition.

When I opened my notebook, for Amsalu to write his name and address on the back page, I noticed a folded bit of paper tucked away there. Examining it, I found that it was the ineffectual chit from the Governor of Lalibela to the priests of Imrahanna Kristos so I tossed it towards a pile of litter on the table. Then Amsalu caught sight of the Amharic script and the countless seals and stamps that bedeck every Ethiopian document, however insignificant, and glancing through it he exclaimed, 'But *this* would have done the police, instead of your passport!' I stared at him, and confessed that *faranjs* don't think of offering chits as substitutes for passports; but he insisted that any officially stamped paper serves the purpose and said that if we brought this chit to the Governor's home I would immediately be freed.

The night wind felt icy as the four teachers walked with me through the village. Approaching the Governor's shack we heard horrible noises emanating from his transistor radio and when Amsalu shouted loudly for a servant to come to announce us no one could hear him. I suggested knocking on the tin door but this appalled my companions, as it is bad manners for the *hoi-polloi* to communicate directly with a Big Man. However, when Amsalu had again shouted unavailingly, several times, I gave up pandering to local etiquette and hammered the tin sheets resoundingly.

At once Ato Balatchaw appeared, wrapped in his *shamma.* He beckoned us crossly into his living-room, where an apologetic Amsalu produced the precious chit—and, realising that I need not discuss his police force with Leilt Aida, the Governor stopped being cross. Five minutes later we were departing, with a written permit for me to proceed to Molale unescorted. It surprised me to find that a piece of highland 'official business' could be transacted so briskly.

*25 March. Molale*

Both geographically and historically there is a certain fitness about trekking through this region towards the end of my journey. In Manz the beauty of these highlands reaches a triumphant crescendo of light, space, colouring and formation; and here one is in the homeland of the House of Shoa, whose head now occupies the Solomonic Throne.

If the highlands in general seem remote from the rest of the world, Manz in particular seems remote even from the rest of the highlands. Its atmosphere is unique. This is partly because of physical differences—well-built stone dwellings replace flimsy *tukuls*, heavy, dark woollen cloaks are used instead of *shammas*, the average altitude is 10,000 feet—and partly because of the character of the people, who seem to have more individuality than most highlanders. They also seem more mentally alert, more physically vigorous and more arrogant. Even within Manz, communication between the three districts has always been difficult because of the chasms that split the plateau and today we crossed three in fifteen miles. This morning crowds were coming to market as we approached the first gorge. It is inhabited by Gelada baboons, scores of whom were sitting near the path saying uncomplimentary things to the passers-by, and at its head is a hundred-foot waterfall which must be gloriously exciting during the rains. Most of the women were wearing brown, or brown and black, ankle-length gowns and the barefooted men, in their long, rough, brown cloaks, looked like so many Franciscans. The more prosperous also wore sheepskin capes around their shoulders for at this height the mornings are bitterly cold.

The ascent from the bottom of the third gorge was exhilaratingly difficult. Assefa and Satan went a long way round while I rock-climbed straight up the smooth, slightly sloping grey cliff. With Addis so near, I am getting an extra, bitter-sweet pleasure from every highland experience.

Beyond the gorges our track wound between low, brown hills, before bringing us on to a wide plain planted with barley —some silver-green, some ripely golden. Here we began to meet the crowds returning from Molale market. Many women

as well as men were riding on mules, who wore silver necklaces and most people greeted me with bows and smiles. I
noticed an unusual variety of skin-colour, from almost black to
palest brown—which is surprising, for unlike most parts of
Shoa Manz was never overrun by the Galla. Perhaps the darker-
skinned inhabitants are the descendants of slaves captured by
the renowned Manze warriors when they were recovering
Galla-conquered territory for their Emperor Menelik II.

On our arrival at this little town, soon after three o'clock,
Assefa abruptly announced that he was too exhausted to walk
another step. Satan was also looking sorry for himself so we
pushed through the still-crowded market-place to a *talla-beit*,
accumulating the inevitable retinue of schoolboys. Ten minutes
later the Director (Headmaster) of the school appeared in the
doorway, expressed disapproval of a *faranj* drinking with the
peasantry and invited me to be his guest for the night.

Ato Beda Mariam lives in a row of stable-like dwellings
behind the three-year-old, two-storied school which is Molale's
biggest building. There are eight grades in this school (twelve
is the maximum) and ten teachers cope with about four hundred pupils. Here again I found that merely knowing the name
of 'Dr Donald' sent my status rocketing. Americans in general,
and the Peace Corps in particular, are unpopular among Ato
Beda Mariam and his staff, as they are among the majority of
the English-speaking Ethiopians with whom I have discussed
them. Yet in Manz Dr Levine is hardly regarded as a *faranj*,
and only those who have experienced the highlanders' aloofness
can appreciate what a compliment this is.

My thirty-two-year-old host has been in charge of this school
for the past five years. His English is excellent and I was
astounded to hear that he only began his schooling at the age
of seventeen. The traditional opposition to state-sponsored
education is so strong in Manz that many of Molale's pupils
have run away from home and are paying for their own education by doing odd jobs in the town; but parental opposition is
lessening yearly because of the infectious illusion that a state-
school education means 'instant wealth'.

Ato Beda Mariam rejoices at this change but I do not. I
disagree with the argument that Ethiopia cannot afford to

postpone the education of the masses until a sufficient number of adequately qualified teachers is available. Apart from two Gondares in a remote settlement, he himself is the first rural teacher I have met who possesses both the ability and the outlook required for this vocation. Nothing in this country depresses me as much as the harm being done to Ethiopia's children by half-baked, cynical, unworthy teachers. I have become so fond of the highlanders that this problem distresses and alarms me as would the illness of a friend. It is a problem common to all 'undeveloped countries', but highland children seem extra vulnerable to the terrible consequences of having a mock-Western education unskilfully thrust upon them. In Asmara or Addis, *faranjs* may study statistics and be impressed by the Emperor's zeal for educating his subjects, but in the little towns and villages one is swamped with despair when one meets either teachers or pupils. Here again one feels guilty on behalf of Western civilisation. What damage are we doing, blindly and swiftly, to those races who are being taught that because we are materially richer we must be emulated without question? What compels us to infect everyone else with our own sick urgency to change, soften and standardise? How can we have the effrontery to lord it over peoples who retain what we have lost—a sane awareness that what matters most is immeasurable?

### 26 March. Sali Dingai

Today we walked only sixteen miles, but the three-hour descent from Manz, into another low, hot river-gorge, and the tough climb to this 9,000-foot plateau have left Assefa semi-invalided and Satan too dispirited even to attempt to go home.

When we left Molale a steely sky hung low and the wind blew harsh, but soon the sun was shining and at midday the bottom of the gorge felt equatorial. Yet a few hours later, as I climbed the escarpment below Sali Dingai, Manz was hidden by dark clouds, thunder was crashing nearby and a sleet-laden gale was tearing at my sweat-soaked shirt. Assefa and Satan were a long way behind so I sat near the edge of the escarpment overlooking the country we had just crossed—a scene made all the more dramatic by swiftly-moving cloud-masses and sulphurous flickerings of lightning. Then, thinking of the beauty that I had seen, even within the past eight hours, I felt very sad. Yet it is not only through their beauty that these highlands have enchanted me. I love them, too, for their challenging brutality, and had I seen the beauty without meeting the challenge I could not now feel so attached to Ethiopia. Its muscle-searing climbs and nerve-racking descents, its powdery dust and vicious thorns, its heat, cold, hunger and thirst, its savage precipices, treacherous paths and pathless forests— these, as much as its wide, proud, chaotic landscapes, are the characteristics that have forged the bond.

Assefa and Satan ascended by a steep, roundabout path that avoided the escarpment. Reunited, the three of us climbed from this broad ledge, over a still higher summit, to the big village of Sali Dingai—an outpost of 'motor-road civilisation'. A new fifteen-mile track links it to the main Asmara–Dessie–Addis road and there is a daily bus-service. Where the track ends a few square shacks and a small school have recently been built; otherwise Sali Dingai remains unspoiled, though one can foresee it changing soon.

By this time Assefa and I had but a single thought and, as we searched for *talla*, a cheerful man emerged from a mud shack and invited us to help celebrate the christening of his fifth son. In the dark, straw-strewn room about forty men sat on mud benches around the walls, fondling rifles, while a minstrel played in the centre of the floor and a tall, elderly woman sang and danced with strange, fierce gaiety.

This invitation was providential, as no one could long remain sad at a highland party. After an enormous meal, accompanied by much *talla*, I found myself holding a half-pint tumbler brimming with *araki*, which normally is served in tiny vessels. I sipped the burning spirit slowly, but was soon cut off from reality by a sentimental haze through which I regarded myself, my host, his fifth son, all his other sons, my fellow-guests, all highlanders, the world in general—and even the prospect of arriving in Addis—with benevolence.

At seven o'clock Samuel, the Director of the school,

waveringly led Assefa and me towards his home. Evidently I was then at the maudlin stage; on looking up at the brilliance of the storm-cleared sky I wanted to weep because in comparison Irish skies seem to have so few stars.

Lots of strong black coffee sobered us and when I was again able to focus I saw that my hostess is a most beautiful and charming young woman. Both she and her husband are Addis-born and educated but here they are living—resentfully—at a level little higher than that of the local peasants.

With sobriety my gloom returned and as I sat dolefully thinking of the motor-road ahead it was ironical to hear Samuel and his wife envying me because within three or four days I will be in Addis.


## 27 March. Addis Ababa

An abrupt ending—but my arrival here without Jock would in any case have been imperfect, and it was almost a relief to have the painful farewell stage cut short.

This morning I found Satan severely lame in both hind legs. Were I a highlander I would have loaded him up regardless and beaten him on his way. Not being a highlander I gave him to Samuel, as a present of doubtful value, and a little boy shouldered my sack to the bus-stop.

It was a wonderful morning, in this high, cool world of clarity, spaciousness and quiet; but such a curious numbness had crept over me that I observed it without feeling it. The bus was due at eight o'clock and I was being seen off by three teachers and half-a-dozen other men. To them I was at last doing the normal thing by getting on a *makeena*, after walking through Manz for some infinitely obscure reason. They had no conception of the significance of the occasion for me and I chatted casually with them while inwardly trying to adjust to the fact that now—already—my trek was ended.

The mini-bus arrived on time and Samuel carefully explained that when we reached the main road I must change on to the big Dessie–Addis bus. He added, wistfully, that by midday I would be in the capital of the Empire; and I politely pretended to be pleased at the thought.

Waiting for the bus to start I took out my notebook and totted up the miles I have walked—according to my pocket pedometer—since landing at Massawah. As I passed the 800 mark, and got to 900, and then 950, I became aware of a childish suspense. At the end I checked and re-checked; but there was no mistake—the final figure was 1,024 miles.

# Epilogue

Addis Ababa means 'New Flower', a misnomer that many *faranjs* find wonderfully funny. However, this malformed infant capital so atrophied my sense of humour that I never saw the joke. My first impression, as the bus topped a ridge some five miles from Addis, was of more tin roofs than usual among more blue-gums than usual, and my permanent impression was of a calamitously *unreal* city. Other recently-modernised non-European capitals seem unreal too, and are all the more enchanting for that. Yet they are unreal only in relation to the Western visitor, whereas Addis Ababa is unreal in relation to Ethiopia.

The gulf between capital and countryside appeared repeatedly during my conversations with Addis' foreign residents. Whether diplomats, businessmen or nurses, the majority expressed identical opinions about Ethiopia and usually the experiences on which their opinions were based differed considerably from those of travellers in the provinces. To most foreigners familiar with the provinces Addis seems like a faked jewel that has been hastily stuck on to the fabric of the Empire and that may fall off any day, since it represents a centralised administration unacceptable to millions of the Emperor's subjects.

Among the city's handicaps are an immaturity for which no one can be blamed, as it was founded only eighty years ago, and a proliferation of architectural excesses for which many people can and should be blamed. Recently a colossal hospital was built in memory of the Duke of Harrar, before any nurses had been trained to staff it, and on going to a vast, avant-garde bank to change travellers' cheques one finds the splendour of the building equalled only by the multitude of clerks with whom one has to deal with while transacting a simple bit of business. All over the city other extravagant, meaningless new buildings rise at random from amidst a huddle of mud shacks, to offend both the eye and the reason of the beholder. Many of the V.I.P.s who visit Ethiopia get no further than Addis and evidently these architectural frolics are partly inspired by a desire to create an impression of imminent prosperity. Much suffering might have been averted by the spending of this money in drought areas.

Another aspect of the inspiration to 'develop' Addis is even more dangerous—the city's use as a screen behind which the Ethiopians themselves hide from the facts of their national life. In the 1960's the simplest way to gratify the old Amharic blind pride is by building a spectacular capital: to lessen trachoma or forestall famine in remote areas would be unobtrusive achievements, giving no impression of Instant Progress. All highlanders are proud of Addis—the many who have never been there as well as the few who can compare it with other capitals. For everyone it is a triumphant symbol of what Ethiopia can do when she tries.

The formidable communication problem presented by the highland terrain is sometimes given as an excuse for this governmental flight from reality. Yet, unlike many other undeveloped countries, Northern Ethiopia is fortunate in having a uniquely healthy climate and a generally self-sufficient population. In *The Christian Romance of Alexander the Great** we read that one day Alexander and his soldiers came to the City of Saints 'where the water is sweeter than the grapes of which wine is made and the stones are of sard, chalcedony, jacinth and sapphire, where there is neither freezing cold nor parching heat, neither summer nor winter, neither oppression nor tears. Instead of snow, manna falleth from heaven. All their wells and rock cisterns are filled with honey, and every beast among them is filled with milk.' Granted this is a Romance, not an agricultural survey, but it does convey truly the feeling of the highlands, where an energetic and responsible government could bring prosperity to most regions.

My six weeks' stay in Addis Ababa was an instructive ordeal,

* An original Ethiopian work, translated by Sir C. Wallis Budge.

though I might have learned a lot more had I not been trapped in the *faranj* ghetto. As time passed the frustration of living *among* a people, yet not *with* them, made me more and more restive. On a few occasions I slunk away from my opulent base to drink in a *tej-beit* down an alleyway, but though I was always treated politely my presence caused embarrassment and a furtive amusement. Addis is not yet on the intercontinental hitch-hiking route and the locals expect *faranjs* to keep to themselves. Then, shortly before flying home I broke loose and went into the mountains for a day to say farewell to the real Ethiopia.

It was a cloudy morning when I set out, heading straight for a mountain to the south-east. The mood of the moment made me feel that any mountain would do—except Entoto, which has recently been afflicted by a motor-road. This was the Sunday after the Orthodox Easter and as I crossed the city every alleyway was bubbling with wedding excitement; when Lent ends one has the impression that half the younger generation are about to be married. Here, as in India, weddings are cripplingly expensive. White banqueting tents stood in scores of tiny compounds, everyone was out in their Easter best, minstrels were rehearsing in *tej-beits*, women were scurrying to and fro with *injara*-baskets on their heads and basins of *wat* in their hands and men were carrying zinc buckets, earthen jars and wooden casks brimming with *talla* or *tej*.

Most of my route lay between tin-roofed shacks and the rough laneways were ankle-deep in thick, black, stinking liquid. So few foreigners ever leave the main streets that hoardes of children followed me, screaming '*Faranj! Faranj!*' Then suddenly I would find myself crossing a broad tarred road, lined with tall new buildings, gaudy petrol stations and glossy advertisement hoardings; these roads were hazardous because of the mechanised wedding processions of the richer citizens, who were driving like things demented (or prematurely drunk) in cars garlanded with flowers and over-loàded with wildly-singing guests. Yet immediately beyond Addis the only signs of a city's nearness are foot-bridges across rivers that elsewhere would have to be forded and a line of electricity pylons.

This pleasant, placidly hilly country had easy, smooth slopes, newly-green meadows, neat little pinewoods and wide planta-

tions of blue-gum saplings whose young leaves trembled like
shot silk, in the gentlest of breezes. The few hamlets were
Amharic, except for one little Galla settlement, and the countryside was neither intensively cultivated nor densely populated.
At one time I walked for an hour without seeing anybody.

The mountain I climbed is over 10,000 feet but the view
from the summit was obscured by haze; yet here I felt again
that familiar, overwhelmed sensation experienced so often
before in this vast, withdrawn highland world. Below me lay
'The New Flower'—its petals tin roofs, its stalks baby sky-
scrapers, its leaves eucalyptus groves—and now it seemed more
than ever a pathetic, futile bid to escape from these rough
solitudes that will long remain the reality at the heart of the
Empire.

Descending by a different route I came to level pasturelands,
dense with mushrooms, which cost thirty shillings for an imported tin in the Addis supermarket. Not since childhood have
I seen so many blobs of white satin half-concealed by thick,
cropped grass. My bush shirt had four capacious pockets and
I spent the next hour filling them all, ritually quartering those
pastures in a state of peaceful obsession.

Now the early afternoon sky had clouded over. The lines
of the surrounding mountains were blurred, the air was moistly
warm and it might have been the sort of August day on which
one wanders through Irish fields absorbed in this same cosy
adventure. Then thudding hoofs broke the stillness and some
forty young horses came galloping towards me from behind a
eucalyptus grove. Three lads followed, riding bareback on
mules and exuding curiosity about my eccentric behaviour.
None of them spoke English, but it was easy to explain that
mushrooms are a *faranj* delicacy. They stared at me, appalled—
then hastily dismounted, the better to dissuade me from eating
the lethal growth. It seems strange that a people with such
limited food resources should never have discovered that certain fungi are edible—though no stranger than the Aran
Islanders' ignorance of the edibility of watercress. However, by
eating half-a-dozen mushrooms on the spot I convinced the
boys that *faranjs* are immune to the poison.

Soon after this I became involved with a wedding party.

While resting on a boulder, at the edge of another pasture, I heard distant singing and saw about twenty men and women marching, running and jumping across a wide expanse of brilliant grass. (This is only an approximate description of their peculiar method of progress: it seemed that they couldn't wait for the dancing to begin at the bride's home.) The men were wearing snow-white *shammas* over grubby European pants and the women were dazzling in white, full-skirted dresses with exquisitely-woven, richly-coloured borders. Two maidens, balancing *injara*-baskets on their heads, led the group, and on the lid of each basket a tall bouquet of shrub and herb fronds swayed gracefully as the girls came prancing through the grass. The older women followed, singing, skipping and laughing with unmatronly abandon, and the men leaped vigorously up and down every step of the way, brandishing their *dulas* over their heads and loudly chanting. (The women's songs were more varied and at intervals they paused to ululate beautifully.) This little procession—so simple and gay against a background of smooth hills, wooded valleys and calm meadows—was among the most charming sights I have ever seen.

As the group passed by me everyone smiled shyly at the surprising spectator. They were going in my direction, so I followed them down a muddy path between tall blue-gums and soon I could hear the fast beat of festive drums and the loud chanting of many men.

Fifteen minutes later we came to a grassy slope below a compound containing a big white tent. The stockade and entrance archway were decorated with clumsily-arranged blue-gum branches and, as we approached, four maidens and a group of older women came to meet us and together the women danced, their wide skirts whirling brilliantly as the drums throbbed more and more frenziedly. Then suddenly I was seized by a pair of laughing girls and a small grinning boy, who conducted me into the compound through throngs of welcoming fellow-guests. This wasn't an invitation, but a most endearing assumption that naturally the passing stranger would like to join the party.

Inside the crowded tent it was stiflingly hot and the atmosphere reeked of sweating bodies, highly-spiced stews and crushed eucalyptus leaves. Leafy branches were strewn on the ground, beneath rows of unsteady benches and long trestle-tables spread with worn *shammas*. Each guest was given a chipped enamel mug for his *talla* and a chipped enamel plate for his *wat*, the *injara* being laid on the table—an enormous folded round for each guest, since it is etiquette to serve more than could possibly be eaten. Obviously this was a poor family. No *tej* or raw beef were served and the *wat* was not elaborate. As the tent only held about a hundred and fifty people, the guests were being fed in two shifts.

There were no English-speakers present and not one of the men smoked; only the enamelware and the women's calf-length skirts (the local mini) marked a city's nearness. Here I realised that for me the worst irritant of Addis was the inability of so many foreigners to regard the Ethiopians as fellow-humans; it is indeed shocking to think that hundreds of complacent Westerners are sitting in the capital drawing fat salaries for 'helping' a people with whom they have so little sympathy that effective help is impossible. (A considerable number of Ethiopians also sit in the capital drawing fat salaries to no good purpose: but that's beside the present point.) Admittedly the foreigners have not created this situation alone. The Amharas are difficult to deal with, both officially and socially; they will accept help only on their own terms and they are blandly certain that every other race is inferior. But an important distinction must be made here. While Amharas tend to look on non-Amharas as their preordained servants, whatever the nominal status of a particular non-Amhara, *faranjs* tend to look on the highlanders as creatures of another species and even when they profess a liking for an individual one can usually detect overtones of condescension. Yet the geographically circumscribed highlanders have an historical excuse for their attitude, whereas we present ourselves to them as the apostles of tolerant enlightenment.

During the feast we managed to exchange a certain amount of information. I learned that this was the bride's home and that the groom was expected to arrive at any moment from his own village, ten hours' ride to the west. There was to be no church ceremony, with a solemnisation of the marriage vows by taking the Eucharist; instead the couple would simply swear in the name of the Emperor 'She is my wife' and 'He is my husband'.

After such civil ceremonies divorce is a simple procedure so, among the peasants, Church ceremonies are favoured only by the clergy themselves, who are forbidden to remarry even if widowed, and by a minority of exceptionally devout families. The third form of marriage, more usual among soldiers and traders than in settled communities, requires no formal vows; the man merely provides his wife with a home, clothes and pocket-money.

Towards the end of the feast, as people were wiping greasy fingers on leaves off the floor, four friends of the bride began to dance in a corner of the tent to the beat of a drum played by a fair-skinned youth. This boy stood slim and taut in white jodhpurs and tunic, looking rather like a sensuous angel and vibrating with a fierce joy as he drummed faster and faster. Soon everyone was clapping in time to the music and frequently the women ululated; but all my attention was on the girls, whose every muscle was brought into supple, vigorous action— sometimes subtly, as they followed each other in a circular, pacing movement, shuddering with energy and ecstasy—then violently, as they advanced towards an imaginary male partner with undisguised sexuality, or dropped to their haunches and remained so for a few moments, convulsively working their shoulder-muscles. The dancers were glistening with sweat when their performance was interrupted by four little boys, who had been watching the bridegroom's route from a hilltop and who rushed breathlessly into the tent to announce his approach.

Hurrying out to join the welcoming party, we saw a procession of five coming slowly through the blue-gums. Only the twenty-year-old bridegroom was riding, on a mule caparisoned with that shabby magnificence so characteristic of all highland festivals; the weary animal, draped in frayed cloth-of-gold, wore high plumes of crimson ostrich feathers between his ears and silver bells were sweetly jangling on bridle and saddle. As highland stirrups are designed to accommodate only the big toe the groom paused here to put on his smart new wedding shoes, which had been slung around the best man's neck.

The bride's friends advanced to greet the party and danced slowly backwards towards the compound, facing the groom and confining themselves to the chaste, stylised movements customary at this stage. On every side men were chanting gravely and groups of women were ululating in turn. Then, as the groom dismounted, all the women united to produce a beautifully trembling wave of sound that seemed to come from some invisible, far-away choir.

Next there was a formal delay. The bride's father must hesitate before receiving the groom, to show affection for his daughter and doubt about the young man's worthiness to be allied with such a notable family. I hoped that the delay would be brief since the groom and his friends, each of whom was carrying a heavy rifle, looked utterly exhausted. Apparently Father-in-law-to-be thought so too, and soon the five were sitting in the tent around an enormous jar of specially brewed 'groom's beer'.

In theory the couple had not yet met, though actually they knew each other quite well, and now six maidens, all dressed alike, filed into the tent to sit in an embarrassed row opposite the groom's party. It was easy to recognise the agitated bride, but by tradition these girls are curtained off from general view and the best man ritually 'finds' the bride and triumphantly carries her on his shoulders to the groom. This was the only unenjoyable part of the ceremony. The wretched fourteen-year-old burst into tears on being presented to her future husband, and he looked almost equally unhappy as he turned away abruptly to accept another horn tankard of *talla*.

The mutual misery of the couple was understandable, since a highland marriage-night is often a semi-public test of the will-power and physical strength of both partners. In some regions the girl is taught to defend her virginity as though she were being threatened with rape: yet she knows that should her husband prove unequal to the occasion—as decent highlanders often do, being inhibited rather than stimulated by their bride's terrified belligerence—he will request his best man to provide the proof of virginity for display to the eagerly-waiting guests. The wedding-night takes place at the home of the groom's family, to which this party would ride next day, so the couple had to live through another twenty-four hours of suspense.

When I announced my departure there were many invitations to stay the night—which I had to decline, as my absence might have caused anxiety in Addis.

Walking home, I reflected that in the capital one can talk to twenty English-speaking Ethiopians during the day and find nineteen so addled by the synthetic urban atmosphere that with them genuine communication on any level is impossible. Yet among non-English-speaking villagers genuine communication can very soon be established, mysteriously but unmistakably, on that basic level where ideas are excluded but sincerity of feeling has full scope. I realised also that in Ethiopia, more than in any other country I know, this sort of rapport must be worked for, unconsciously. (Probably it would forever elude one if consciously pursued.) Remembering my first weeks in the country, and comparing them with that afternoon, I marvelled at the contrast. Granted the people around Addis are a little less ingrown than the isolated peasants of the north, yet this does not fully explain the change in my relationship with the highlanders. Superficially it was a change that I alone had wrought; but if these strange, aloof Tigreans and Amharas had not revealed a fundamental responsiveness, through countless tiny details, I could never have built my side of the bridge.

A traveller who does not speak their language cannot presume to claim any deep understanding of the Ethiopian highlanders. But it is the gradual growth of affection for another race, rather than the walking of a thousand miles or the climbing of a hundred mountains, that is the real achievement and the richest reward of such a journey.

# Index

277

# *Acknowledgements*

I owe gratitude

To Her Highness Leilt Aida Desta, whose sympathetic co-operation made many rough ways smooth.

To the scores of highland peasants without whose hospitality I could not have survived.

To His Excellency Sir Thomas Bromley and Lady Bromley; Mr Robert Swann, Councillor; Mr George Peel, Consul, British Embassy, Addis Ababa, who generously gave every assistance to the Irishwoman.

To Major and Mrs John Bromley, British Consulate, Asmara, whose friendship supported me throughout my trek.

To Mr and Mrs Marcel Landey, of E.C.A., who for five weeks were my long-suffering hosts in Addis Ababa.

To the many other Ethiopians and *faranjs* who assisted and encouraged me in a variety of ways.

And to The Honourable Jock, whose fidelity, intelligence and endurance were for three months my main support.